CHILD LABOUR IN HOTEL INDUSTRY

CHILD LABOUR IN HOTEL INDUSTRY

By

Dr. S.W.P. Prabakaran

M.A., M.Phil., PG. Dip., I.R.L.W, Ph D.
Project Manager
A Poverty Reduction & Empowerment Project
Government of Tamil Nadu
D.R.D.A. Collectorate
Tirunelveli – 627 011
(Tamil Nadu)

DISCOVERY PUBLISHING HOUSE PVT. LTD.
NEW DELHI-110 002

Published by:
Tilak Wasan
DISCOVERY PUBLISHING HOUSE PVT. LTD.
4831/24, Prahlad Street, Ansari Road
Darya Ganj, New Delhi-110002 (India)
Phone : +91-11-23279245, 43764432
Fax : +91-11-23253475
E-mail : parul.wasan@gmail.com
discoverypublishinghouse@gmail.com
info@discoverypublishinggroup.com
web : www.discoverypublishinggroup.com

***First Edition:* 2011**
ISBN: 978-81-8356-906-4

Child Labour in Hotel Industry

Printed at:
Shree Balaji Art Press
Delhi

Foreword

We pick up a good bargain with an auto driver for Rs. 5 and Rs. 100 with a housemaid. These two acts undoubtedly contribute to child labour. It is not the generic that this has brought about rather specific. This distinction is evident since the author has dealt with the child labour in the hotel industry in Tirunelveli District of Tamil Nadu.

Every dropout from a school is a potential child labour. The child labour and the right to education are incompatible. This makes no difference in the hotel industry. Despite, the child labour act enacted in the year of 1986. The hotel and domestic child labour have come to focus for the past two decades.

The study discloses poverty, indebtedness, social customs and the attitude of parents towards education. However, they are evidently denied their right to education. The child labour in the hotel industry drifts to delinquents or social deviants. This is primarily because a sort of sub-culture is created. The child labour in this industry considers their supervisors and peers as their role-models. This again greatly has a telling effect on their future. The major findings point out to the shrinking job opportunities in agriculture, and the accessibility to hotel industry. It shows their utter backwardness in terms of depleted income, non-availability of jobs and fall prey to the exploitation of the hotel owners.

The diseases they contact, the habits they inculcate and the vicious activities they indulge in, will clearly open our eyes to the realities. The report is critical of the lack of educational awareness and concomitant income supplements.

I fervently hope that this report in a book form would be a reference material to the students and the intelligentsia alike. India, our country aspiring to be a super power will certainly not tolerate this social evil. If this book ventures us to eliminate child labour, the success and the development of India are in sight, I hope.

Dr. G. Karunanithi
Professor and Head
Department of Sociology,
Manonmaniam Sundaranar University
Tirunelveli – 627 012
Tamil Nadu

Preface

Child labour has assumed serious proportions in developing societies as economic needs force the children to indulge in work. It has been estimated by the International Labour Organization (ILO) that a third of Asia's 38 million working children belong to India. The child workers in India are mainly employed in the unorganized sectors such as agriculture, cottage industries and tertiary service sectors. The incidence of child labour shows variations among the major States of India. For instance, Andra Pradesh has the largest population of child labour, whereas Kerala has the lowest. It is evident from the data that the number of working children has been increasing over time, and that their working conditions have been getting worse. Especially, the hotel working children are subjected to harassment and sexual exploitation in their work place. They are put to work at the early childhood and are denied their rights to get education as well as playing at that age.

Child labour as a social problem has become an important component of welfare consciousness among the public, social organizations and the State. The problem of child labour is mankind's belated recognition that children are important, and that care for each stage of a child's growth is imperative if a nation is to prosper. In the present study, an attempt has been made to find out the socio-economic factors which play a significant role in pushing children into the labour force and the repercussions of early employment. The study discloses that poverty, indebtedness, social customs and attitude of parents to education are the main reasons which force children to work as labourers.

India is not able to tackle the problem of child labour even after 63 years of Independence. In spite of a tremendous scientific and technological advancement that India is registering every year, millions of children in the country are denied the right to education and lead a life of dignity.

This study highlights how the child labour in hotel based workers are deprived of their education and other childhood activities. It examines their working conditions to what extent they are exploited by the hotel owners, managers and masters, denial of basic rights, health hazards and unhealthy practices. Further, this book provides a detailed insight how they are turned into delinquents, and how they fall prey to sub-culture. It recommends that government should enforce compulsory primary education to check the problem of child and also insists that the parents should be prepared to sacrifice their lives for the betterment of their children.

S.W.P. PRABAKARAN

Acknowledgements

First of all I should submit shower my glorification on the graceful feet of the Almighty for the strength and wisdom he has given me to complete this work.

I am grateful to my teacher and guide, Dr. G. Karunanithi, Professor and Head of the Department of Sociology, Manonmaniam Sundaranar University, Tirunelveli, for his able guidance to complete my work. His fund of scholarship and experience, his critical acumen and above all, the parental affection with which he treated me have been undoubtedly major sources of inspiration and encouragement.

I am indebted to Professor V. Sankarasubramanian, Professor and Head, Department of English Madura Collage, Madurai, for his valuable comments on my work, which indeed helped me to develop and make it a lucid presentation.

I express my sincere thank to Dr. A. Nihamathullah, M.A., Ph.D., Reader in English, Sadakathullah Appa College, Tirunelveli, for his useful comments on my work.

I also express my thanks to Mr. A. Chellaperumal, Anthropologist in the Department of Folklore, St. Xavier's College, Palayamkottai, for his very useful comments to develop the arguments analytically and critically.

I am indebted to my father, Thiru. S.W. Paul Pandian, for his sustained encouragement and kind help in extending financial support throughout my research.

I am extremely thankful to my brother-in-law, Mr. G. Jeyakumar, Manager, State Bank, and my father-in-law Prof. Moses Govintha Narayanan and my mother-in-law Mrs. Lakshmi Narayanan, for providing me with moral and financial support to complete my work.

I would like to express my sincere thanks to Dr. A. Selvakumar, Reader, Department of Commerce, Pope's College, Sawyerpuram, for his useful suggestions during my fieldwork.

I am very much thankful to Mr. Sudalaimuthu, Assistant Professor in Sociology, Devendran College of Physiotherapy, Palayamkottai and Mr. Pandaram, for their sincere and able assistance during my field work.

I am thankful to Mr. Senthil Kannan and Mrs. Murugeswari, for their timely help in computer processing the data.

I am also thankful to Dr. M. Ramakrishnan, Dr. N. Kannan, and Dr. R.Maruthakutti, [Department of Sociology, Manonmaniam Sundaranar University for their encouragement to complete the work.

I would like to express my thanks to Mr. J.Paul Bhaskar, Chairman, Peace Trust, Dindigul, Fr.Antony Cruz, Director, Tirunelveli Social Service Society (Saranalayam), Tirunelveli, and Mr. B. Nalachandrasekaran, Director, Navajeevan Trust, Tirunelveli, for having provided me with relevant literature for my research.

I thank my wife Mrs. Chitra for her assistance and support in several ways in completing the research work.

Last but not least, I am very much thankful to my friends Mr. Dhinesh, Manager, Jack Xerox, and Mr. V. Sankar, DTP Operator, Mr. N. Sasikumar and Mr. Krishnakumar, for having typed several drafts of the manuscript and taking photocopies of the report in an impressive manner.

S.W.P. PRABAKARAN

Contents

CHAPTER 1

Introduction

CHILD LABOUR IN HOTELS IN TIRUNELVELI DISTRICT OF TAMIL NADU

In the Third Millennium of 2001, child labour continues to be a universal problem challenging human rights. It is a serious social problem, especially in the third world countries. However, the developed countries too face this problem though to a lesser extent.

Children are the future citizens of a society. So it is the prime duty of parents to look after them, protect them and provide them with good care for their physical and mental development. In a welfare state, it is an important duty of the government to promote children's welfare through different schemes and policies so that they are not exposed to hazards which may damage their growth and ultimately damage the social, economic and political development of the society.

In India, there are 37 crores (370 millions) of children below the age of fourteen years. They are one-third of the total population of India. Of these, 120 to 170 millions are working and about ten million children are bonded labourers. About 20 per cent of the country's total production is contributed by the working children. Of the total number of child workers, 80-90 per cent are domestic workers and children are also engaged in agricultural operations.

Mostly due to economic necessity and poor living conditions, children are forced by their parents to take up work even at their tender age. They work under poor physical conditions detrimental to their health and welfare. Undoubtedly the employment of children at an early age hampers the development of their efficiency and stunts their mental, physical and psychological growth. Consequently, the socio-economic and cultural growth of the country is affected severely.

Child labour has become an important component of welfare. The problem of child labour is mankind's belated recognition that children are important and that care for each stage of every child's growth is imperative if the nation is to prosper.

DEFINITION OF CHILD LABOUR

Childhood can be defined in terms of age, but the problem of defining child labour is not as simple and straightforward as it may appear because it encompasses three difficult concepts to define: *child, work and labour*.

In the context of child labour, a working definition of a *child* may be a person below the age of 14 years set by the Minimum Age Convention, 1973.[1]

J.C. Kulshreshtha observes that there are three essential features which help one in detecting and identifying child labour. First, the child should be employed in gainful occupation; second, the work to which he or she is exposed must be dangerous to his or her health; third, it must deny him or her the opportunity of development. Hence, any work extracted by a father from his child by making him or her work in fields or business places for long hours is covered under this definition, but work by students at school workshops cannot be called *child labour.*[2]

According to I.S. Singh, the term *child labour* not only applies to the children working in industries but also to children working in all forms of non-industrial occupations which are injurious to their physical, mental, moral and social development.[3]

The Committee on Child Labour (*1979*) says that children are involved also in Cashew Processing and Manufacturing of Coir Products, Machine Tool Repair Shops and Petrol Pumps, Domestic Work, serving in Hotels, Restaurants, Canteens, Tea Stalls, Rag Picking, Construction, Wayside Establishments, selling newspaper and vegetables. This list covers only some of the establishments employing child labour.[4]

K.K. Khatu *et.al.* (1994) define child labour in various ways:

> those children who are doing paid or unpaid work, in factories, workshops, establishments, mines and in the service sector such as domestic labour. Since the law prohibits the employment of children below the age of 14, in factories, and other hazardous employments, all such children, except those who work in the service sector or as domestic labour, can be assisted legally.[5]

They differentiate child labour from the *street children* as follows:

> Children living on and off the streets, such as shoe-shine boys, rag–pickers, newspaper-vendors, beggars, etc. The problem of street children, for instance, is somewhat different from that of child labour in factories and workshops. For one thing, most children have homes to go back to in the evenings or nights, while the street children are completely alone and are at the mercy of their employers, night and day. They live in the *dhaba* (small eating-place), on the pavement, in the bus depot or on the railway platform. They are at the mercy

> of criminals, drug addicts and the police. They are basically on the run. Although the street children work full-time and are deprived of education, their problem is more acute than that of the children working in a factory and living at home.[6]

They also make a distinction between child labour and *bonded children*:

> those who have either been pledged by their parents for paltry sums of money or those working (mainly in rural India) to pay off inherited debts of their fathers. The bonded children are in many ways the most difficult to assist, because they are inaccessible. If the *dhabas* owner has bought them, they cannot escape. If the middle-class housewife has paid for them, they cannot run away. If the landlord in the village owns them, they will spend their life in servitude till they get married, and can in turn sell their children.[7]

Again, they point out the difference between *child labour* and *working children*:

> those who are working as part of family labour in agriculture and in home-based work. If children are working 12-14 hours a day along with their parents at the cost of their education their situation is similar to that of children working for employers. In fact children, particularly girls, are expected to take on work burdens by parents in complete disproportion to their strength and abilities.[8]

This differs from the view of P.V. Gopujkar and Dhole who say that the working children are those under 14 years of age and who do some work and receive returns in cash or kind or save money by rendering services for which the family will have to pay otherwise. These children may or may not continue the work with their schooling.[9]

On the other hand, child labour are employed children who have a contractual relationship with their employers. Mostly they are full-time workers. In case they are unpaid domestic workers, they assist their parents in work or they attend to the assigned work regularly but at their convenience.

According to the Operation Research Group (ORG), "A working child is that child who was enumerated during the survey as a child falling within the 5-15 age bracket and who is at remunerative work, paid or unpaid, and busy in the hours of the day within or outside the family."[10]

Helmer Folks defines child labour as "any work of children that interferes with the full physical development of their opportunities for a desirable minimum of education."[11]

According to Kulshereshtha, the term *child labour* itself may be used as a synonym of *employed child or working child.* This may be explained as employment of children in gainful occupation for material contribution to the income of the family.[12] The term *child labour* refer to children who are mostly full time workers and are denied education, recreation, play and other childhood activities, whereas the term *working children* applies to the children who are mostly part time workers and who may or may not continue their studies.

V.V. Giri uses the term *child labour* in quite an analytical manner. According to him, the term *child labour* is commonly interpreted in two different ways, first, as an economic practice and secondly, as a necessary social evil. In the first context, it signifies employment of children in gainful occupations with a view to adding to the labour force of the family. In assessing the nature and extent of this social evil, it is necessary to take into account the characteristics of any job in which the children are engaged, the dangers to which they are exposed, and opportunities of development which they have been denied. In other words, child labour is a social evil when the jobs are hazardous and the opportunities for normal mental and physical development are denied them.[13]

R.S. Goyal writes that generally the term *child labour* refers to the employed child as well as the working child. It signifies employment of children in gainful occupation with a view to adding to the household income. However, it must be noted that children do not always work for monetary gain. It is not unusual to find them as unpaid workers particularly in household industries. They contribute substantially to the labour force in their families. Moreover, they spend much of their time in household maintenance activities.[14]

According to I.S. Singh, the term *Child Labour* applies to children working in all forms of non-industrial occupations which are detrimental to their physical, mental, moral, and social development.[15]

B.M. Otta defines child labour as "any activity performed by a child in the productive process in a more or less regular or casual basis with or without any remuneration attached to it."[16]

After considering the demographic, social and economic implications of child labour, D.A. Naidu, defines child labour as "that act which deprives them of educational opportunities, minimizes their chances for vocational training, stunts their physical growth, hampers their intellectual development and forces them to remain as unskilled labourers with low wage all their life".[17]

Taking all the definitions into consideration, the investigator defines child labour to provide a guideline to understanding the children employed in hotels:

> Child labourers in hotels are those below the age of 14 years. They are full time workers and are paid for their work for the duration of 12-14 hours a day. Some of them are bonded children who are pledged to the hotel owners by their parents for a sum of money.

The population of the sample children drawn from the hotels in Tirunelveli District conforms to this definition.

The UNICEF has listed the characteristics of child labour and their nature of work as follows:

(i) Starting full-time at too early an age (e.g. in manufacturing industries, shoe shining, etc.) many children start full-time work even before reaching the age of 9 or 10 years.

(ii) Working too long within or outside the family and unable to attend school due to lack of time and excessive fatigue (e.g. in shop and domestic services).

(iii) Work that results in erosive physical, social and psychological strain upon the child (e.g. coolies, rickshaw-pullers, etc).

(iv) Work and life in the streets in unhealthy and dangerous conditions (e.g., rag picking, newspaper selling at crossings, etc.).

(v) Inadequate remuneration for work outside the family (e.g., auto-repairs, teashops and domestic service).

(vi) Too much responsibility is entrusted to children when parents, especially fathers, have died, or are incapacitated, and children have to look after younger siblings.

(vii) Work that inhibits the children's self-esteem, as in bonded labour and prostitution, and in less extreme cases the negative perception of street children.[18]

CHILD LABOUR AS A SOCIAL PROBLEM

Child labour is a social problem from the sociological point of view. The reason is that it tends to interfere with normal family life and results in the breakdown of social control. It also seriously interferes with the education, play and recreation of children. It subjects them to several health problems, which, in turn, interfere with their personality development and thwarts their preparation for adult responsibility.

Nevertheless, normal work given to a child turns to be a healthy practice in the process of socialization. Mukta Mittal, who is in support of this view, says:

> all forms of work by children cannot be considered deleterious. In fact, work plays an important role in the development of a child, if it involves purpose, plan and freedom. The function of work in childhood should be primarily developmental and not economic, and children's work as a social good is the direct anti-thesis of child labour as a social evil.[19]

Child labour is a social problem in the sense that child workers are subjected to economic exploitation and health problems. To employers, child labour is profitable because the wages of child labourers are low, their complaints are fewer and they accomplish in some industries and occupations as much as adults do. The employers have therefore, no qualms in exploiting the children in order to safeguard their interests. They ignore the needs of the children for real physical and mental growth and development. Gurupadaswamy, in his report submitted to the Government of India in 1979, observes: "Child labour assumes the character of a social problem inasmuch as it hinders, arrests or distorts the natural growth processes and prevents the child from attaining the full-blown manhood."[20]

Mukta Mittal observes:

> Every child labour is a child with all the needs of other children. He needs opportunity for growth not only physical, but in mind and personality, through all the activities and experience which properly belong to childhood. When business of wage earning or of participation in self or family support conflicts directly or indirectly with the business of growth and education the result is child labour. The function of work in childhood is primarily developmental and not economic and children's work as a social good is direct anti–thesis of child labour as a social evil.[21]

Thus, in the modern times, child labour is a social problem obstructing the normal development of children. The act of protecting and promoting the interests of working children has become a subject of paramount importance. Therefore, any civilized society cannot afford to overlook this duty. It has been rightly pointed out in the preamble to the Children Act, 1960 that:

> Children are the most vulnerable group in any population and in the need of the greatest social care. On account of their vulnerability and dependence, they can be exploited, ill treated and directed into undesirable channels by anti-social elements in the community. The State has the duty of according proper care and protection to children at all times as it is on their physical and mental well–being that the future of the nation depends.[22]

It is, thus, evident from the discussion that child labour is a serious problem confronting world societies. Rodgers and Standing say that the greater the degree of the drudgery involved in the work, the less the possibility of the children acquiring knowledge and skill through their work. They also observe that children's participation in labour force activities tends to reduce their potential for educational development. They point out that the work assigned to children weakens their resistance to illness and decreases their life expectancy. According to them, the high level of adult unemployment and widespread poverty push children into unskilled, unsafe and low-income labour market.[23] It is believed that the elimination of child labour will be able to solve these problems.

CHILD LABOUR AS AN ECONOMIC PURSUIT

Child Labour is an economic practice. Poor parents compel their children to work. They start earning at the age of six or seven, and keep contributing substantially to the family income. Thus, from the parents' point of view, putting children to work is a realistic practice. For many parents of working class families, a majority of their children are extra earners augmenting the family income. Whether the children's earning for their family is justified or not, it has become a tradition handed down form generation to generation. In the view of Elias Mendelievich, "This idea stems not so much from poverty as from the traditional belief that there is no point in making any plans beyond those for satisfying the family's immediate basic needs."[24] Therefore, a majority of the parents do not care to better the prospects of their children. They are ready to exploit them. As a result of this, children become an integral part of the household economy. This turns out to be a curse on their life.

There is some element of truth in the statement of Mendelievich. It is sometimes observed that the children are getting a pleasant life from their earnings. So, they are compelled to go for job at an early age. As long as they are not compelled to go to school, they are happy. Also, their parents do not have the leisure to think of their future

India has the largest child labour force employed in mostly hazardous industries. The Child Labour (Prohibition and Regulation) Act, 1986, was enacted to ban child labour in industries and regulate its conditions. However, this problem continues to exist without much alteration. The main reason for the prevalence of this problem all over India is perhaps the failure to stringently enforce this Act.

It is mostly parents from poor families and the so-called low castes who force their children to work as early as possible instead of allowing them to go to school and enjoy a carefree childhood. Gangrade observes:

> "for them, uneducated children are an asset and the desire to educate them becomes a double liability because of, first, the loss of earning of the child who does not work, and second, the expenditure involved in education, however low it may be."[25]

Particularly in developing countries, children are employed at an early age instead of being given primary education. In some cases, they have to take the responsibility of supporting their old unemployed sick parents.

CHILD LABOUR IN HAZARDOUS INDUSTRIES

The practice of employing children in hazardous work affects their physical as well as mental health. They are made to work for hours together every day. Normally, they work 10-12 hours per day. They might contract occupational diseases even during their childhood. They are especially susceptible to respiratory diseases such as chronic bronchitis and tuberculosis.

Child workers are employed in certain places on jobs an adult worker refuses to take up. Neera Burra observes that in certain occupations, workers are allowed to come into contact with harmful substances like chemicals as in the case of balloons, glass, match and fireworks and lock industries. These industries emit fumes, dust or cotton fluff that damage the lungs or other organs of the body. Children working in such industries are exposed to various health hazards.[26] Besides the nature of their occupation, malnutrition and under-nutrition double the health problems.[27]

The government has identified certain hazardous industries employing child labour. They include: the match industry of Sivakasi, Tamil Nadu, the diamond polishing industry of Surat, Gujarat, the precious stone polishing industry of Jaipur, Rajasthan, the glass industry of Ferozabad, Uttar Pradesh, the carpet industry of Mizapur-Bhadohi, Uttar Pradesh, the carpet industry of Jammu and Kashmir, and the slate industry of Mandsaur, Madhya Pradesh, and Markapur, Andra Pradesh. It is relevant here to refer to a report on child labour that suggests that the elimination of this problem would increase the employment opportunities for at least fifteen million unemployed adults.[28]

However, it is important to note that it may lead a number of families to succumb to starvation if the major income earned by the child workers is stopped. Therefore, alternative measures for earning should be given to those families by the Government. Table 1.1 shows the health problems of child labour involved in various occupations.

Table 1.1: Health Problems by Occupation

Sl. No.	Occupation	Health Hazards
1.	Beedi Industry	Chronic Bronchitis and Tuberculosis
2.	Glass Industry	Bronchitis, Asthma, TB, Eye defects
3.	Handloom Industry	Asthma, TB
4.	Zari and Embroidery	Eye defects
5.	Gem Cutting and Diamond Cutting	-Do-
6.	Construction	Stunts growth of the child
7.	Rag picking	Tetanus, Skin diseases
8.	Pottery	Asthma, Bronchitis, T.B.
9.	Stone quarries/Slate quarries	Silicosis

Source: *Children are in Darkness: A Manual on Child Labour in India* (Hyderabad: Rural Labour Cell of Academy of Gandhian Studies, 1988, p. 13.

MAGNITUDE OF CHILD LABOUR

An estimate made by the International Labour Organisation in 1998 points out that developing countries alone account for 120 million working children in the age group of 5-14 years. Of these, 61 per cent are found in Asia, 32 per cent in Africa, and 7 per cent in Latin America.

Though child labour is prevalent all over the world it is alarmingly widespread in South Asia where it is reported that about 29 million children are engaged as work force.[29] In industrialized India, children are employed in cotton and jute mills and coalmines as wageworkers. However, at present, several thousands of children are employed mostly in cottage industries such as beedi works, match works, fire works, agarbatti manufacture, handloom weaving, leather tannery, glass bangle making, carpet weaving, matweaving, carpentry, pottery, tailoring and the like. The major sector employing a large number of children is agriculture. In urban areas, children work as domestic servants, and they are found to work in hotels and restaurants, automobile, tinkering and fuelling stations, small workshops and repair-shops and brick-kilns or construction sites.

In the third world countries, of the total work force, the working children constitute 30.12 per cent in Bangladesh, 55.10 per cent in Bhutan, 16.09 per cent in Brazil, 42.30 per cent in Ethiopia, 41.27 per cent of in Kenya, 45.18 per cent in Nepal, 25.75 per cent in Nigeria, 17.67 per cent in Pakistan, 62.22 per cent in Thailand, 24.00 per cent in Turkey. Although India has the largest child labour population in the world, the proportion of working children to the total labour force is lower in India than in many other developing countries. Child labour constitutes 14.37 per cent of the total labour force in India.[30]

According to the estimates of non-government organizations (NGOs), the number of child labourers could be between 44 and 100 million. According to an estimate of the International Labour Organization (1996), there are 12.66 million full time and 10.50 million marginal child workers. The UNICEF India Country Programme, 1999-2002, reports that the population of child labour in India constitutes about 100 million in 1999. Whatever the actual figure of child labour, this phenomenon in India is on the rise and it shows that India has a substantial number of working children. Hence, the country needs to take various measures on a war footing to curb this social evil.[31]

Various surveys disclose that the number of working children in the world is about 200 millions.[32] The National Sample Survey (1999-2000) shows that 523 male and 237 female child workers in rural areas are working per thousand population, whereas in urban areas, the figure is 513 male and 117 female child workers per thousand population.[33] The year-wise population of child workers worked out by various agencies is furnished in Table 1.2.

Table 1.2: Magnitude of Child Labour in India

Sl. No.	Source	Year	Number in Millions
1.	Census of India*	1971 1981 1991	10.74 13.60 11.29
2.	UNICEF in India**	1999-2002	100
3.	ILO*	1975 1996	15.10 23.17
4.	National Sample Survey Organisation (N.S.S.O), India*	1987-88 1993-94	17.60 13.50
5.	Planning Commission, Government of India*	1983	17.36
6.	Operations Research Group Baroda, India*	1983	44

Source: * Helen R. Sekar. *Child Labour in India: A Study in Retrospect and Prospect* (Noida: V.V. Giri National Labour Institute, 1997) p. 20.

** UNICEF In India, 1999-2002, *Challenges and Opportunities*.

According to the 1991 Census, 11.3 million child workers were working all over India. It also shows that Andhra Pradesh has the highest proportion of child workers (1.7 million), Uttar Pradesh is in the second position (1.4 million) and Madhya Pradesh occupies the third position (1.35 million). It is also reported that 78-85 per cent of them, in rural areas, are employed in agriculture and allied activities.[34]

Nevertheless, the remaining proportions of them are engaged in various economic activities as shown in Table 1.3.

Table 1.3: Percentage of Child Labour in Different Economic Activities

Sl. No.	Name of the Activity	1981	1991
1.	Cultivators	35.95	35.20
2.	Agricultural Labourers	42.76	42.50
3.	Livestock, Forestry, Fishing, Hunting, Plantations, etc.	6.130	–
4.	Mining and Quarrying	0.23	–
5.	Manufacturing, Processing, Servicing and Repairs	8.63	9.10
6.	Construction	0.72	–
7.	Trade and commerce	2.20	–
8.	Transport, Storage and Communication	0.29	2.30
9.	Other workers	2.92	10.20

Source: Helen R. Sekar, *Child Labour Legislation in India*, cited above, p. 24.

The data in the table disclose that the proportions of children engaged in agricultural operations in their own lands in 1981 (35.95%) and 1991 (35.20%) are almost the same. A similar trend is found while comparing the proportions of children engaged in agricultural operations in others' land as labourers in 1981 (42.76%) and 1991 (42.50%). But the proportion of children engaged in other occupations is rather negligible.[35]

According to a study sponsored by the UNICEF in April 1992, as many as one lakh children are working as domestic servants in Delhi and about 40,000 children are working as porters and labourers. Besides, there are 30,000 children working as shop assistants and the same number of them are employed in *dhabas* and shops. The number of child rag pickers, newspaper sellers and others constitute 1,80,000. About 20,000 children are working as assistants to mechanics in automobile workshop.[36]

It is clear from Table 1.4 that Andhra Pradesh, Madhya Pradesh, Maharashtra, Uttar Pradesh, Karnataka and Bihar are the States in order according to the numerical strength of child labour. It also shows the types of child labour in terms of main workers and marginal workers. However, Table 1.4 clearly shows the proportion of child labour in those States, their drop out rate and the proportion of those under poverty line.

Table 1.4: **Child Labour by Their States, Drop-out Rate and Proportion Below Poverty Line in 1991**

Sl. No.	States	Percentage of child labour	Drop-out rates	Percentage of Below the poverty line
1.	Andhra Pradesh	14.3	71.68	31.7
2.	Bihar	8.1	79.08	40.8
3.	Gujarat	4.5	61.60	18.4
4.	Karnataka	8.3	66.1	32.1
5.	Madhya Pradesh	12.5	55.78	36.7
6.	Maharashtra	11.4	59.87	29.2
7.	Orissa	5.1	64.86	44.7
8.	Rajasthan	6.0	66.35	24.4
9.	Tamil Nadu	7.1	48.22	32.8
10.	West Bengal	4.4	75.41	27.1
11.	Uttar Pradesh	10.5	51.20	35.1
12.	All India	–	–	29.9

Source: Helen R. Sekar, *Child Labour Legislation in India*, cited above, p. 21.

Table 1.4 shows that Andhra Pradesh has the highest proportion of child labourers (14.3%) in India. As a result of this, their dropout rate (71.68%) and their proportion below poverty line (31.7%) are also high as compared to such categories of children in other States.

Madhya Pradesh occupies second position as for as the proportion of child labour (12.5) is concerned. But the rate of dropouts in Bihar, Gujarat, Karnataka, Maharashtra, Orissa, Rajasthan and West Bengal is high. The proportion of those living below poverty line in these States and in Tamil Nadu and Uttar Pradesh is considerably high. The decade-wise and state-wise distribution of child workers are given in Table 1.5.

According to the 1991 Census, the total workforce of children in India is 1,12,85,349 in the age group of 0-14 years. Of these workers, 54.85 per cent are boys and 45.15 per cent are girls. Of the total number of child workers, 80.40 per cent are main workers and 19.52 per cent are marginal workers (Refer Table 1.6 & 1.7). Among the total number of child workers, 90.85 per cent are rural workers. Out of these rural child workers, 48.36 per cent are rural boys and 42.50 per cent are rural girls. Of the rest of 9.04 per cent of urban child workers, 6.49 percent are boys and 2.65 per cent are girls.[37]

In Tamil Nadu, the total workforce of children is 578,889. Of those children, 48.22 per cent are boys and 51.78 per cent are girls. Out of them, 90.34 per cent are main workers and 9.63 per cent are marginal workers (refer Tables 1.6 and 1.7). Among them, 82.35 per cent are rural workers and 17.65 per cent urban workers. Of the 82.35 per cent of rural child workers, 37.35 per cent are boys and 45 per cent are girls. On the other hand, the urban boys constitute 10.88 per cent and urban girls constitute 6.77 per cent.

Table 1.5: State-wise Distribution of Child Workers: 0-14 Age Group According to 1971, 1981, and 1991 Census

Sl. No.	State/Union Territories	Child Workers in the age group of 0-14 (Million)				
		1971	1981	1991		
				Main Child Workers	Marginal Child Workers	Total Child Workers
1.	Andhra Pradesh	15.13	14.30	16.93	5.66	14.73
2.	Assam	2.23	0.00	2.86	3.07	2.90
3.	Bihar	9.85	8.08	8.76	6.66	8.35
4.	Gujarat	4.82	4.52	4.11	6.83	4.64
5.	Haryana	1.28	1.42	0.98	0.94	0.97
6.	Himachal Pradesh	0.66	0.73	0.34	1.16	0.50
7.	Jammu & Kashmir	0.65	1.89	0.00	0.00	0.00
8.	Karnataka	7.52	8.30	9.01	7.18	8.65
9.	Kerala	1.04	0.68	0.31	0.28	0.31
10.	Madhya Pradesh	10.34	12.45	10.99	16.10	11.99
11.	Maharashtra	9.19	11.42	8.87	11.92	9.47
12.	Manipur	0.15	0.15	0.15	0.14	0.15
13.	Meghalaya	0.28	0.33	0.34	0.18	0.31
14.	Nagaland	0.13	0.12	0.18	0.02	0.15
15.	Orissa	4.58	5.15	3.58	5.77	4.01
16.	Punjab	2.16	1.59	1.46	0.47	1.27
17.	Rajasthan	5.46	6.01	5.40	12.88	6.86
18.	Sikkim	0.15	0.06	0.06	0.02	0.05
19.	Tamil Nadu	6.63	7.15	5.76	2.58	5.13
20.	Tripura	0.16	0.18	0.15	0.13	0.15
21.	Uttar Pradesh	12.34	10.52	12.61	12.03	12.49
22.	West Bengal	4.76	4.44	6.53	5.37	6.31
23.	Andaman & Nicobar Islands	0.01	0.01	0.01	0.02	0.01
24.	Arunachal Pradesh	0.17	0.13	0.13	0.03	0.11
25.	Chandigarh	0.01	0.01	0.02	0.00	0.02
26.	Dadra & Nagar Haveli	0.03	0.03	0.03	0.08	0.04
27.	Delhi	0.16	0.19	0.29	0.03	0.24
28.	Daman and Diu	0.07	0.07	0.01	0.01	0.01
29.	Goa	0.04	0.01	0.05	0.00	0.00
30.	Lakshadweep	0.00	0.00	0.00	0.00	0.00
31.	Mizoram	0.00	0.05	0.07	0.45	0.15
32.	Puducherry	0.03	0.03	0.03	0.01	0.02
	Total	**100.00**	**100.00**	**100.00**	**100.00**	**100.00**

Source: Census Reports 1971,1981 & 1991, Government of India.

Table 1.6: State-wise Distribution of Main Child Workers According to 1991 Census

Sl. No.	State/ Union Territory	Main Child Workers						Total No. of Child Workers
		Rural			Urban			
		Male	Female	Total No. of Workers	Male	Female	Total No of Workers	
1.	Andhra Pradesh	13.89	22.62	17.29	12.50	17.43	13.80	16.93
2.	Assam	3.69	1.94	3.01	1.17	2.94	1.64	2.86
3.	Bihar	11.09	6.35	9.25	5.20	2.97	4.61	8.76
4.	Gujarat	4.11	3.77	3.97	5.90	3.41	5.24	4.11
5.	Haryana	1.21	0.57	0.96	1.33	0.65	1.15	0.88
6.	Himachal Pradesh	0.26	0.53	0.37	0.09	0.13	0.10	0.34
7.	Jammu & Kashmir	0.00	0.00	0.00	0.00	0.00	0.00	0.00
8.	Karnataka	7.81	10.15	8.72	10.52	13.95	11.43	9.01
9.	Kerala	0.25	0.30	0.27	0.53	1.15	0.69	0.31
10.	Madhya Pradesh	0.01	12.80	11.57	5.82	6.72	6.06	10.99
11.	Maharashtra	6.64	12.03	8.74	9.82	10.41	9.97	8.87
12.	Manipur	0.11	0.22	0.15	0.07	0.23	0.11	0.15
13.	Meghalaya	0.35	0.39	0.36	0.08	0.22	0.11	0.34
14.	Nagaland	0.14	0.26	0.19	0.06	0.09	0.07	0.18
15.	Orissa	4.15	3.22	3.79	1.76	1.95	1.81	3.58
16.	Punjab	2.07	0.26	1.36	2.77	0.83	2.26	1.46
17.	Rajasthan	5.00	6.47	5.57	4.06	3.65	3.95	5.40
18.	Sikkim	0.05	0.08	0.06	0.03	0.06	0.04	0.06
19.	Tamil Nadu	4.21	6.82	5.23	8.82	14.44	10.30	5.76
20.	Tripura	0.17	0.13	0.15	0.07	0.22	0.11	0.15
21.	Uttar Pradesh	15.78	6.94	12.22	18.93	7.40	15.89	1.26
22.	West Bengal	7.98	5.62	6.44	6.69	9.04	7.31	6.53
23.	Andaman & Nicobar Islands	0.01	0.00	0.01	0.02	0.01	0.02	0.01
24.	Arunachal Pradesh	0.10	0.20	0.14	0.05	0.11	0.06	0.13
25.	Chandigarh	0.00	0.00	0.00	0.18	0.12	0.16	0.02
26.	Dadra & Nagar Haveli	0.02	0.04	0.03	0.01	0.02	0.01	0.00
27.	Delhi	0.04	0.01	0.03	3.08	1.16	2.57	0.03
28.	Daman and Diu	0.01	0.01	0.01	0.01	0.02	0.01	0.00
29.	Goa	0.02	0.03	0.02	0.17	0.28	0.20	0.04
30.	Lakshadweep	0.00	0.00	0.00	0.00	0.00	0.00	0.00
31.	Mizoram	0.05	0.09	0.06	0.10	0.23	0.13	0.07
32.	Puducherry	0.01	0.01	0.01	0.17	0.16	0.17	0.03
	Total	**100.00**	**100.00**	**100.00**	**100.00**	**100.00**	**100.00**	**100.00**

Source: Census Reports 1991, Government of India.

Table 1.7: State-wise Distribution of Marginal Child Workers According to 1991 Census

Sl. No.	State/ Union Territories	Marginal Child Workers						Total No. of Child Workers
		Rural			Urban			
		Male	Female	Total	Male	Female	Total	
1.	Andhra Pradesh	5.59	14.56	5.62	6.19	1.85	3.43	5.66
2.	Assam	3.30	8.06	3.16	0.63	0.17	0.33	3.06
3.	Bihar	6.30	17.88	6.77	3.08	1.11	1.93	6.66
4.	Gujarat	3.26	20.49	6.83	5.64	2.02	3.52	7.11
5.	Haryana	0.80	2.59	0.95	0.63	0.10	0.25	0.94
6.	Himachal Pradesh	1.77	2.64	1.19	0.50	0.08	0.20	1.16
7.	Jammu & Kashmir	0.00	0.00	0.00	0.00	0.00	0.00	0.00
8.	Karnataka	7.11	18.73	7.21	6.28	1.63	3.17	7.18
9.	Kerala	0.54	0.42	0.25	1.47	0.27	0.59	0.28
10.	Madhya Pradesh	17.11	41.41	14.84	10.25	3.24	5.89	16.10
11.	Maharashtra	13.54	29.35	11.85	17.83	2.86	6.90	11.92
12.	Manipur	0.17	0.24	0.11	0.60	0.26	0.43	0.14
13.	Meghalaya	0.29	0.38	0.18	0.09	0.02	0.04	0.18
14.	Nagaland	0.04	0.03	0.02	0.01	0.00	0.00	0.02
15.	Orissa	5.26	15.77	5.90	2.20	0.62	1.17	5.77
16.	Punjab	0.31	1.35	0.47	0.69	0.10	0.25	0.47
17.	Rajasthan	10.34	36.01	13.08	4.60	2.33	3.68	12.88
18.	Sikkim	0.02	0.03	0.01	0.07	55.64	0.02	0.02
19.	Tamil Nadu	1.47	7.10	2.45	3.38	0.02	2.45	2.58
20.	Tripura	0.17	0.33	0.14	0.03	4.82	0.03	0.13
21.	Uttar Pradesh	13.36	29.28	11.79	18.25	1.19	9.34	12.03
22.	West Bengal	0.98	11.37	5.34	8.93	0.00	2.78	5.37
23.	Andaman & Nicobar Islands	0.05	0.04	0.02	0.02	0.00	0.00	0.02
24.	Arunachal Pradesh	0.04	0.09	0.04	0.01	0.00	0.00	0.03
25.	Chandigarh	0.00	0.00	0.00	0.04	0.00	0.01	0.00
26.	Dadra & Nagar Haveli	0.11	0.03	0.08	0.01	0.12	0.01	0.08
27.	Delhi	0.01	0.01	0.01	1.14	0.02	0.37	0.03
28.	Daman and Diu	0.01	0.02	0.01	0.07	0.03	0.04	0.01
29.	Goa	0.04	0.06	0.03	0.14	0.00	0.07	0.03
30.	Lakshadweep	0.00	0.00	0.00	0.01	1.22	2.87	0.00
31.	Mizoram	0.54	0.15	0.26	7.19	0.02	0.04	0.45
32.	Puducherry	0.00	0.01	0.00	0.08	25.59	50.20	0.01
	Total	**100.00**	**100.00**	**100.00**	**100.00**	**100.00**	**100.00**	**100.00**

Source: Census Reports 1991, Government of India.

The Census data show that during 1961-71, the number of child workers in India declined from 14.5 million to 10.8 million. In 1981, it went up again. But in 1991 it again declined. These ups and downs express a more definitive, conceptual and statistical problem than any changes in the incidence of child labour as such.

The status of child workers in India demands the attention of social scientists and administrations. Andhra Pradesh has the largest population of child labour, whereas Nagaland has the lowest. It is also a fact that there are more boys than girls among child workers. Nevertheless, in certain occupations, more girls than boys are employed.

In Tamil Nadu, the concentration of child workers is high in Vellore, Erode, Coimbatore, Ramanathapuram, Trichy, Madurai, Virudhunagar, Tuticorin and Tirunelveli districts. This shows that the problems of children are more serious in these districts than in other districts.

In Tamil Nadu, 32 per cent of child workers are non-agricultural workers engaged in various jobs. For instance, several thousands of children work in the fireworks and matchworks in Sivakasi town in Virudhunagar District. In a similar way, several thousands of children are engaged in *beediworks*[38] in Tirunelveli, Vellore and Trichy districts.

CAUSES OF CHILD LABOUR

The Ministry of Labour, Government of India, maintains that poverty, lack of adequate awareness among parents to educate their children, illiteracy, large size family, unemployment and the state of landlessness are the causes of child labour.[39] It is relevant to discuss these causes separately.

(i) Poverty

Unequal distribution of wealth or income, unbalanced economic development, scanty resources flow to rural areas for employment generation and agricultural development, chronic and acute poverty and the like contribute to the genesis of this problem. The problem owes its origin to frequent crop failures, recurring droughts, sloppiness, the state of landlessness among agricultural workers, distressed living conditions, bondage and the like. Though it is a universal problem, it is more pronounced in underdeveloped and developing countries than in developed countries. It is directly linked to socio-economic and cultural factors.

Most child labourers belong to economically and socially backward families. Therefore, the poverty of family is the main reason forcing children to work. The insufficient income of parents forces their children to work to augment their family income in order to satisfy basic needs.

According to the Gurupadaswamy Report (1979), chronic poverty is the most important factor for the prevalence and perpetuation of child labour. Nearly half the population of India is below the poverty line. In this situation, the child, since its very appearance, is endowed with an economic mission.[40]

Economic compulsions weigh so heavily on poor parents that they do not mind colluding with employers in violating the laws and placing their children under risks of inhuman employment situations. Poverty and child labour always go hand in hand and tend to reinforce each other.[41]

In addition to poverty, the low and irregular income of the family is an important cause of child labour. A survey carried out by the Baroda-based Operations Research Group (ORG) demonstrates that poverty and the absence of regular income compel children to go to work rather than to school.[42] Mohsini also stresses that poverty is the breeding ground for child labour.[43]

The children of farmers' families start learning and functioning as participants and productive members of the family and community. Therefore, they form an integral part of the agricultural household economy. They receive training for various work roles and gradually start making a contribution to their family income.[44] A large section of children in India do agricultural operations. Besides their association with childhood activities, they have to necessarily assist their parents in all agricultural operations to improve their economic condition. The poverty of the family drives them to their lands in the early hours of the morning instead of to schools. The children go for agricultural work in and around their villages, besides attending to work on their small pieces of land. The landowners, instead of giving a just wage, exploit them economically.

Pati, who deals with child labour in dry agricultural lands in India, point out that during three or four months of the monsoon season, children do play a key role in augmenting the overall income of the family, without attending schools. In dry seasons, they are engaged in animal grazing and harvesting minor crops for family consumption. Consequently their schooling is severely affected and finally they end as dropouts.[45]

An econometric analysis by Sarojini Mishra shows that there is a negative correlation between children's work participation rate and literacy ratio. But there is a positive correlation between child labour on the one hand and school dropout rate and the high incidence of poverty on the other hand. She observes that rural poverty has a positive effect on high work participation of boys as well as girls in Orissa.[46] In 1981, the Labour Bureau of the Ministry of Labour undertook a macro-level diagnostic study on Child Labour in Organised and Unorganised Sectors. The study finds that extreme poverty and lack of opportunity for education and regular income are the main reasons for the prevalence of child labour.[47]

Sinha's study on working children in various jobs in Calcutta concludes that poverty is the major cause of child labour. About 91.25 per cent of children left their village due to poverty.[48]

A majority of child labour hails from lower castes, because a great proportion of children are associated with agricultural activities and a great majority of them belong to the Scheduled Castes, Scheduled Tribes and Other Backward Classes. Another study of child labour in six villages in the Warangal District, Andhra Pradesh, shows that 75 per cent of child labour belong to the Scheduled Castes and Scheduled Tribes. Similarly, in the match industry in Tamil Nadu, most of the children employed are from the Scheduled Castes.[49]

(ii) Unemployment

The availability of prospective employment is also an important cause of child labour. For instance, in certain regions, where the green revolution represents an increasing trend in agricultural productivity, children get into the labour market to a great extent. When the wages rate increases along with gross production, parents force their children to agricultural operations, such as ploughing, sowing, weeding, threshing, transplanting, irrigating, harvesting, manuring, and the like. In addition to this, children help their parents in certain activities like digging roots, collecting fruits, guarding crops, grazing cattle, and carrying meals to the work place. That is how agriculture has been a major source of employment to rural child workers. Helen Sekar estimates that in rural areas, children work for 211 days a year on an average, compared to men's 277 days and women's 156 days.[50]

The problem of child labour is inter-related to the problem of unemployment and poverty. It is also related to the living wages of adult workers. The very inadequacy in wages of adults compels them to send their children to work for compensation. The employers take advantage of this weakness by providing work for the children on low wages. A report of the International Labour Organisation (ILO) indicates that the problem of child labour is not the problem of itself, but it is the problem of the maintenance of the child and the living wages of the adult wage earner so that they should maintain their family at adequate standards.

Generally the owners of cottage industries prefer children because they form cheap labour. For instance, in Sivakasi, a large industrial town in South Tamil Nadu, the owners of matchworks and fireworks employ a large number of children besides recruiting a limited number of adult workers. In the absence of regular employment for adult workers, they have no alternative except to send their children to work.

(iii) Illiteracy and Ignorance of Parents

In India, the lower socio-economic groups like the Most Backward Classes, Scheduled Castes and Scheduled Tribes, are mostly illiterates or just literates. A majority of them can think only about the present. They are satisfied with what they gain at present by the earning of their children, but do not think about the benefits that they will get in future by educating them.

Kanbargi finds a strong association between illiteracy and work participation. He identifies three reasons for child work participation: competing demand made on children's time by school attendance and work participation, insufficient income of parents leading to inability to meet the cost of schooling, and inability to forgo some small income from the productive work of children.[51]

Tripathty's study finds that 11.22 per cent of the child labour left school due to the lack of interest of their parents in their children's education and also the lack of interest on the part of the children themselves in attending school.[52] Since most of the parents are illiterates, they do not attribute value to education. They seem to be ignorant of the values of education because they have a notion that earning at an early age would promote the life of their children rather than learning.

(iv) Literacy and Child Labour

High literacy rate goes with a low rate of child labour participation. For instance, Kerala, which has the highest rate of literacy, has the lowest rate of child labour participation. On the contrary, Andhra Pradesh, which has a low rate of literacy, has a high rate of child labour participation. Grub and Lazarcen assume that children's employment prevents them from going to schools.[53]

(v) Large Family

Large families with comparatively less income cannot have happy notions in their mind. As a result of this, they do not protect and encourage the childhood of their children. If a family is limited and well planned, there will be no need for sending the children to the labour market. They would educate their children willingly, but illiterate and ignorant parents think otherwise.

If the family is small, the parents can provide all facilities to their children, which are necessary for their mental, physical and social growth. Ashok Mitra points out that most of the people in India have the opinion that a large family is an asset. They believe that more hands result in more work that in turn results in more production. This is perhaps the reason why parents prefer to have large families.[54] S.Vijayagopalan's study based on 500 children working in the carpet industry in the Bhadati and Mirzapur belt of Uttar Pradesh concludes that a large family is the major cause of child labour (85% of his respondents belonged to large families and 50 per cent belonged to the economically weaker section). The study suggests that along with legal steps, suitable welfare measures should be initiated for ameliorating the economic conditions of the weaker sections of society.[55]

(vi) Child Labour is Cheap

With the advent of industrialization, the tendency among the employers is to have quick and large profits at low costs. Hence, in every country, there is enrolment of children in a large number of factories. They are paid very low wages, subjected to too many hours of work, and made to work in hazardous conditions. Child labour exists not because children are more capable workers but because they can be hired for lower wages. Thus the preference for child labour by many employers is mainly due to its cheapness and the tendency of the children to be obedient and willing workers. Employers have developed the ancient commodity approach towards these working children. At present, employers think that the children in their work place can do a lot of work and their labour is very cheap in comparison to adult labour. In fact, it ensures them more margin of profit on less investment. Jerome Davis says: "besides the compulsion of poverty within the family, is the stimulus of the manufacturer who desires to secure cheap labour and more profit."[56] Tripathy observes in his survey that there is greater prevalence of cheap labour from among the Scheduled Castes and Scheduled Tribes and their counterparts from other castes.[57] An empirical study undertaken by the Asian Workers' Development Institute discloses that the lower the position in the caste ladder, the larger the incidence of child labour. In other words, the lower the caste of child workers the greater the chance of hazardous jobs handled by them and the greater the acceptance of menial jobs.[58]

(vii) Culture and Tradition

The children of an overwhelming majority of the country's population are committed to the culture of work to avoid begging. For instance, studies conducted in the metropolitan city of Mumbai show that 41 per cent of the children are working in line with their family tradition.[59] In a similar way, Kakar observers that sometimes family tradition and profession induce children to work. While children work they slowly learn their traditional occupation. This is one of the ways to make children work and contribute substantially to their family income.[60]

In many hereditary professions, the elders are keen on their children learning their profession and continue the family's tradition. As a matter of fact, one of the former Chief Ministers of Tamil Nadu wanted to make this a basic principle in elementary education. He felt that if the children spent half the time in traditional education and the rest in formal education, they would have a double advantage. But this scheme was interpreted as an effort at the preservation of the traditional ways in order to deny children of the lower castes their legitimate share in modern education and the advantages it offered.

CONSTITUTION RELATING TO CHILD LABOUR

The following articles of the Indian Constitution reflect the national concern to eradicate child labour:

Article 23

Prohibition of Traffic in Human beings and Forced Labour

(i) Traffic in human beings and begging and other similar forms of forced labour are prohibited and any contravention of this provision shall be an offence punishable in accordance with the law.

Article 24

Prohibition of Employment of Children in Factories, etc.

No child below the age of fourteen years shall be employed to work in any factory or mine or engaged in any other hazardous employment.

Article 39 (e) and (f)

Certain Principles of Policy to be Followed by State

The State shall, in particular, direct its policy securing:

(e) that the health and strength of workers, men and women, and the tender age of children are not abused and that citizens are not forced by economic necessity to enter avocations unsuited to their age or strength.

(f) that children are given opportunities and facilities to develop in a healthy manner and in conditions of freedom and dignity and that childhood and youth are protected against exploitation and against moral and material abandonment.

Article 45

Provision for Free and Compulsory Education for Children

The State shall endeavour to provide, within a period of ten years from the commencement of this Constitution, free and compulsory education to all children until they complete the age of fourteen years.

HISTORY OF CHILD LABOUR LEGISLATION IN INDIA

The Factories Act, 1948, raised the minimum age of employment in factories to 14 years.

Employment of Children (Amendment) Act, 1949, raised the minimum age of children to 14 years for employments in establishments governed by this Act.

Employment of Children (Amendment) Act, 1951, (as a result of the ILO Convention relating to night work by young persons) prohibited the employment of children between 15 and 17 years at night in railways and ports and also provided for requirement of maintaining a register for children under 17 years.

The Plantations Labour Act, 1951, prohibited the employment of children under 12 years in plantations.

The Mines Act, 1952, prohibited the employment of children under 15 years in mines.

The Act stipulates two conditions for underground work:

(i) The workers must have completed 16 years of age ; and

(ii) they must obtain a certificate of physical fitness from a surgeon.

The Factories (Amendment) Act, 1954, included prohibition of employment of persons under 17 years at night ("night" was defined as a period of 12 consecutive hours and which included hours between 10 p.m. and 7 a.m.)

The Merchant Shipping Act, 1958, prohibits children under 15 years to be engaged to work in any capacity in any ship, except in certain specified cases.

The Motor Transport Workers Act, 1961, prohibits the apprenticeship/training of a person under 14 years.

The Beedi and Cigar Workers (Conditions of Employment) Act, 1966, prohibits:

(i) the employment of children under 14 years in any industrial premises manufacturing *beedis* or cigars and;

(ii) persons between 14 and 18 years to work at night between 7 p.m. and 6 a.m.

Employment of Children (Amendment) Act, 1978, prohibits employment of a child below 15 years in occupations on railway premises such as cinder-picking or clearing of ash pit or building operations, in catering establishments and in any other work which is carried on in close proximity to or between the railway lines.

The Child Labour (Prohibition and Regulation) Act, 1986, prohibits the employment of children in seven occupations and eighteen processes, which have been listed in Parts A & B of the Schedule of the Act, of any person who has not completed fourteen years of age.

Highlights of the Child Labour (Prohibition and Regulation) Act, 1986

The Child Labour (Prohibition and *Regulation) Act, 1986,* was the culmination of efforts and ideas that emerged from the deliberations and recommendations of various committees on child labour. Significant among them are the *National Commission on Labour (1966-69), The Gurupadaswamy Committee on Child Labour (1979), and The Sanat Mehta Committee (1984).*

The Child Labour (Prohibition and Regulation) Act aims to prohibit the entry of children into hazardous occupations and to regulate the services of children in non-hazardous occupations.

Aims of the Act

- to ban the employment of children who have not completed 14 years of age in specified occupations and processes;
- to lay down a procedure to make additions to the schedule of banned occupations or processes;
- to regulate the working conditions of children in occupations where they are not prohibited from working;
- to lay down penalties for employment of children in violation of the provisions of this Act, and other Acts which forbid the employment of children; and
- to bring about uniformity in the definition of Child in related laws.

Proposed Amendments to this Act pertain to:

- the definition of Hazardous Occupation;

- the replacement of Child Labour with Unemployed Adult;
- the definition of the Duty of the Parent/Guardian;
- to specify the right of Trade Unions and Panchayats to bring action against employers;
- the establishment of Child Labour Rehabilitation-cum-Welfare Fund;
- the utilisation of the Welfare Funds;
- the application for release of the Welfare Fund;
- the appeal from the directions of the Welfare Commissioner.

The Commission on Child Labour emphasized the elimination of child labour and the universalization of elementary education. It felt that these were inseparable processes. It also felt that except in certain circumstances, the prohibition of child labour should be secured through the law. As a result of this, The Child Labour (Prohibition and Rehabilitation) Act, 2002, came into existence. This Act recognises the need to prohibit the employment of children in all employment and the regulation of the working conditions for children in all employment. It intends to ensure that no child is deprived of a future by being deprived of the right to education and other child rights. It considers every child out of school as a child involved in labour. It seeks to tackle the problem of child labour by ensuring universal education. It also seeks to ensure that each of these children gets education.

The Shops and Establishments Act, 1947

The minimum age prescribed for child labour under the Shops and Establishments Acts (which are States Acts enacted and enforced by the respective States and Union Teritories) varies in different States and Union Territories. The age of a child for employment in shop or establishment is 12 years in the following States/Union Teritories:

> Goa, Daman and Diu, Rajasthan, Orissa, Delhi, Madhya Pradesh, Jammu and Kashmir, Tripura, Uttar Pradesh, Bihar and Karnataka. The age of employment in a shop or establishment is 14 years in the following States/Union Teritories:
>
> > Andhra Pradesh, Assam, Tamil Nadu, Kerala, Punjab, Haryana, Himachal Pradesh. In the State of Maharashtra, the minimum age for employment of a child in a shop or establishment is 15 years. Night work for children and young persons is also prohibited under the State Laws relating to Shops and Commercial Establishments. Children and young persons are allowed to work between 6.00 a.m. and 7.00 p.m. in Andhra Pradesh, Gujarat, Maharashtra, Tamil Nadu and Pondicherry; 7.00 a.m. to 7.00 p.m. in Bihar and Kerala; 7.00 a.m. to 9.00 p.m. in Jammu & Kashmir and Madhya Pradesh; 6.00 a.m. to 8.00 p.m. in Karnataka; 6.00 a.m. to 10.00 p.m. in Orissa and Rajasthan; and 6.00 a.m. to 8.00 p.m. during winter and 7.00 a.m. to 9.00 p.m. during summer in Delhi. They cannot be employed after 8.00 p.m. in West Bengal and Tripura.

Hotel Industry and Catering Establishments Act, 1958

This act stresses the eradication of child labour from Catering Establishments, Hotels and Restaurants. It defines certain relevant technical terms as follows:

A Catering Establishment is a restaurant or residential hotel and includes any society registered under any law for the time being in force but does not include a restaurant or canteen attached to, or run or managed by, any educational institution.

A Child means a person who has not completed sixteen years of age.

An Employee is a person wholly or principally employed directly or through any agency whether for wages or not in, or in connection with, the business, of any catering establishment, but does not include a member of the employer's family.

A Restaurant means any premises on which a business is carried on in terms of the supply of refreshments or meals to the public or a class of the public for consumption.

Wages means the basic wages, dearness allowance, the cash equivalent of the meals and tiffin supplied to the employees free of charge and the value of any other amenity or of service or of any concessional supply of food grains or other articles which can be computed in terms of money, but does not include a bonus.

A Young Person is a person who has completed sixteen years of age, but has not completed eighteen years of age.

Sec.7: Daily and Weekly Hours of Work in Catering Establishments

According to Section 7 of the Act, no young person shall be required or allowed to work in any catering establishment for more than five hours a day. In a similar way, no other employee shall be required or allowed to work in any catering establishment for more than nine hours a day or for more than 48 hours a week.

Sec. 17: Prohibition of Employment of Children

According to Section 17 of the Act, no child shall be required or allowed to work in any catering establishment.

Sec. 18: Prohibition of Employment of Women or Young Persons during Night

According to Section 18 of the Act, no woman or young person shall be required or allowed to work whether as an employee or otherwise in any catering establishment between the hours of 9 p.m. and 5 a.m.

The Government of India directed all State Governments to implement the Supreme Court directive of December 10, 1996, and work towards concretizing an action plan. As per the directions of the Supreme Court, any employer who employs children to work will have to pay a compensation of Rs. 20,000 for every employed child. An Inspector appointed will ensure that an offending employer pays the amount which will be deposited in a Child Labour Rehabilitation-cum-Welfare Fund. Since the income may not be enough to dissuade parents or guardians from seeking employment for the child, the responsibility will be with the State Government to either ensure a job for an adult in the affected family or deposit an amount of Rs. 5,000 for each child in the fund.

As per the rehabilitation measures, the Court has directed payment of interest on the corpus of Rs. 25,000 to the family of the child withdrawn from the work and arrangement of compulsory free education for children below the age of 14 years. But at present the implementation of the Apex Court's direction is in question.

However, according to the Child Labour Act, Catering Establishments do not come under the purview of the prohibited list. According to the Act, child labour can be regulated in terms of prescribing limited number of working hours, fixing reasonable wages according to the nature and extent of work, providing required facilities to carry out the work and the like. An Establishment may be a *commercial establishment, workshop, farm, residential hotel, restaurant, eating house, theatre or other places of public amusement or entertainment.* Thus, the Department of Labour can only proceed under the Child Labour Act for regulation. There is no age bar regulating the employment of children. Further, hotels and restaurants governed by the Catering Establishments Act do not require to be registered under the Factories Act. They need a license from a local-government authority and should be registered to enable them to carry on business under the Tamil Nadu Catering Establishments Act.

By implication, it is only *Sec.17* of the Tamil Nadu Catering Establishments Act, 1958, which prohibits the employment of children below 16 years of age to work in any catering establishment. If it is violated, a sum of Rs. 50 is collected as penalty. Nevertheless, hotels and restaurants employ children with impunity and find that paying this fine is more practical and profitable. The point made here is that while the penalty for employing child labour prohibited from employment under the Child Labour Act is Rs. 40,000 today including a contribution of Rs. 5000 by the State, for the Catering Establishment Act, the penalty of Rs. 50 for employing children (up to 16 years) is ridiculous. The employment of children under the Child Labour Act working in *Establishments, which* include *a residential hotel, restaurant, eating house, theatre or other place of public amusement or entertainment* is regulated for children up to 14 years. The penalty provided under sec.14 (3) *is simple imprisonment, which may extend to one month without or with fine, which may extend to ten thousand rupees or with both.*

At the World Summit for Children held on 30 September 1990, it was agreed to end the practice of child labour. The Summit also focused its attention on the welfare of the children pursuing legitimate employment. It further recommended various strategies to deal with the problem of child labour in general and healthy upbringing of children in particular.[61]

Article 32, in the Convention on the Rights of the Child adopted by the General Assembly of the United Nations on 20 November 1989 declares that:

1. State parties recognize the right of the child to be protected from economic exploitation and (also) from performing any work that is likely to be hazardous or to interfere with the child's education, or to be harmful to the child's health or physical, mental, spiritual, moral or social development.

2. State parties shall take legislative, administrative, social and educational measures to ensure the implementation of the present article. To this end, and having regard to the relevant provisions of other international instruments, state parties shall in particular:

   (a) provide for a minimum age or minimum ages for admission to employment;

   (b) provide for appropriate regulation of the hours and conditions of employment; and

   (c) provide for appropriate penalties or other sanctions to ensure the effective enforcement of the present Article.[62]

After Independence, the Indian Constitution was also committed to the protection and promotion of the interest of the child, which found expression through Articles 23, 24, 39E, 39F, and 45. The Government of India also set up various committees such as the Labour Investigate Committee, 1954, the Harbans Singh Committee, 1976-77, the Gurupadaswamy Committee, 1979, the Sanat Mehta Committee, 1983, and the L.M. Singhevi Committee, 1989. These Committees highlighted the nature and magnitude of child labour in different sectors, which employ child labour. All the Committees strongly recommended that a uniform law has to be enacted in order to tackle the problem of child labour. However, each Committee had its specific recommendations, which culminated in the Child Labour (Prohibition and Regulation) Act, 1986, which prohibits the employment of children below 14 years of age in certain occupations and processes.

In a radical departure from the earlier approach of dealing with child labour through legislation alone, the *National Labour Policy* was formulated in 1987 to look at the problem from a broader perspective. The main focus was on general development programmes for the benefit of child labour and their families and also project-based action plans in areas of high concentration of child labour so as to reduce the incidence of child labour, and thereby encourage the elimination of child labour.

REFERENCES

1. Laxmi Devi, *Child Labour* (New Delhi: Anmol Publications, 1999) p. 2.
2. Jinesh Chandra Kulshreshtha, *Child Labour in India* (New Delhi: Ashish Publishing House, 1978), p. 2.
3. I.S. Singh, *Child Labour* (New Delhi: Oxford & IBH, 1992), p. 7.
4. *Report of the Committee on Child Labour, 1979* as cited by Mukta Mittal, *Child Labour in Unorganised Sector*, (New Delhi: Anmol Publications, 1994), pp. 11-12.
5. K.K. Khatu, *et.al.*, *Working Children in India, 1983* as quoted in *Child Labour Impact, Assessment* NORAD (New Delhi: Royal Norwegian Embassy, 1994), p. 10.

6. *Ibid*, p. 10.
7. K.K. Khatu *et.al.*, *Working Children in India*, 1983 as quoted in *Child Labour Impact, Assessment, op. cit.*, p. 10.
8. *Ibid*, p. 10.
9. P.V. Gopujkar and V.S. Dhole, *A Summary of the Study of Working Children in Tribal Area of Maharashtra,* (Paper Presented at a Seminar on Child Labour and Health), p. 182.
10. Kishi Kumar, *Definition, Concept and Overview of Child Labour* (A Paper Presented at a Workshop Organized by the National Institute of Public Co-operation and Child Development, New Delhi, 1995.), p. 4.
11. Folks, Helmer, *National Child Labour Committee, 1969*, As Quoted in Mukta Mittal, *Child Labour in Unorganised Sector* (New Delhi: Anmol Publicaions Pvt. Ltd., 1994), p. 7.
12. J.C. Kulshreshtha, *Child Labour in India*, As Quoted in S.K. Tripathy, *Child Labour in India* (New Delhi: Discovery Publishing House Pvt. Ltd., 1989), p. 11.
13. V.V. Giri, *Labour Problem in Indian Industries*, As Quoted in Mukta Mittal, *Child Labour in Unorganised Sector*, op.cit., p. 8.
14. R.S. Goyal, *Problems of Child Labour in India in Rehabilitation of Child Labour in India* ed. R.N. Pati (New Delhi: Ashish Publishing House, 1991), p. 153.
15. I.S. Singh, Child Labour, *op.cit.*, p. 7.
16. Braja Mohan Otto, *Child Labour As An Adjunct to Domestic Mode of Production in Rehabilitation* of *Child Labour in India*, ed. R.N. Pati, *op. cit.*, p. 196.
17. D.A. Naidu, *Some Micro-Determinants of Child Labour in Rural South India: A Provisional Analysis* (Paper Presented at a Seminar on *Child Labour and Health* Organised Jointly by Tata Institute of Social Sciences and World Health Organisation, Bombay, 1982).
18. UNICEF, *Facts and Need of Child Development*, As Quoted in S.N. Tripathy, *Migrant Child Labour in India* (New Delhi: Mohit Publications, 1997) p. 28.
19. Mukta Mittal, *Child Labour in Unorganised Sector*, *op.cit.*, p. 4.
20. T.N. Kitchlu, *Child Labour: Current Scenario*, in *Child Labour in India: Issues and Policy Options*, ed. S.N. Tripathy (New Delhi: Discovery Publishing House Pvt. Ltd., 1996), p. 109.
21. Mukta Mittal, *Child Labour in Unorganised Sector*, *op.cit.*, p. 4.
22. *Ibid.*, p. 5.
23. Gerry Rodgers and Guy Standing, *The Economic Roles of Children: Issues for Analysis in Child Work* in Rodgers and Standing, ed., Poverty and Underdevelopment (Geneva: International Labour Organisation, 1981), p. 10.
24. Elias Mendelievich, *Introduction: Child Labour at Work* (Geneva: International Labour Organisation, 1979) p. 4.
25. K.G. Gangrade, *Child Labour in India*, as quoted in Elias Mendelievich, Introduction: Children at Work, Op. cit,.p. 81.
26. Neera Burra, *Born to Work* (Bombay: Oxford University Press, 1995) pp. 231-236.
27. *Report of the Director General, International Labour Conference, 69th Session* (Geneva: International Labour Organisation, 1983) p. 16.

28. *Report of the Committee on Child Labour* (Government of India: Ministry of Labour, 1979), p. 8.

29. Jan Videk, "World's Working Children Need Protection Against Exploitation" in *Eastern Economist* 18 (October 1978) pp. 822-823.

30. *Child Labour: Challenges and Response*—A *Status Report on Indian Initiative Towards the Elimination of Child Labour* (NOIDA: National Resource Centre on Child Labour Institute, 1996), p. 8.

31. Mahaveer Jain, *Elimination of Child Labour in India: The Government Initiative* (NOIDA: Published by National Resource Centre on Child Labour, V.V. Giri Labour Institute, 1996), p. 1.

32. *The Hindu*, March 4, 1997, p. 14.

33. Helen R. Sekar, *Child Labour Legislation in India: A Study in Retrospect and Prospect*, (Noida: National Resource Centre on Child Labour, V.V. Giri Labour Institute, 1997) p. 20.

34. *Census of India*, 1991.

35. Helen R. Sekar, *Child Labour Legislation in India, op.cit.*, p. 21.

36. Mohd. Mustafa and Onkar Sharma, *Child Labour in India: A Bitter Truth* (New Delhi: Deep & Deep Publications, 1997) p. 21.

37. *Census Report*, 1991, Government of India.

38. *Beedi* is a locally made cigarettes Widely used by labour.

39. *Ministry of Labour*, Government of India, 1979, As Quoted in Nazir Ahmad Shah, Child Labour in India, (New Delhi: Anmol Publications, 1992), p. 35.

40. *Report of the Committee on Child Labour*, 1979, as quoted in S.K. Tripathy, *Child Labour in India, op.cit,*. p. 8.

41. C. Francis, *Eradication of Child Labour: Need for an Integrated Approach in Social Action* Vol. 46, October-December, 1996, pp. 457-458.

42. Roy Bhaskar, *An Adult Wages for Tiny Hands*, as quoted in Satya Sundaran, *Child Labour: Facing the Harsh Reality*, in *Social Action* Vol. 44, July-September, 1994, p. 40.

43. Mohsini, *Poverty Vs. Child Labour* As Quoted in U.C. Sahoo, *Child Labour in Agrarian Society*, (New Delhi: Rawat Publications, 1995), p. 70.

44. A.N. and Amerijit Singh, *Child Labour in India in the Indian Worker*, 29 (October, 1980), p. 61.

45. R.N. Pati, (ed.), *Rehabilitation of Child Labour in India* As Quoted in Basudeb Sahoo, Labour Movement in India (New Delhi: Rawat Publications, 1999) p. 69.

46. Sarojini Mishra, *Economics of Child Labour in the Informal Sector of Orissa*, as cited by Basudeb Sahoo, *Labour Movement in India, op.cit.*, p. 71.

47. *Report on Child Labour in Indian Industries*, Labour Bureau, As Cited by I.S. Singh, *Child Labour, op.cit.*, p. 12.

48. S.K. Sinha, *Child Labour in Calcutta*, As Cited by Basudeb Sahoo, *Labour Movement in India, op.cit.*, p. 71.

49. Walter Fernandes, Neera Burra, Tara Anand, *Child Labour in India: Poverty, Exploitation and Vested Interest* As Cited by Walter Fernandes, *Child Labour and the Processes of Exploitation* in *The Indian Journal of Social Work* Vol, LIII, No. 2 (April 1992) p. 180.

50. Helen R. Sekar, *Child Labour Legislation in India*, *op.cit.*, p. 27.

51. Kanbargi, Ramesh, *Child Labour in the Indian Subcontinent: Dimensions and Implications*, as cited by Basudeb Sahoo, *Labour Movement in India*, *op.cit*, pp. 68-69.

52. S.K. Tripathy, *Child Labour in India*, as cited by Basudeb Sahoo, *Labour Movement in India*, *op.cit.*, p. 85.

53. W.N. Grub and M.Lazarcen, *Education and the Labour Market in Work and Schooling*, as cited by Basudeb Sahoo, *Labour Movement in India*, *op.cit.*, p. 68.

54. Ashok Mitra, *Issues in India's Population Policy, Demography-India* as cited by T.N. Tripathy, *Migrant Child Labour in India* (New Delhi: Mohit Publications, 1997), p. 12.

55. S. Vijayagopalan, *Child Labour in Carpet Industry*, as cited by Basudeb Sahoo, *Labour Movement in India*, *op.cit.*, p. 70.

56. Jerome Davis, *Workers Problems and Modern Industry*, as cited by Nazir Ahmad Shah, *Child Labour in India*, op.cit., p. 37.

57. S.K. Tripathy, *Child Labour in India*, as cited by Basudeb Sahoo, *Labour Movement in India*, *op.cit.*, p. 85.

58. *Ibid.*, pp. 84-85.

59. NIPC, *Working Children in Bombay*, as cited by S.K. Tripathy, Child Labour in India, *op.cit.*, p. 35.

60. S. Kakar, *Childhood in India Traditional Ideals and Contemporary Reality*, as cited by Basudeb Sahoo, *Labour Movement in India*, *op.cit.*, p. 68.

61. *Convention on the Rights of the Child: World Declaration and Plan of Action from the world Summit for Children* (UNICEF India Country office, 1991), p. 20.

62. Convention on the Right of the Child, *op.cit.*, p. 58.

CHAPTER 2

Review of Literature

This chapter deals with the review of literature on working children in three sections. The first section explains various aspects of child labour in different units or sectors. For instance, the poverty, illiteracy of parents, adult unemployment, large family, death of father or mother or both and the like are identified as main causes of child labour. Mostly children are drawn from Backward Castes, Scheduled Castes and Scheduled Tribes. The second section deals with child labour in hotel industries in terms of types of hotel in which they are employed, types of work, duration of work, wage pattern, age and experience of the employed children, working conditions, exploitation, health problems, unhealthy practices, welfare measures provided by hotels and the legal aspect of child labour. The third section analyses the applicability of certain theories to the unhealthy practices among the sample children.

SECTION I

Most of the studies on child labour point out that poverty is the main cause of this problem. A report on Socio-economic conditions of labour in India by the Labour Investigation Committee (1946)[1], a study on child labour by Khandekar and Mandakini (1970)[2], a study of working children in urban Delhi by the ICCW (1977)[3] a report on child Labour in Indian Industries (1981)[4], and child labour studies by Savithri (1985)[5], Parveen Nangia(1987)[6], Singh (1990)[7], Sushila Srivastava and Bhanumathi (1990)[8], Mir (1991)[9], Ramesh Kanbargi (1991)[10], Nazir Ahamed Shah (1992)[11], Geeta Lal (1997)[12], Ojha (1997)[13], and Dinamalar, a Tamil daily (2000)[14] clearly mention that the poor economic condition of parents leads the children to various types of work for the family even at their tender age.

Certain studies on child labour disclose that the illiteracy of the parents is also an important cause of child labour. For instance, studies by Khandekar and Mandakini

(1970)[15], Savithri (1985)[16], Mir (1991)[17], and Nazir Ahamed Shah (1992)[18], stress that the illiteracy of parents is mainly responsible for the employment of children to support their family financially. Since the parents are illiterates, they may not be able to realize the value of education.

The studies by Savithri (1985)[19], Mir (1991)[20] and Suda Priya Das (1999)[21] identify adult unemployment as an important cause of child labour. The skilled adult workers remain unemployed because they do not get suitable employment in their places. In other words, they hesitate to do certain types of work because they can be performed by any unskilled worker. In such circumstances, the employers would prefer to absorb as many children as possible for the sake of economy.

Some studies show that the large family contributes to the increase of child labour. For instance, studies conducted by Ramesh Kanbargi (1991)[22], N.A. Shah (1991)[23], Nazir Ahamed Shah (1992)[24], Ojha (1997)[25] and Vijayalakshmi (1999)[26], disclose that the parents put their children to work to earn in order to sustain their large families.

Another important cause as specified by Savithri (1985)[27], Srivastava and Bhanumathi (1990)[28], Pratima and Majumdar (1991)[29], and Ojha (1997) [30] is that the death of father or mother or both turns the children to be workers.

Generally, all these studies show that the children are drawn from Backward Castes, Schedule Castes and Schedule Tribes. They also point out that the families with child labour are economically and socially weak. This is reflected in studies carried out by Balamurugan (1995)[31], Geeta Lal (1997)[32], Ojha (1997)[33], Baskar (1997)[34] Sudha Priya Das (1999)[35], Mishra (1999)[36], and Soundra Pandian (1999)[37] and the *Dinamalar* (2000).[38]

SECTION II

Several studies have attempted to classify the hotels into different types. For instance, a study of the working children in urban Delhi by the Indian Council of Child Welfare (1977)[39], and other studies on child labour by Prakash Kothari (1985)[40], Sushila Srivastava and Bhanumathi (1990)[41], Pati and Swain (1991)[42], Prembhai (1992)[43], Pichholia (1992)[44], Walter Fernandes (1992)[45], Damodaran (1995)[46], Vijayalakashmi (1999)[47] and Soundra Pandian (1999)[48] have classified the hotels based on certain criteria. The types of hotel classified by them include A, B and C grade hotels, domestic and catering sectors, *dhabhas*, small restaurants and tiffin-tea-stalls. All these types of hotels employ children for various jobs.

Some studies explain the types of work done by children in hotels. The studies by Sushila Srivastava and Bhanumathi (1990)[49], Balamurugan (1995)[50], Baskar (1997)[51], Vijayalakashmi (1999)[52] and Soundra Pandian (1999)[53] discuss the types of work the children do in hotels.

According to some studies, the duration of work done by children employed in various sectors including hotels is 12-16 hours a day. Besides the reports on children by the Labour Investigation Committee (1946)[54], the Indian Council of Child Welfare (1977)[55], the Committee on Child Labour (1979)[56], I.S. Singh (1980)[57] the Harban Singh Committee (1987)[58] and the studies on child labour by Srivastava and Bhanumathi (1990)[59], Pati and Swain (1991)[60] and Prembai (1992)[61], Murthy (1992)[62], Singh (1992)[63], Nazir Ahamed Shah (1992)[64], Mahalaksmi (1995)[65], Geeta Lal (1997)[66], Vijayalakashmi (1999)[67], Paul Baskar (1997)[68], Mishra (1999)[69], and Soundra Pandian (1999)[70] disclose that the children work for more than 10-12 hours a day.

The wage pattern of working children is discussed in several studies. For instance, a study of working children in Urban Delhi by the Indian Council of Child Welfare (1977)[71], a report by the Committee on Child Labour (1979)[72], Musafir Singh (1980)[73], a Report on Child Labour in Indian Industries (1981)[74], Prakash Kothari (1985)[75], Harban Singh Committee report (1987)[76] on child labour, Sushila Srivastava and Bhanumathi (1990)[77] and studies on child labour by Ramesh Kanbargi (1991)[78], Pati and Swain (1991)[79], Priya Das (1991)[80], Prembai (1992)[81], Pichholia (1992)[82], Murthy (1992)[83], George (1992)[84] I.S. Singh (1992)[85], Nazir Ahamed Shah (1992)[86], Sarojini Mishra (1999)[87], Ojha (1997)[88], Geeta Lal (1997)[89], Paul Baskar (1997)[90], Vijayalakashmi (1999)[91], Soundra Pandian (1999)[92] uniformly mention that the children are paid low wage for long hours of work.

Some other studies explain the age of employed children. The report of the Committee on Child Labour (1979)[93], the report on Child Labour in Indian Industries (1981)[94] and studies on child labour by Pati and Swain (1991)[95], Pratima and Majumdar (1991)[96], Singh (1992)[97], Nazir Ahamed Shah (1992)[98], Balamurugan (1995)[99], Mahalaksmi (1995)[100], Geeta Lal (1997)[101], Ojha (1997)[102], Paul Baskar (1997)[103], Sudha Priya Das (1999)[104], Vijayalakshmi (1999)[105], Soundra Pandian (1999)[106], and Sarojini Mishra (1999)[107] find that the children are mostly in the age group of 7-14 years. However, the report of the Committee on Child Labour make a categorical suggestion that the age of the child at the time he/she is sent to work should be increased to 14 years from 12 years.

Some specific studies deal with the educational level of children employed in hotels. They show that most of these children are either illiterates or drop-outs or have primary education up to Vth standard.

A report on Child Labour by the Labour Investigation Committee (1946)[108], the Harban Singh Committee (1987)[109] and studies by Pratima and Majumdar (1991)[110], Kanbargi (1991)[111], Pichholia (1992)[112], Singh (1992)[113], Murthy (1992)[114], Balamurugan (1995)[115], Damodaran (1995)[116], Mahalaksmi (1995)[117], Geeta Lal (1997)[118], Paul Baskar (1997)[119], Karunanithi (1998)[120], Sudha Priya Das (1999)[121], Sarojini Mishra (1999)[122], and Vijayalakashmi (1999)[123] recommend that the Government should run night schools to offer non-formal and vocational education to the children employed in the hotel industry and this facility should also be extended to children employed in other sectors.

Some studies deal with certain unhealthy practices and illegal activities among the children working in hotels. These studies show that most of the children prefer to see films that glorify violence. They also prefer to see films which are meant for adults only. They have contact with sex-workers and pimps. Sometimes, they act as contact persons for sex-workers. They are motivated by the customers, gamblers and rowdy element to indulge in stealing and smuggling. They are also motivated by them to drink alcohol, smoke and use intoxicating drugs at their early age. Sometimes, they are picked up by the police for selling *ganja* (an intoxicating drug) and alcohol. The studies conducted by Prakash Kothari (1985)[124], Sushila Srivastava and Bhanumathi (1990)[125], Walter Fernandes (1992)[126] and Paul Baskar (1997)[127] deal with this problem.

The reports on child labour by the Indian Council of Child Welfare (1977)[128] and the Committee on Child Labour (1979)[129] and some other studies on child labour by Singh (1990)[130], Pati and Swain (1991)[131], George (1992)[132], Damodaran (1995)[133], Ojha (1997)[134], Paul Baskar (1997)[135], Karunanithi (1998)[136], Vijayalakashmi (1999)[137], and bring out the health problems of the children employed in hotels and other cottage industries. They also show that these children work in unhygienic and polluted environment. They are afflicted with physical deformities and weak eyesight. Many of them suffer from gastrointestinal disorders and skin diseases.

A few studies have gone into the pledging system prevailing in hotels. Most of the parents have taken an advance sum of money from the owners of the hotels on a condition that their children should continue to work till the advance is repaid. The parents often fall prey to the tactics of the middlemen and send their children with a hope that their future would be bright. On the contrary, their children are subjected to economic exploitation which would lead them to an uncertain future. For instance, studies on child labour by Prembai (1992)[138], Paul Baskar (1997)[139], and Vijayalakshmi (1999)[140]explain this aspect.

Studies by Prakash Kothari (1985)[141], Walter Fernandes (1992)[142], and Paul Baskar (1997)[143] discuss the sexual exploitation of child workers prevailing in hotels. The children are often subject to sexual exploitation by their adult co-workers, masters and owners. The children working in wayside *dhabas* are physically punished and sexually abused. They are even forced to play pimp for the underworld or other gangsters. The sex-workers who visit hotels regularly turn to grown up children if they do not get customers.

Different studies conducted by Singh (1980)[144], Sushila Srivastava and Bhanumathi (1990)[145], Geeta Lal (1997)[146], Vijayalakashmi (1999)[147] and Soundra Pandian (1999)[148] explain the welfare schemes for children employed in hotels. They find that the owners do not provide the children with uniform, bonus, medical facilities and other welfare measures and do not permit them to avail themselves of leave. However, they are provided with food thrice a day and accommodation within the hotel. They have to stay in a common room with poor lighting and ventilation, and share a common toilet which is unclean and stinky.

Some other studies on child labour deal with the experience of the children employed in hotels. They found that most of them have no experience at all and some of them have 2-4 years of experience in hotel jobs. Especially studies undertaken by Singh (1992)[149], Geeta Lal (1997)[150], Soundra Pandian (1999)[151] lay special stress on this aspect.

The report of the Labour Investigation Committee (1946)[152], report of the Committee on Child Labour (1979)[153], report on Child Labour in Indian Industries (1981)[154], Savithri (1985)[155], report of the Harban Singh Committee (1987)[156], and studies on child labour carried out by Karunanithi (1998)[157] and make specific recommendations regarding the laws and welfare measures for the children employed in hotels and other sectors. They suggest that there is a need for a single model legislation on child labour in India, so that there will not be anomalies on issues like minimum wages, working hours, medical facilities, penalties for offences and the like. They also stress the need to involve social workers, voluntary organizations and trade unions and parents to facilitate the enforcement of legislative measures and to bring about a positive change in the social attitude to child labour. The Government and voluntary organizations have to organize medical camps to identify the specific health problems of children employed in hotels and other industries. They further recommend that the primary and middle schools are to be provided with facilities to draw the attention of children and to educate them.

SECTION III

It is observed during the field-work that some hotel owners make use of the children as brokers to bring more customers to the hotels by informing them that they get easy access to bars and sex-workers. Over a period of time, the children gain the confidence of the sex-workers. Besides the socio-economic factors involved in the deal between sex-workers on the one hand and children on the other had, it is relevant to analyse the relationship between the two groups based on the social exchange theory from Peter Blau's point of view.

He says that the term *social exchange*, refers to voluntary actions of individuals that are motivated by the returns they are expected to bring and typically in fact bring from others.[158] He observes that "only social exchange requires trusting others to discharge their obligations; the individual who gives another an expensive gift must trust him to reciprocate in proper fashion."[159]

Blau distinguishes between social exchange and economic exchange. According to him, "the former entails unspecified obligations and generates feelings of personal obligation, gratitude and trust, but the latter rests on a formal contract that stipulates the exact quantities to be exchanged."[160] He notes that "only social exchange tends to engender feelings of personal obligation, gratitude, and trust; purely economic exchange as such does not."[161]

He further adds: "In contrast to economic commodities, the benefits involved in social exchange do not have any exact price in terms of a single quantitative medium of exchange, which is another reason why social obligations are unspecific."[162] Moreover, social exchange is more personalized than economic exchange.

He also points out that "If either or both should come to think that the advantages one gains from the transaction are greater than those of the other, one will feel obligated to supply additional favors to the other who will feel justified in accepting or even requesting favours."[163]

Thus, Blau regards social life as a market place in which actors negotiate with each other in order to make a gain, a material benefit or a psychological reward. The individual who receives some benefits is obligated to reciprocate in order to continue receiving them in the future. Hence, the norm of reciprocity serves as a starting mechanism of social interaction and group structure.

Based on this, Francis Abraham summarizes Blau's exchange theory as follows:

(i) A person who enters into a particular social activity expects a reward.

(ii) The more he receives a valuable reward in return for an activity, the more he will emit that particular activity.

(iii) The more a particular activity brings expected rewards, the less valuable additional rewards become and the less likely the emission of the particular activity.

(iv) A person who receives a benefit in a social interaction is expected to reciprocate.

(v) Reciprocal obligations cement bonds of social interaction. Social obligations cement bonds of social relationship and lead to social integration.

(vi) Violation of reciprocal obligations invites negative sanctions from the deprived parties.[164]

Blau's social exchange theory is found suitable to explain the reciprocal relations or obligations between the children as brokers on the one hand and the sex-workers on the other. The social exchange between them is explained in detail in Chapter 9.

Delinquent Subculture

The concept of a Delinquent Subculture is found to be applicable to groups of hotel employees including children. This concept applies to criminal acts of deviants as well as non-criminal acts that the members of a dominant culture view as unethical, immoral, peculiar, sick, or otherwise outside the bounds of respectability.

The concept, culture, refers to a set of values and norms that guide the behaviour of the members of a group. The prefix sub-indicates that the culture often emerges in the midst of a more inclusive group. A subculture is a subdivision within the dominant culture which has its own norms, beliefs, and values. It emerges when a group of people in similar circumstances find themselves isolated from the mainstream. As a result of this, they organize themselves for mutual support. Since it exists within a larger society, it shares some of its values with that society. Nevertheless, the lifestyle of the members of a subculture is significantly different from the lifestyle of their counterparts from the dominant culture.[165]

The term Delinquent Subculture refers to a system of values and beliefs encouraging the commission of delinquencies, awarding status on the basis of such acts, and specifying typical relationships to persons who fall outside the delinquents' social world.[166]

Several sub-cultural theories in criminology were developed in order to account for delinquency among lower-class males, especially the teenage gangs. According to sub-cultural theorists, delinquent subcultures, like all subcultures, emerge in response to special problems that the members of a dominant culture do not face.[167]

Walter B. Miller develops the notion that lower or working-class values would result in a delinquent subculture. He finds the origin of the delinquent subculture in the values of the working-class. According to him, these working-class values emerge from the shaking-down process of immigration, internal migration, and vertical mobility. For instance, he observes, toughness is one of the characteristics of a person from lower-class culture. Since acting tough and being tough are often defined as delinquency by the agencies of law enforcement, the stress on toughness would amount to a delinquent subculture. It is, thus, clear that the lower-class culture is characterized by distinctive values, which vary notably from the dominant culture represented by middle class values.[168]

It is reported that conformity with certain lower-class values may lead to violation of law. Miller observes:

> "Engaging in certain cultural practices which comprise essential elements of the total life pattern of lower class culture automatically violates certain legal norms."[169]

If a delinquent subculture is to persist, there must be devices for passing the norms, values and rules for delinquency on to newcomers, who may be children or immigrants from other areas where the subculture does not exist.[170]

Conklin examines six focal concerns of the lower-class as follows:

> The focal concern of trouble refers to situations that bring unwelcome or complicating involvement with official authorities. The issues of staying out of trouble, and getting into trouble are of daily concern to the lower class. According to him, the lower class avoids illegal behaviour in order to avoid trouble rather than because it is committed to a law-abiding way of life. Although the low class seeks to avoid violating the law, it sometimes accords status to those who do violate the law. A second focal concern is toughness, the concern with masculinity, physical prowess, bravery, and daring. A third is smartness, the capacity to outwit or con others and the ability to avoid being duped oneself. . . . Another focal concern. The lower class is excitement, the concern with thrills, risks, and the avoidance of boredom. . . . Another focal concern the lower class is fate, a concern with luck, fortune, and jinxes . . . Related to this concern with external control is the sixth focal concern, autonomy. This refers to a desire to be one's own master, which is often expressed as the idea that "no one's going to push me around."[171]

Richard A. Cloward and Lloyed E. Ohlin also concentrate on lower-or working–class youth. They attach more importance to the criminality of the lower-class juvenile because it illustrates the existence of gangs or subcultures, which support and approve the actions of delinquents. In other words, the lower-class delinquents are likely to receive the support and approval of non-delinquents and other adult members of their class. Like Robert K. Merton, Cloward and Ohlin see most of the working-class boys as goal oriented, and also view their problem as a discrepancy between the available means and the desired ends. They call this theory *differential opportunity structure.* [172]

In formulating their theory, they rely extensively on Merton's ideas of the *Anomie Theory* which argues that crime results form exclusion form legitimate means of achieving success, and on Sutherland's *Differential Association Theory* which stresses that criminal behaviour is learned from group relationships. According to their theory, crime occurs because of blocked legitimate opportunities. However, the type of criminal behaviour depends on the place and peer group with which an individual is associated.[173]

Cloward and Ohlin list three types of illegal opportunity or three delinquent subcultures, which may be available to the lower-class juvenile. They are:

> . . . the criminal subculture, which contains rules for the pursuit of material gain by means such as theft, extortion, and fraud and the conflict subculture which contains rules for the achievement of status through manipulation of force or the threat of force. The other subculture, the retreats subculture, contains rules favoring the consumption of drugs. The basic notion here is that the subcultures are invented when aspirations are frustrated and when the frustration is diagnosed as due to the conditions of the social order rather than to personal attributes of the interacting but frustrated population.[174]

The criminal activities of lower-class (working-class) juveniles may be analysed from the view point of Cloward and Ohlin. Their theory, *differential opportunity structure*, is found to be relevant in order to explain the criminal behaviour of the children employed in hotels. They disclose that the occurrence of crime is mainly due to the closure of legitimate opportunities. The criminal behaviour of an individual depends on play group and peer group with which he or she is associated. This means that they learn the criminal behaviour from those groups. Of the three types of subcultures identified by them, the *criminal subculture* seems to be more applicable to the children who do act as brokers to get customers for female sex-workers, than *conflict subculture* and *retreatist subculture*. This may perhaps be explained in terms of the role of the children in prostitution. According to the Immoral Traffick (Prevention) Act, 1956 [under Section 3, sub clause (i)], the brokers or pimps are also subject to punishment irrespective of their sex and age. The studies discussed above are related, in one way or the other, to the present study. However, the present study differs from these studies in several respects. It has certain special features, which come with evidence in the succeeding sections.

The present study gives primary importance to the level of exploitation of working children. It analyses how they are exploited by the owners, masters, supervisors and co-employee in hotels. In addition to that, it explains how they are pledged by their parents and the terms and conditions of pledging.

The study also attempts to trace the working conditions and the types of work they do in hotels. Besides, a special focus has been maintained on the types of their unhealthy practices.

Some of the studies reviewed here have a considerable similarity at a general level as well as specific levels. This study attempts to survey a wider area of child labour in hotels and aims at studying their different dimensions. In the first Instance, the socio-economic profile of the child labour is discussed in the following chapter.

REFERENCES

1. *The Labour Investigation Committee 1946*, as cited by Parveen Nangia, *Child Labour Causes—Effect Syndrome* (New Delhi: Janak Publishers, 1987), p. 12.
2. Khandekar and Mandakini *A Report on the Situation of Children and Youth in Greater Bombay* (Bombay: Tata Institute of Social Sciences, 1970), pp. 6-11.
3. *Study of the Working Children In Urban Delhi: A Report* (New Delhi: Indian Council of Child Welfare, 1977). pp. 11-19.
4. Praveen Nangia, *op.cit.*, pp. 15-16.
5. S. Savithri, *A Survey of Child Labour in Tamil Nadu* in *Child Labour and Health: Problems and Prospects.* In: Usha S. Naidu and Kamini R. Kapadia (Eds.), (Bombay: Tata Institute of Social Sciences, 1985), pp. 41-64.
6. Parveen Nangia, *op.cit*., p. 12.
7. I.S. Singh, *Child Labour in India: Socio-Economic Perspective* (Delhi: Shipra Publications, 1990).
8. Sushila Srivastva and R. Bhanumathi, *Child Workers in Farming, Domestic and Catering Sectors*, Social Welfare, 37 (October 1990), pp. 24-26.
9. A. Mir, Child Labour With Special reference to Carpet Industry of Kashmir: A Social-Legal Study (Unpublished Ph.D., Thesis, Kashmir University Library, Srinagar, 1991).
10. Ramesh Kanbargi, *Child Labour in the Indian Sub-Continent: Dimensions and Implications* (New Delhi: Sage Publications, 1991).
11. Nazir Ahamed Shah, *Child Labour in India* (New Delhi: Anmol Publications, 1992).
12. Geeta Lal, *Child Labour in India: An Over View*, Social Change, 27, No 3-4 (September-December 1997): 57-65.
13. J.M. Ojha, *Mental Health of Working Children and Their Needs Social Welfare* ed. A.S. Kohli, (New Delhi: Anmol Publications, 1997), pp. 11-17.
14. *Dinamalar*, Dated 27 May, 2000, p. 16.
15. Khandekar and Mandakini, *op.cit.*, pp. 6-11.
16. S. Savithri, *op.cit.*, pp. 41-64.
17. A. Mir, *op.cit.*

18. Nazir Ahamed Shah, *op.cit.*

19. S. Savithri, *op. cit.* pp. 41-64.

20. A. Mir, *op.cit.*

21. Sudha Priya Das, *Child Labour in Cuttack City*, as cited by Basudeb Sahoo, *Labour Movement in India* (New Delhi: Rawat Publicarions, 1999), pp. 87-89.

22. Ramesh Kanbargi, *op.cit.*

23. N.A. Shah, A Study of Child Labour in Unorganised Sector in Kashmir (Unpublished Ph.D., Thesis, Kashmir University Library, Srinagar, 1991).

24. Nazir Ahamed Shah, *op.cit.*

25. J.M. Ojha, *op.cit.*, pp. 11-17.

26. S. Vijayalakshmi, *Working Conditions of Children Employed in Unorganised Sector: A Study in Sivakasi*, In: *Social Welfare* ed, A.S. Kohli, *op.cit.*, pp. 18-24.

27. S. Savithri, *op.cit.*, pp. 41-64.

28. Sushila Srivastva and R. Bhanumathi, "Child Workers in Farming Domestic and Catering Sectors", *Social Welfare* 41 (October 1990): 24-26.

29. Pratima Nath and P.P.K. Majumdar, *Working Children in Calcutta*, in *Rehabilitation of Child Labour in India* ed. R.N. Pati, (New Delhi: Ashish Publishing House, 1990) pp. 165-170.

30. J.M. Ojha, *op.cit.*, pp. 11.17.

31. B. Balamurugan, *Child Labour in Hotel Industry in Tiruchy City* as cited by R.Vidyasagar, *A Status Report on Child Labour in Tamil Nadu: Based on An Annotated Bibliography of Studies and Surveys on Child Labour in Tamil Nadu for UNICEF, 1995,* pp. 18-19.

32. Geeta Lal, *op.cit.*, pp. 57-65.

33. J.M. Ojha, *op.cit.*, pp. 11-17.

34. Paul Baskar, *Resting Centres for Restaurant Child Workers*, (Annual Report of Peace Trust at Dindugal, Tamil Nadu, submitted to East France, 1997).

35. Sudha Priya Das, *op.cit.*, pp. 85-87.

36. Sarojini Mishra, *op. cit.*, pp. 85-87.

37. M. Soundra Pandian, *A Study on Working Children In Hotel Industry in Chennai*, Proceedings of a *Workshop on Street Children* (Department of Sociology, Gandhigram Rural Institute-Deemed University, 1999).

38. *Dinamalar*, Dated 27 May, 2000.

39. *Study of the Working Children In Urban Delhi: A Report* (New Delhi: Indian Council of Child Welfare, 1977).

40. Prakash Kothari, S*exual Exploitation of Working Children*, In: *Child Labour and Health Problems & Prospects,* ed. S.Usha Naidu and Kamini R. Kapadia, (Bombay: Tata Institute of Social Sciences, 1985), pp. 191-192.

41. Sushila Srivastva and R. Bhanumathi, *op. cit.*, pp. 24-26.

42. R.N. Pati and S.N. Swain, *op. cit.*, pp. 77-99.

43. Prembhai, *Report on Child Labour in the Carpet Industry*, (Submitted to the Supreme Court) as cited by Walter Fernandes *Child Labour and the Processes of Exploitation, The Indian Journal of Social Work*, 53 (April 1992): 171-190.

44. K.R. Pichholia, *Child Labour in Metro Politian City; A Study of Ahmedabad*, As Cited by I.S. Singh, *Child Labour*, *op.cit.*, p. 11.

45. Walter Fernandes, "Child Labour and the Processes of Exploitation", *The Indian Journal of Social Work*, *op. cit.*, pp. 171-190.

46. A. Damodaran, *Living and Working Condition of Child Labour in Small Hotels and Tea Stalls in Coimbatore*, as cited by R.Vidyasagar, *A Status Report on Child Labour in Tamil Nadu*, *op.cit.*, p. 20.

47. S.Vijayalakshmi, *op.cit.*, pp. 18-24.

48. M. Soundra Pandian, *A Study on Working Children In Hotel Industry in Chennai,* Proceedings of a Workshop on Street Children, op.cit.

49. Sushila Srivastva and R. Bhanumathi, *op.cit.*, pp. 24-26.

50. B.Balamurugan, *op.cit.*, p. 20.

51. Paul Baskar, *op.cit.*

52. S.Vijayalakshmi, *op.cit.*, pp. 18-24.

53. M. Soundra Pandian, *op. cit.*

54. *The Labour Investigation Committee 1946*, *op.cit*. p. 12.

55. *Study of the Working Children In Urban Delhi: A Report*, *op.cit.*, pp. 11-19.

56. *Report of the Committee on Child Labour, 1979* As Cited by Parveen Nangia, *Child labour Causes-Effect Syndrome*. op. cit., pp. 14-15.

57. I.S. Singh, *op.cit.*

58. Harban Singh Committee, *Report on the problem of child labour in Various Factories and Industries in Ramanathapuram District*, As Cited by Parveen Nangia, *Child labour Causes-Effect Syndrome*, op.cit., pp. 12-13.

59. Sushila Srivastva and R. Bhanumathi, *op.cit.*, pp. 24-26.

60. R.N. Pati and S.N. Swain, *op.cit.*, pp. 77-99.

61. Prembhai, *Report on Child Labour in the Carpet Industry*, (Submitted to the Supreme Court) as cited by Walter Fernandes, *Child Labour and the Process of Exploitation, The Indian Journal of Social Work*, *op.cit.*, pp. 171-190.

62. G.K, Murthy and T.J. Rani, *Wages of Child Labour* As Cited by I.S. Singh, *Child Labour*, *op.cit.*, p. 13.

63. I.S. Singh, *op.cit.*

64. Nazir Ahmad Shah, *op.cit.*

65. Mahalaksmi, *Child Labour in Hotel at Trichy Town*, As Cited by R.Vidyasagar, *A Status Report on Child Labour in Tamil Nadu*, op.cit., p. 30.

66. Geeta Lal, *op.cit.*, 57-65.

67. S. Vijayalakshmi, *op.cit.*, pp. 18-24.
68. Paul Baskar, *op.cit.*
69. Sarojini Mishra, *op.cit.*, pp. 87-89.
70. M. Soundra Pandian, *op.cit.*
71. *Study of the Working Children In Urban Delhi: A Report*, *op.cit.*
72. *Report of the Committee on Child Labour*, 1979 As Cited by Parveen Nangia, *op.cit.*, pp. 14-15.
73. Musafir Singh, V.D. Kaura and S.A. Khan, *Working Children in Bombay—A Study* (New Delhi: National Institute of Public Co-Operation and Child Development, 1980).
74. *Report on the Child Labour in Indian Industries, 1981*, As Cited by Parveen Nangia, *Child Labour Causes-Effect Syndrome*, *op.cit.*, pp. 15-16.
75. Prakash Kothari, *op.cit.*, pp. 41-64.
76. *The Labour Investigation Committee 1946,* As Cited by Praveen Nangia, *op. cit*, p. 12.
77. Sushila Srivastva and R. Bhanumathi, *op.cit.*, pp. 24-26.
78. Ramesh Kanbargi, *op.cit.*
79. R.N. Pati and S.N. Swain, *op.cit.*, pp. 77-99.
80. Sudha Priya Das, *op.cit.*, pp. 85-87.
81. Prembhai, *Report on Child Labour in the Carpet Industry*, (Submitted to the Supreme Court) as cited by Walter Fernandes, *op. cit.*, pp. 171-190.
82. K.R. Pichholia, *op.cit.*, p. 11.
83 G.K. Murthy and T.J. Rani, *op.cit.*, p. 13.
84. K.N. George,*op.cit.*, p. 10.
85. G.K. Murthy and T.J. Rani, *op.cit*, p. 13.
86. Nazir Ahamed Shah, *op.cit.*
87. Sarojini Mishra, *op.cit.*, pp. 87-89.
88 J.M. Ojha, *op.cit.*, pp. 11-17.
89 Geeta Lal, *op.cit.*, pp. 57-65.
90 Paul Baskar, *op.cit.*
91. S. Vijayalakshmi, *op.cit.*, pp. 18-24.
92. M. Soundra Pandian, *op.cit.*
93. *Report of the Committee on Child Labour, 1979* as cited by Parveen Nangia, *op.cit.*, pp. 14-15.
94. *Report on the Child Labour in Indian Industries, 1981*, *op.cit.*, pp. 15-16.
95. R.N. Pati and S.N. Swain, *op.cit.*, pp. 77-99.
96. Pratima Nath and P.P.K. Majumdar, *op.cit.*, pp. 165-170.
97. I.S. Singh, *op.cit.*
98. Nazir Ahmad Shah, *op.cit.*

99. B.Balamurugan, *op.cit.*, p. 20.

100. Mahalaksmi,*op.cit.*, p. 20.

101. Geeta Lal,*op.cit.*, pp. 57-65.

102. J.M. Ojha, *op.cit.*, pp. 11-17.

103. Paul Baskar, *op.cit.*

104. Sudha Priya Das, *op.cit.*, pp. 85-87.

105. S.Vijayalakshmi, *op.cit.*, pp. 18-24.

106. M. Soundra Pandian, *op.cit.*

107. Sarojini Mishra, *op.cit.*, pp. 87-89.

108. *The Labour Investigation Committee 1946,* as cited by Parveen Nangia, *op.cit.*, p. 12.

109. Harban Singh Committee, *Report on the Problem of Child Labour in Various Factories and Industries in Ramanathapuram District*, As Cited by Parveen Nangia, *op.cit.*, pp. 12-13.

110. Pratima Nath and P.PK. Majumdar, *op.cit.*

111. Ramesh Kanbargi, *op.cit.*

112. K.R. Pichholia, *op.cit.*, p. 11.

113. Sarojini Mishra, *op.cit.*, pp. 87-89.

114. G.K. Murthy and T.J. Rani, *op.cit.*, p. 13.

115. B. Balamurugan, *op.cit.*, p. 20.

116. A. Damodaran, *op.cit.*, p. 20.

117. Mahalaksmi, *op.cit.*, p. 20.

118. Geeta Lal, *op.cit.*, pp. 57-65.

119. Paul Baskar, *op.cit.*

120. G.Karunanithi, "Plight of Pledged Children in Beedi Workers", *Economic and Political Weekly* 33 (February 1998) pp. 450-452.

121. Sudha Priya Das, *op.cit.*, pp. 85-87.

122. Sarojini Mishra, *op.cit.*, pp. 87-89.

123. S.Vijayalakshmi, *op.cit.*, pp. 18-24.

124. Prakash Kothari,*op.cit.*, pp. 191-192.

125. Sushila Srivastva and R. Bhanumathi, *op.cit.*, pp. 24-26.

126. Walter Fernandes,*op.cit.*, pp. 171-190.

127. Paul Baskar, *op.cit.*

128. *Study of the Working Children in Urban Delhi: A Report*, *op.cit.*, pp. 11-19.

129. *Report of the Committee on Child Labour, 1979*, as cited by Parveen Nangia, *op.cit.*, pp. 14-15.

130. I.S. Singh, *op.cit.*

131. R.N. Pati and S.N. Swain, *op.cit.* pp. 77-99.

132. K.N. George, *op.cit*., p. 10.
133. A. Damodaran,*op.cit*., p. 20.
134. J.M. Ojha, *op.cit*., pp. 11-17.
135. Paul Baskar, *op.cit*.
136. G.Karunanithi, *op.cit*., pp. 450-452.
137. S.Vijayalakshmi, *op.cit*., pp. 18-24.
138. Prembhai, *op.cit*., pp. 171-190.
139. Paul Baskar, *op.cit*.
140. S.Vijayalakshmi, *op.cit*., pp. 18-24.
141. Prakash Kothari, *op.cit*., pp. 191-192.
142. Walter Fernandes, *op.cit*., pp. 171-190.
143. Paul Baskar, *op.cit*.
144. I.S. Singh, *op.cit*.
145. Sushila Srivastva and R. Bhanumathi, *op.cit*., pp. 24-26.
146. Geeta Lal, *op.cit*., pp. 57-65.
147. S. Vijayalakshmi, *op.cit*., pp. 18-24.
148. M. Soundra Pandian, *op.cit*.
149. I.S. Singh, *op.cit*.
150. Geeta Lal, *op.cit*., pp. 57-65.
151. M. Soundra Pandian, *op.cit*.
152. *The Labour Investigation Committee 1946*, as cited by Parveen Nangia, *op.cit*., p. 12.
153. *Report of the Committee on Child Labour, 1979*, Ibid., pp. 14-15.
154. *Report on the Child Labour in Indian Industries, Ibid.*, pp. 15-16.
155. S. Savithri, *op.cit*., pp. 41-64.
156. Harban Singh Committee, *op.cit*., pp. 12-13.
157. G. Karunanithi, *op.cit*., pp. 450-452.
158. Peter M. Blau, *Exchange and Power in Social Life* (New York: John Wiley & Sons, Inc, 1964), p. 91.
159. *Ibid*., p. 94.
160. *Ibid*.
161. *Ibid*.
162. *Ibid*, p. 94-95.
163. *Ibid*, p. 103.
164. M. Francis Abraham, *Modern Sociological Theory: An Introduction* (Calcutta: Oxford University Press, 1997) p. 156.

165. Freda Adler, Gerhard O.W.Mueller and William S. Laufer, *Criminology* (New York: Mcgraw-Hill, Inc.1991), pp. 135-136.

166. *International Encyclopedia of the Social Sciences* 10th ed. (1972), S.V. *Delinquency: Sociological Aspects*, by Stanton Wheeler.

167. *Ibid.*

168. Walter B. Miller, *Lower Class Culture As a Generating Milieu of Gang Delinquency*, As Cited in Edwin H. Sutherland and Donald R. Cressey, Criminology (New York: J. B. Company, 1978), p. 107.

169. *Ibid*, p. 107.

170. *Ibid*, p. 109.

171. John E.Conklin, *Criminology*, op.cit., p. 199-200.

172. Katherine S. Williams, *Criminology* (New Delhi: Oxford University Press, 2001), p. 355.

173. Cloward and Ohlin, *Criminology*, op.cit., p. 355.

174. Cloward and Ohlin, *Delinquency and Opportunity*, As Cited in Edwin H.Sutherland and Donald R. Cressey *Criminology*, op.cit., pp. 108-109.

CHAPTER 3

Methodology

This comprehensive study is about children at the age of fourteen and below fourteen years, who are working and living in hotels. They are from three different areas: district headquarters, tourist centres and rural taluks of Tirunelveli district. This study focuses on the socio-economic condition of child labour in these places and their exploitation by their owners, masters and co-employees. It also deals with their health problems. A few empirical studies have been conducted in the area of child labour in hotels, restaurants, *dhabas* and tea stalls in certain parts of India. However, they are not in-depth and elaborate studies. The present study highlights issues such as how the parents pledge their children to hotel owners and how they get accustomed to certain unhealthy practices such as smoking, drinking, taking drugs and intoxicants, reading pornographic books, seeing blue films and establishing contacts with sex-workers.

OBJECTIVES OF THE STUDY

In view of these observations, the following objectives have been formulated carefully:

1. To highlight the socio-demographic profile of child labour in selected hotels.
2. To examine their working conditions.
3. To evaluate to what extent they are exploited by the hotel owners, managers, and masters.
4. To understand their health problems in their occupational context.
5. To study their unhealthy practices in the hotels.

FIELD OF STUDY

In order to fulfil these objectives, the district of Tirunelveli in Tamil Nadu was selected for this study. This district is located in the south-eastern part of Tamil Nadu. It is triangular in shape. It lies between 8°05′ and 9°30′ of the northern latitude and 77°30′ and 78°25′ of the eastern latitude. The district is bounded by Virudhunagar district in the north and Tuticorin district in the east and Quilon district (Kerala) in the west and Kanyakumari district in the south. It is located at about 610 km south of Chennai, the capital of the state of Tamil Nadu. According to the topography of the district, it can be divided into three regions. The northern part consists of black soil mostly depending on seasonal rain for agriculture. The normal annual rainfall is 814 mm. The central part of the district is irrigated by the river Thambraparani flowing from the Western Ghats and the southern part is a red loamy area.

Tirunelveli district has been divided into three divisions for administrative purposes - Tirunelveli, Cheranmahadevi and Tenkasi. It is divided into nine taluks, nine municipalities and nineteen panchayat unions. This district has 435 village panchayats and 568 revenue villages. The total geographical area is 6823 sq.km (ha). The total population of the district is 2,801,194 comprising 1,372,082 males (48.98%) and 1,439,112 female (51.37%). According to the 2001 census, the total literate population is 1,917,338 (68.45%) comprising 1,041,964 males (37.19%) and 875,274 females (31.25%). The total urban literate population is 968,844 (34.58%), whereas the total number of their rural counterparts is 948,394 (33.85%). There are several industries in this district such as Engineering (25), Textile (75), Mining (6), Forest-based (35), Chemical (5), Animal Husbandry (10), Agro-based (25), and Aerated Drinks (4). The total cropped area of Tirunelveli district is 2,12,889 ha. In the district, two perennial rivers, six seasonal rivers, Thambaraparani Anaicuts and 16 Chithar Anaicuts form the irrigational sources for agricultural and electricity purposes. There were 251,257 cultivators in the district according to the 2001 Census. It comprises of 10.04 per cent of the total population. There were 228,915 (13.39%) rural cultivators, and their counterparts from the urban area were 22,342 (2.81%). The total agricultural labourers numbered 349,096. It represents 13.95 per cent of the total population. The rural agricultural labour population is 306,481 (17.93%) and their counterparts from the urban area number 42,588 (5.36%). The main workers number 110643, representing 44.20 per cent of the total population· There are 74,326 marginal workers who account for 2.97 per cent of the total population. Non-workers in Tirunelveli District are 1,321,463, i.e., 52.81 per cent of the total population. In the rural area, there are 826,227 (48.35%) workers and in the urban area there are 495,236 (62.43%) workers. It is also important to highlight the forced child labour prevalent in this district.

In the district, people do not get agricultural work all over the year. Only during the seasonal time, village people get agricultural work. The cultivators and landowners whose lands are on the riverbed take one or two harvests per year. During the non-seasonal months, the agricultural workers remain unemployed or underemployed. Therefore, for agricultural workers, the home-based *beedi* industry and match industry are suitable alternative professions. Problems such as poverty, unemployment, illiteracy, and ignorance force the parents to send their children to hotels for work, of course among other avenues of work and livelihood.

Table 3.1: Proportion of Working Children of 5-15 Years in Tirunelveli District, 2000

No.	Area	Beedi Workers			Other Workers		
	Municipality	Boys	Girls	Total	Boys	Girls	Total
1.	Tirunelveli	1.39	61.33	36.95	98.61	38.67	63.05
2.	Palayamkottai	0.43	35.93	20.95	99.57	64.07	79.81
3.	Melapalayam	33.45	89.16	71.50	66.55	10.84	28.80
4.	Sankarankoil	0.20	7.68	4.63	99.80	92.32	95.37
5.	Tenkasi	6.13	57.42	37.08	93.87	42.58	62.92
6.	Kadayanallur	2.58	45.71	27.08	97.42	54.29	62.92
7.	Shenkottai	0.67	84.05	53.45	99.33	15.95	46.55
8.	Puliyankudi	24.19	66.90	49.59	75.81	33.10	50.41
	Blocks						
1.	Palayamkottai	1.46	40.66	28.58	98.54	59.34	71.42
2.	Manur	1.23	74.89	47.42	98.77	25.11	52.58
3.	Sankarankoil	-	7.92	4.28	100.00	92.08	95.72
4.	Cheranmahadevi	9.25	24.46	17.54	90.75	75.54	82.46
5.	Pappakudi	0.27	64.48	43.14	99.73	35.52	56.86
6.	Ambasamudram	28.76	56.34	44.36	71.24	43.66	55.64
7.	Kadayam		74.39	44.82	100.00	25.16	55.18
8.	Nanguneri		62.73	33.83	100.00	37.27	66.17
9.	Kalakkadu	22.81	73.63	48.90	77.19	26.37	51.10
10.	Valliyoor	1.57	45.12	24.35	98.43	54.88	76.65
11.	Rathapuram	1.57	45.12	24.35	98.43	54.88	75.65
12.	Alangulam	24.39	9.78	78.53	75.61	10.22	21.47
13.	Keelapavoor	5.12	93.28	62.76	94.88	6.72	37.24
14.	Tenkasi		72.66	49.50	100.00	28.34	50.41
15.	Shenkottai	0.11	75.96	51.48	99.89	24.04	48.52
16.	Kadayanallur	0.57	67.54	40.45	99.43	32.46	59.55
17.	Vasudevanallur	1.66	41.18	26.69	98.34	58.82	73.31
	All together	**5.49**	**56.26**	**37.10**	**94.57**	**43.74**	**62.90**

Source: District Collectorate, Tirunelveli.

Table 3.1 shows that the proportion of workers engaged in beedi making is significantly high in Melapalayam and Shenkottai Municipalities of Tirunelveli District, they have been famous for that work for several decades. In Puliyankudi Municipality also the *beedi* making has been one of the main occupations for a sizable section of families. That is perhaps the reason only a majority of children are engaged in this work.

Similarly, the *beedi* making is widely prevalent in Pappakudi, Kalakkadu, Alangulam, Keelapavoor and Tenkasi Blocks of Tirunelveli District. This is supported by the significant proportion of children engaged in this work in those blocks.

However, in 2001, 1406 male children were employed in 1232 hotels situated in nine taluk headquarters of Tirunelveli district. Since the present study included the children employed in hotels, they were selected by using sampling procedure.

SELECTION OF RESPONDENTS

A sample of not less than one-third of child workers were drawn from each big hotel in nine taluks for investigation. Thus, a sample of 475 child workers was selected on the basis of simple random sampling by the Tippets Table.

Table 3.2: Taluk-wise Big Hotels in Tirunelveli District During 2001

Sl. No.	Taluk-wise location of hotels	A, B, and C Grade Hotels	Big Hotels (A and B Grade only)	Total population of Child labour in A, B and C Grade Hotels	Total Sample of child labour
1.	Tirunelveli	482	30	505	150
2.	Palayamkottai	166	7	125	35
3.	Ambasamudram	103	12	98	60
4.	Nanguneri	23	9	88	45
5.	Tenkasi	125	17	242	85
6.	Shenkottai	117	6	102	30
7.	Sankarankoil	129	7	112	35
8.	Sivagiri	15	4	48	20
9.	Rathapuram	72	3	86	15
	Total	**1232**	**95**	**1406**	**475**

Source: Commercial Tax Office, Municipalities, Town Panchayat Office, and Tirunelveli.

SAMPLING FRAME

Stage 1. All the Taluk headquarters of Tirunelveli district were selected for the study.

Stage 2. From each taluk headquarters all big hotels were covered for the study.

Stage 3. From each big hotel, not less than one-third of the working children were selected as samples on the basis of simple random sampling.

Stage 4. A sample of 475 children selected for the study were surveyed.

TOOLS OF DATA COLLECTION

An interview schedule was chosen as the tool to collect data because the respondents, by and large, belong to the low educational category and were found to be totally incapable of responding to a questionnaire. Before going in for data collection, the author conducted a pilot study in three areas. For this, a sample of 30 child workers were selected at random from Tirunelveli (10), Tenkasi (10) and Sankarankoil (10). Based on this study, the interview schedule was restructured with some additions and omissions.

The modified interview schedule was administered to collect data from the respondents. The data collected for the present study were primary in nature. The questions in this section were based on the objectives of the study. The interview schedule mainly focused on age, nativity, educational qualification, religion, community, migration, shifting from one hotel to another, years of experience in hotel job, order of birth, family particulars, awareness about their work details, exploitation, health problems and recreation. Since the researcher belongs to Tirunelveli district, he is very familiar with the nine taluks. Another reason is that the researcher has already worked as Research Investigator in two major projects on child labour in beedi industry. Therefore, he could closely observe the nature and behaviour of the working children.

With this experience, the researcher conducted the interviews with the child workers in hotels after obtaining the permission of their employers. It is important to mention that three hotel owners are well known to the researcher and therefore his task of conducting the study in those hotels was easy. He was able to collect the necessary and relevant information from the children. He had to stay in several hotels for a day or two paying rent. While doing so, he used to ask room boys quite often to bring him some eatables or hot drinks. He made use of such occasions to interview them after giving them tips. He was particular in interviewing different room boys on different occasions. Some times, he was permitted to meet the children in their rest rooms, which are situated mostly on the first floor of the hotels. Mostly the data were collected from the respondents while interviewing them in the workers' rest room after their work was over. Sometimes, it was done in the hotel room as the researcher was denied permission to meet the children in their rest room. The completed schedules were verified immediately after the interview in order to avoid any lapse. However, the researcher revisited certain hotels in order to fill in the gaps of information. The survey was conducted in the eleven months from January to November 2000.

OBSERVATION

The observation method was applied to collect certain relevant data in order to facilitate the study. Though necessary data were collected by careful administration of the interview schedule, the author could learn the working conditions and the interaction between the working children and their masters, owners and co-workers through the observation method. The pressure on the working children imposed by the hotel owners and co-employees, the seriousness of the health problems of the working children, legal measures and the like were observed by the researcher. In this work, certain pertinent information gained by the observation method has been included in appropriate places. The author being an inhabitant of the study area, his first hand knowledge of the child workers in hotels and his observation of several activities of these workers in the area were also useful to the study. However, the assistance of other persons such as village level workers was also sought to establish rapport with the hotel owners and managers wherever possible and necessary.

CASE STUDY

In addition to these tools of data collection, the case study method was also used to collect detailed information from experienced child workers, hotel owners and co-employees who were capable of giving certain interesting and relevant information. This has, directly or indirectly, supported certain observations made in the field. In addition to this, a few richly experienced children were also interviewed and treated as resourceful respondents for case studies, because they were knowledgeable and spontaneous. This qualitative information has enriched the study in several ways.

DATA PROCESSING AND ANALYSIS

After the fieldwork, the filled up schedules were carefully scrutinised and edited in order to ensure accuracy, consistency and completeness. The researcher did the coding of data manually. The classification, tabulation and further statistical treatment of data were done through computer. The data were qualitative and quantitative in nature. Qualitative data were converted into percentages. Most of the analyses were based on the responses presented in the form of frequency tables. The data thus tabulated were systematically processed and interpreted on the basis of the objectives formulated. These interpretations were carefully studied and necessary conclusions were drawn. The data were analysed by appropriate statistical tests, such as average, chi-square and analysis of variance.

COLLECTION OF SECONDARY DATA

In addition to the data collected from the child workers, hotel owners masters and co-workers from the sample hotels, relevant information was also collected through a series of discussions with local NGOs, especially the Navajeevan Trust and the Tirunelveli Service Society at Tirunelveli and the Peace Trust of Dindigul. Information regarding types of hotels, sanitary conditions in the hotels, was collected from the Income-tax Office, Tirunelveli, the Labour Welfare Office, Tirunelveli, and the Sanitary Inspectorate, at the Tirunelveli Corporation.

LIMITATIONS OF THE STUDY

Every research study suffers from certain constraints and limitations. The present study has the following constraints and limitations:

This work has limited its scope to the study of *Child Labour in the Hotel Industry*. It is limited to nine taluks of the district where there is high concentration of big hotels and child labour. It has also limited the study to full time (non-schooling) child workers in this industry. It has limited the number of the samples to 475 in order to facilitate an in-depth study.

Despite these limitations, the study attempts to throw some light on the objectives formulated. Based on the findings, the study has brought valid inferences and finally provided concrete suggestions.

SCHEME OF PRESENT RESEARCH REPORT

The present study has branched off into ten chapters as given below:

The first chapter deals with child labour as a problem, the concept and definition of this problem, its magnitude, causes and child labour constitution and legislation.

Chapter 2 entitled "Review of Literature" presents a review of various related works and the uniqueness of the present study.

Chapter 3 discusses the methodological aspects like the objectives, sample design, tools of data collection, collection of secondary data, data processing and analysis, limitations of the study, and the scheme of the present research report.

Chapter 4 explains the Profile of Hotel Industry in Tirunelveli district. It also deals with the definition of hotels, their characteristic features and functions and important tourist places. It also deals with details concerning big hotels taluk-wise and their turnover and the role of employers and employees in hotels.

Chapter 5 describes the socio-economic profile of working children. It presents the variations among the child workers in respect of variables such as employment in area-wise distribution of hotels, employment in hotels located in tourist and non-tourist places, age, religion, community, nativity, educational qualification, experience in hotel jobs, migration from one hotel to another hotel, individual income, family income, parents' education, and size of family.

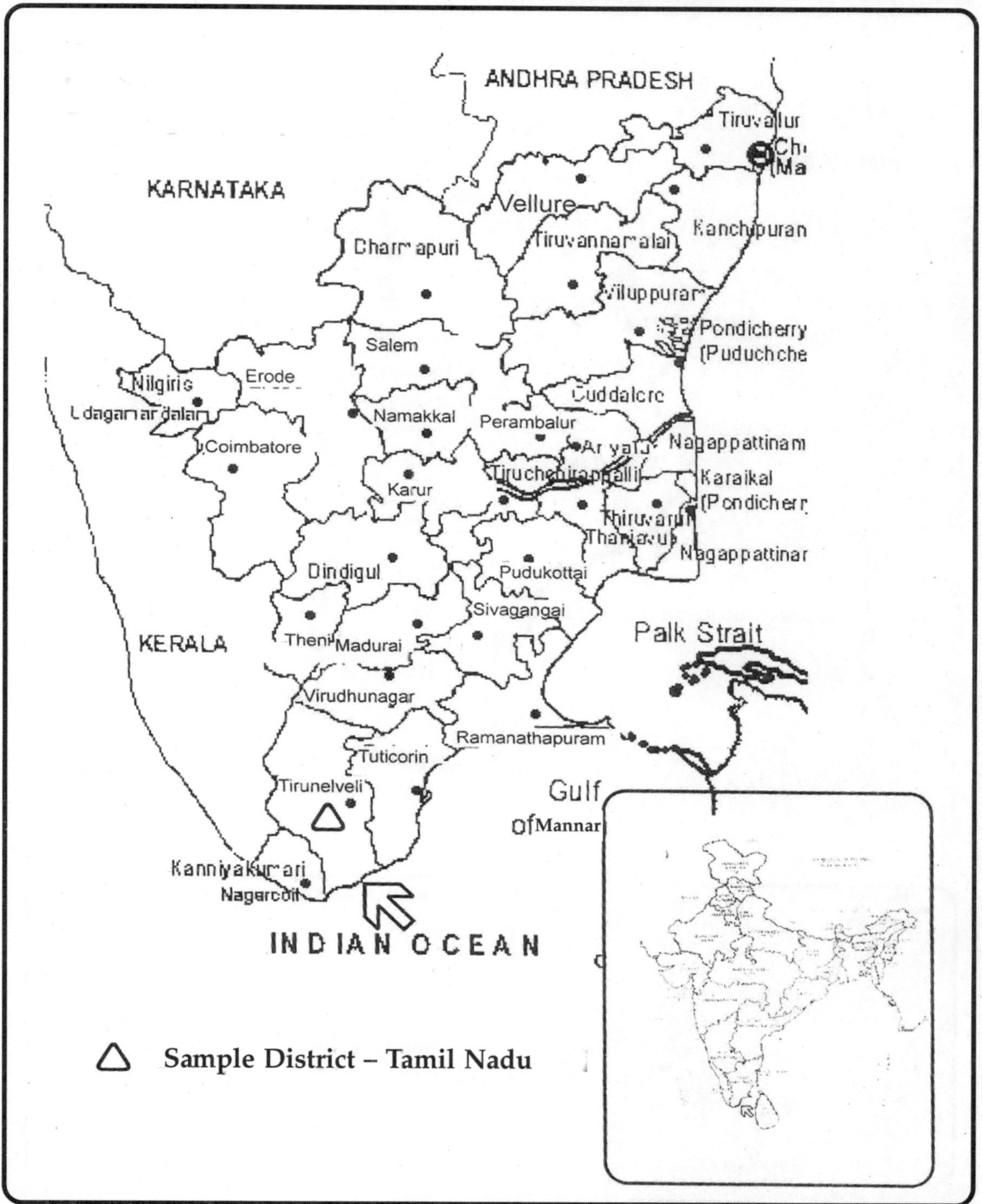

Fig. 3.1: Tamil Nadu Administrative division 2001

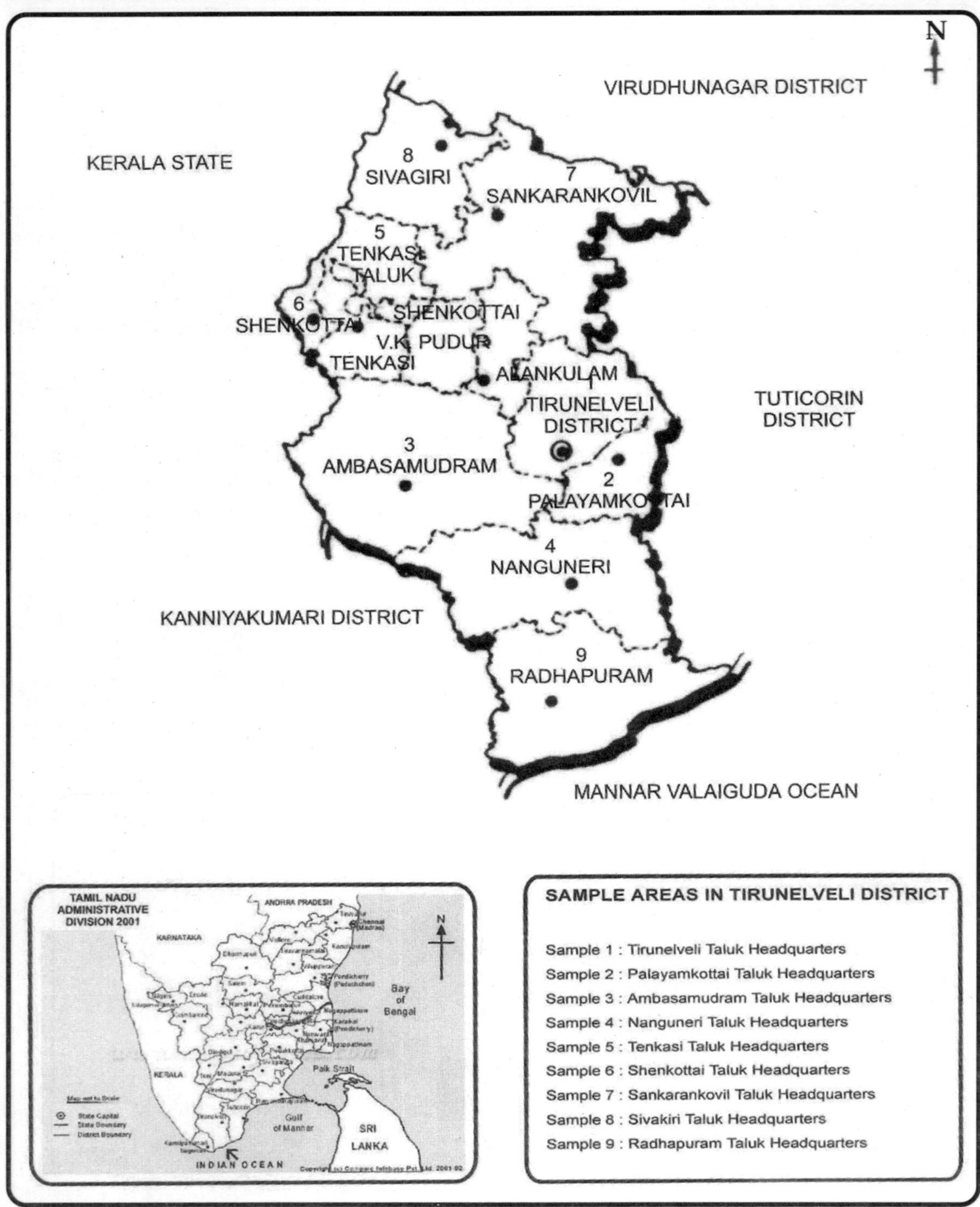

Fig. 3.2: Tirunelveli District Map

Chapter 6 discusses the workers' awareness of work details in hotel jobs. It also discusses the children's liking and dislike of hotel jobs and the reasons thereof.

Chapter 7 analyses the working conditions and exploitation of child labour. It also discusses the working conditions including the duration of work, workload, extra work and wage. Then it explains how they are exploited and punished by the management, employees and adult co-workers. It also deals with the willingness of parents to pledge their children, and with the sexual abuse these workers are subjected to.

Chapter 8 focuses on health problems and presents a general appraisal of diseases affecting the children, their food habits and the physical atmosphere.

Chapter 9 accounts for the unhealthy practices of child labour, especially their habits of smoking, drinking, using of drugs and other intoxicants, reading pornographic books, seeing blue films, masturbating and sex with sex-workers.

The last chapter gives a critical account of the major findings of the study and also provides suitable suggestions and recommendations to tackle the problem of child labour.

CHAPTER 4

Profile of Hotels in Tirunelveli District

Before studying child labour in hotels, it is important to be informed about the hotels and the employment of children in them. Hotels have long been an important element in the economy of several countries. They are directly linked to, and are an integral part of, various economic activities. In particular, the relationship between tourism and hotels is very crucial to understanding the role of hotels in the process of the economic development of a state.

The *Encyclopedia Americana* (1972) defines a hotel as follows:

> a building for public accommodation that furnishes lodging and usually provides meals, beverages, and many personal services. Hotels are often after entertainment; rooms for meetings, banquets, or bills; shops of various kinds; commodious lobbies; and cafes, bars, and restaurants. A small hotel is often called an inn. A motel is one that provides parking space in or adjacent to building for guests' automobiles. Hotels are generally grouped into four main categories: commercial or transient hotels, resort hotels, residential hotles, and motels or motor hotels.[1]

According to *Webster's Dictionary* (1989), a hotel is "a commercial establishment offering lodging to transients and often having restaurants, public rooms, shops, etc. that are available to the general public."[2]

A hotel has a wide range of business activities. Its functions can be grouped into four:

(i) providing living accommodation;

(ii) supplying food, drinks, etc. for immediate consumption;

(iii) providing transportation, recreational and entertainment facilities;

(iv) any other functions incidental or ancillary to any of these activities.

A hotel is a fixed, immobile installation. Its product cannot move to the consumers. It is unique in that the consumers enter into the hotel and consume the food products within it. But a factory or plant never permits the customer to enter its boundary, except as visitors. Hotels are categorised in terms of stars according to the size and facilities available. A hotel is multidimensional in its operations and versatile in its objectives. It constitutes an important sector of the tourist infrastructure of the economy. It can be an individual concern or an international business. It can employ family members of its owner or can create thousands of jobs. It can be a small or a multi-million enterprise. It can be a labour-intensive as well as capital-intensive industry.

HOTEL INDUSTRY AND ECONOMY

The contribution of any sector of economic activity to the economic system is measured by the value of its output or *value added*. In hotel industry, "value added" refers to the sales minus the cost of bought-in goods and services. It includes the payments to the factors of production such as wages, salaries, depreciation and profits and excludes all non-labour and non-capital purchases and stock appreciations.

In the context of the economy, two features of the hotel industry are worth emphasizing:

(i) each unit of the demand for hotel products generates a high percentage of value added within the industry; and

(ii) each unit of value added produced by this industry demands a higher input of labour and raw materials.[3]

These two inter-related features clearly reflect the linkage effect and nature of hotles as a service industry, which is relatively labour intensive.

HOTEL INDUSTRY AND TOURISM

The enormous increase in tourism in the twentieth century has caused the hotel business to outgrow national boundaries and become global in character. Hotel industry is indispensable for the success of tourism. It is said that *no hotel no tourism.* The relationship between hotels and tourism can be expressed in two ways:

(i) hotel industry provides basic ingredients of the total supply of the tourism sector; and

(ii) its bulk of business demand comes from tourism.

Thus, the hotel industry and tourism reinforce each other and are complementry to each other. They together make substantial contribution to economic development. Hotel industry plays a pivotal role in the development of tourism. It has tremendous potentialities for earning foreign exchange, yielding tax revenues, providing employment, promoting the growth of ancillary industrial activities and overall development of industrially backward regions through its linkage effects. In Tamil Nadu, there are beautiful tourist places which attract people from across India and also across the world.

The Tourism Corporation of Tamil Nadu has expanded its activities with the opening of hotels and restaurants. There has been an improvement in the performance of the hotel division during the year 1991-92 with a turnover of Rs. 800 lakhs. The Tourism Corporation has earned a foreign exchange of Rs. 9.9 crores during 1999-2000, and there was no loss of foreign exchange.[4] The Corporation also spends over Rs. 20 lakhs every year on advertising and publicity. The official estimates show that 1.86 million tourists visited India in 1992 as compared to 1.7 million in 1991. South India experienced a healthy growth in foreign tourist traffic up to 14 per cent in 1992. Kerala, Tamil Nadu and Karnataka recorded the largest growth in tourist arrivals. The Government of India has now consciously decided to promote the "Sunny South" as a Tourism destination.[5]

Tourist arrivals in Tamil Nadu registered an increase of 15 per cent in 1991 over 1990. The Tamil Nadu Tourism Industry is already perking up to cater to the rise in both foreign and domestic tourist traffic. Over Rs. 80 crores investment in 25 hotels was cleared in 1991-92 and about 2500 rooms will finally be added.

Table 4.1 shows that in 2001, 7.37 lakhs foreign tourists and 238.12 lakhs domestic tourists visited Tamil Nadu. So most of the hotel owners are concentrating on hotel business in tourist places. They earning is high within a short period.

Table 4.1: Tourist Arrivals in Tamil Nadu

Year	Foreign Tourists (in Lakhs)	Domestic Tourists (in Lakhs)
1987*	3.19	62.36
1988*	3.62	62.32
1989*	3.69	62.71
1990*	3.09	97.58
1991*	3.34	112.27
2001**	7.73	238.12

Source: * *Economic Times*-Data Bank-1993.

** M.R. Thangamani, *Tourism: An Introduction*, *op.cit.*, p. 398.

In Tirunelveli District, there are a number of tourist places streen all over the district. They attract tourists from all over the State and also from other States and abroad. The following Table shows the particulars about the tourist places.

Table 4.2 discloses that Tirunelveli occupies the first place in terms of number of hotels. Tenkasi is in the second place and Courtallam is in the third place in this regard. For the present study the hotels are classified into three categories:

(i) hotels with boarding only (B grade);

(ii) hotels with boarding and lodging (A grade);

(iii) hotels with lodging and canteen (B1 grade).

Table 4.2: Important Tourist Places and Hotels in Tirunelveli District, 2000

Sl. No.	Tourist Places	Famous for	Kilometres from Tirunelveli	Total number of A,B, and C Grade Hotels
1.	Courtallam* (near Shenkottai)	Water falls	58	187
2.	Tenkasi*	Temple	53	205
3.	Papanasam (near Ambasamudram)	Falls and Dam	48	62
4.	Mundanthurai	Wildlife	53	13
5.	Kalakadu	Wildlife Sanctuary	40	24
6.	Thirukarankudi	Temple	47	12
7.	Kunthankulam	Birds	32	17
8.	Athankari Pallivasal	Darha	78	19
9.	Tirunelveli	Temple	2	282
10.	Krishnapuram (near Palayamkottai)	Temple	13	66
11.	Moondradaippu	Bird Sanctuary	15	12

Note: * Tenkasi and Courtallam are nearby places. (5 kilometres apart from each other).

Sources: Department of Tourism, Chennai, and Tirunelveli Corporation Office.

The first category of Type I hotels (B Grade) consists of dining section only where the consumers are served breakfast, lunch and supper. The second category of Type II hotels (A Grade) consists of a spacious dining hall where a variety of breakfast, lunch and supper is provided. It is normally busy between the early hours of the morning and late night. In addition to this, it consists of different types of rooms for accommodation. The occupants are accustomed to hotel service and have the facility of dining in their rooms. The third category of Type III hotels (B1 Grade) provide lodging facility only. However, a canteen on the premises supplies limited items of eatables and hot drinks like coffee and tea all the time.

Table 4.3 shows that the number of big hotels is higher in Tirunelveli than in other places. However, Tenkasi and Ambhasamudram take the second and the third ranks respectively in this regard. The annual turn over increases with the increase of hotels in the selected places.

Table 4.3: Taluk-wise Big Hotels and Hotel Turnover in Rupees in Tirunelveli District, 2000

Sl.No	Taluks	No. of Big Hotels	Total Turnover from 1999-2000 (Rs.)
1.	Tirunelveli	30	2,88,14,943
2.	Tenkasi	17	42,47,081
3.	Ambasamudram	12	29,42,704
4.	Nanguneri	9	16,39,575
5.	Sankarankovil	7	7,41,738
6.	Palayamkottai	7	35,96,644
7.	Shenkottai	6	5,52,512
8.	Sivagiri	4	4,31,526
9.	Rathapuram	3	3,20,468
	Total (Nine Taluks)	**95**	**4,32,87,191**

Source: Commercial Tax Office, Tirunelveli.

Besides the B grade hotels (Type I – Boarding only) in Tiurnelveli District, there are a few A grade hotels (Type II – Boarding and Lodging) situated in the Tiurnelveli Junction area. Especially, B grade hotels (Type I) are numerous in Town Panchayat and Municipality areas. In this district, hoteliers belonging to the Reddiar and Pillai communities (which are characterized as Forward Communities) run most of the A and B grade hotels.

In addition to these types of hotel, there are hundreds of stalls on road sides providing tea or coffee and tiffin items. Many such stalls are located at bus stands, railway station areas, marketing and commercial centres. Mostly Muslims (Backward Caste) own these stalls. If they are not the owners, they are the stall masters because they are specialists in preparing certain non-vegetarian food items greatly relished by the labourers.

A few A grade hotel owners (Type II) in Tirunelveli area have branch hotels within the area. They are styled as open restaurants, garden restaurants and fast food restaurants. They have also started canteens, sweets and bakery stalls.

ROLE OF EMPLOYERS AND EMPLOYEES IN HOTELS OWNER

In some hotels, especially in Type I hotels, the owners exercise complete control over their hotels and directly supervise every activity. For instance, they give orders to the masters, assistant cooks and kitchen assistants regarding the menu and preparation and taste of various food items. They also have direct contact with grocery shops and vegetable shops. In most of the hotels the owners have separate rooms to look after day to day income and expenditure. Nevertheless, in most of the Types I, II and III hotels, the owners entrust the resposibility of managing several activities with the managers.

MANAGER

In hotels, the managers play a crucial role because they coordinate the work of all the other hotel employees. They see to the needs of customers. They work out viable strategies to get more profit as the owners are, by and large, profit-oriented. Their salary ranges between Rs. 3,000 and 7,000 per month.. They are provided with allowances for housing and two wheelers. They are assisted by an assistant manager, especially in big hotels. The assistant manager is assisted by two supervisors, one for the morning shift and another for the evening shift. The manager is in charge of clearing the electric bill, telephone bill and water charge. Most of the managers stay in the rooms exclusively allotted to them in the hotels. Occasionally they visit their families.

SUPERVISOR

The role of the supervisors is to give instructions to the servers and the children attending to the various jobs and also to see that they carry out their work sincerely and neatly. Their salary ranges from Rs. 2,000 to 5,000 per month. Most of the supervisors stay in the rest room of the hotels along with the masters and other employees. They visit their families once in a while.

MASTER

The term *Master* generally refers to the head cook who is responsible for preparing the various food items. He is assisted by four or five cooks in the kitchen. He is keen on maintaining the quality and taste of the food items. Every day he prepares the menu for tiffin and lunch in consultation with his owner and manager. His salary ranges from Rs. 5,000 to 7,000.

SUPPLIER

The role of suppliers is to serve the customers, that is, to supply without delay the available food items required by the customers. Normally they are adult. Their salary ranges from Rs. 750-2,000 per month. In addition to this, they get tips from the customers which might amount to Rs. 30-50 per day. Most of them stay in the rest rooms of the hotels along with the other employees.

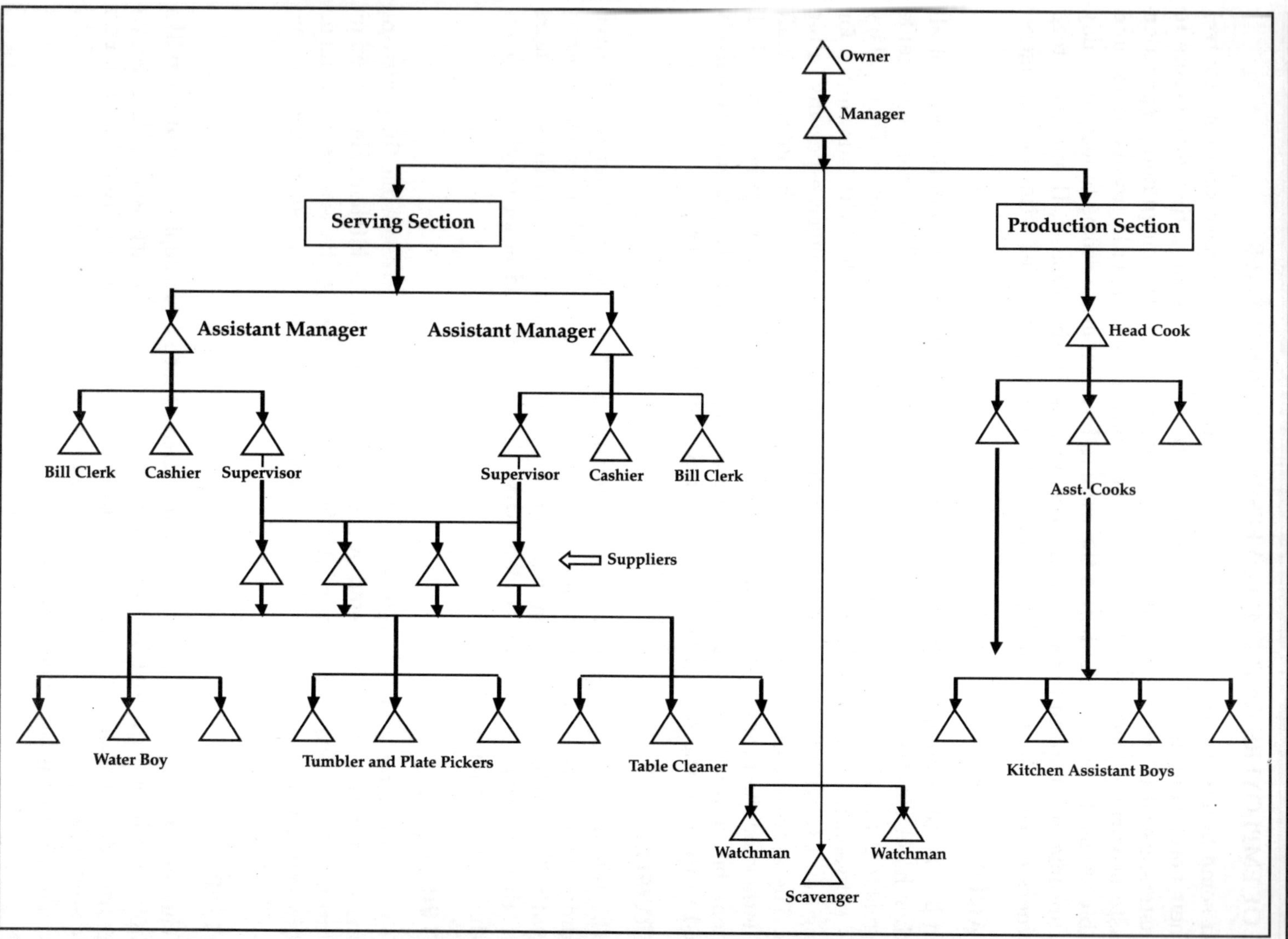

Fig. 4.1: TYPE – I Hotel (Board only) Occupational Structure

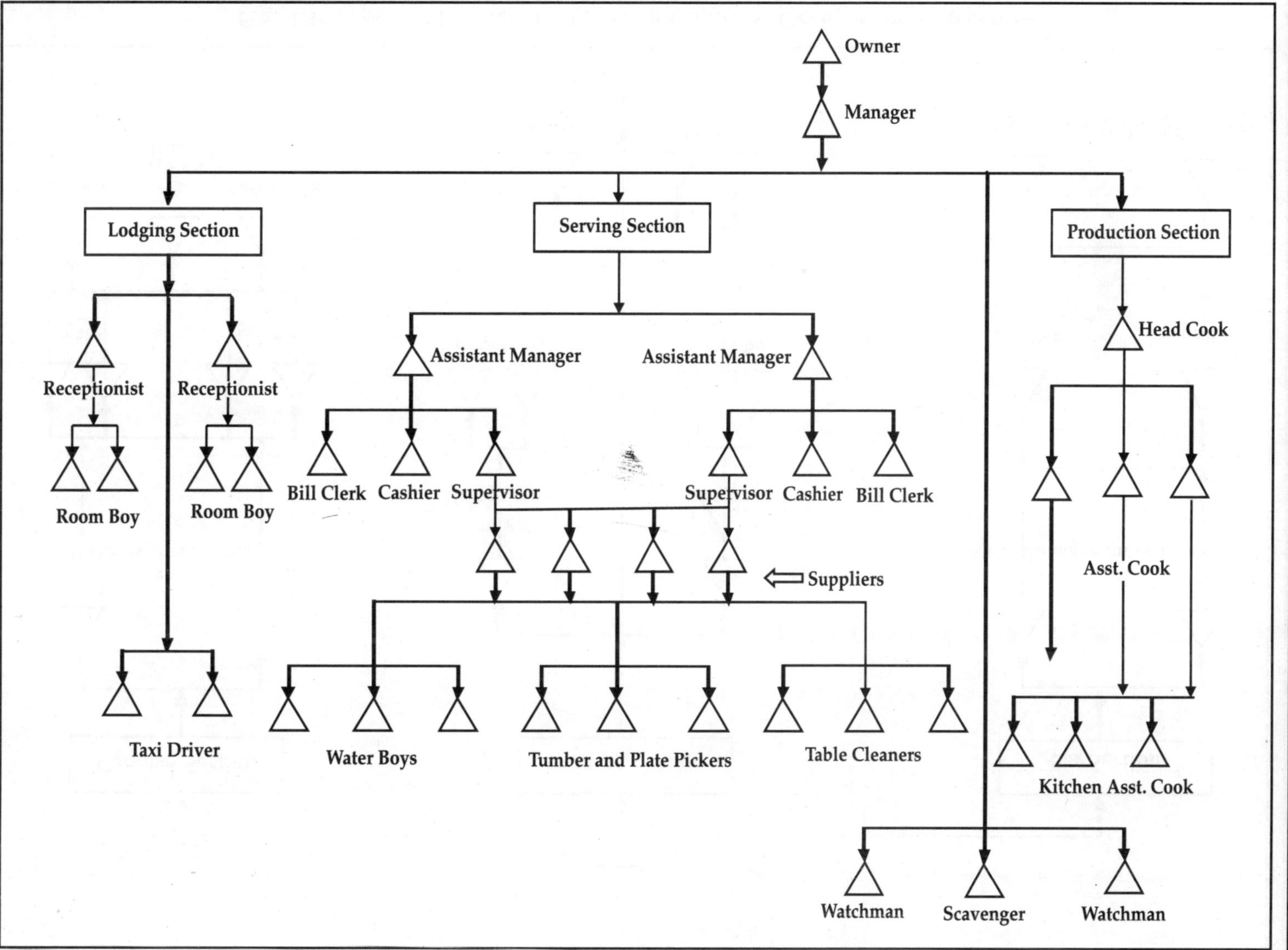

Fig. 4.2: Type – II Hotel (Board and Lodging) Occupational Structure

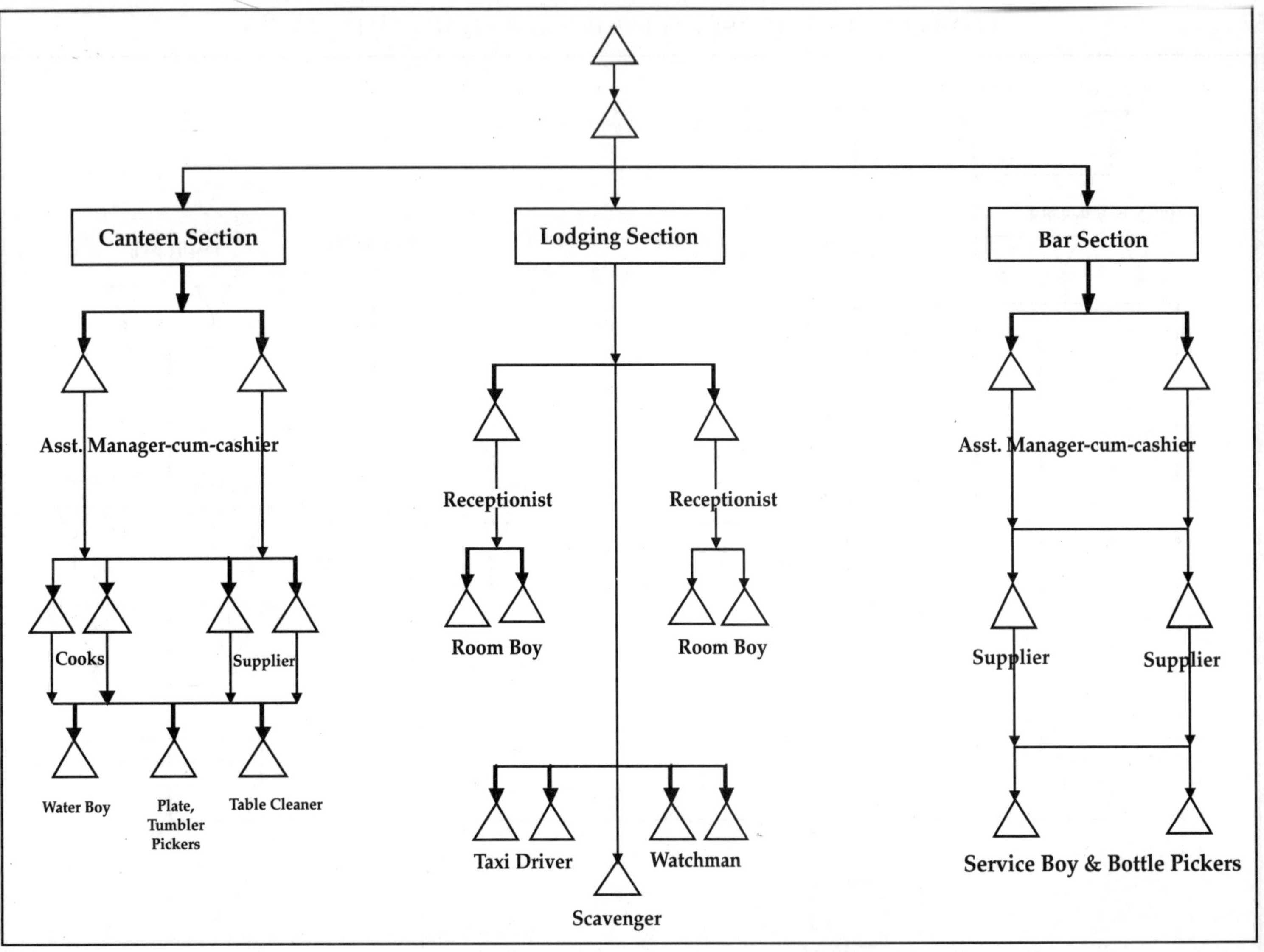

Fig. 4.3: Type – III Hotel (Lodge with Canteen) Occupational Structure

PHYSICAL CONDITION OF KITCHEN AND DINING HALL

In most of the hotels, the production units (kitchen and store room) are not spacious and ventilated. The lights are not bright. The kitchen rooms are littered with vegetable waste and the raw materials which are left over after preparing the food items. Moreover, fumes and smoke cause breathing trouble and suffocation. The unused vegetables in the store room rot causing an unpleasant smell. One may find that there is spill of oil and water all over the kitchens and because of this, the floor is slippery. On the contrary, in most of the hotels, the dining halls are kept clean in order to please the customers.

REFERENCES

1. *Encyclopedia Americana*, 1972 ed., S.V. Hotel.
2. *Webster's Unabridged Dictionary of the English Language*, 1989 ed., S.V. Hotel.
3. Pragati Mohanty, *Hotel Industry and Tourism in India* (New Delhi: Ashish Publishing House, 1994), p. 8.
4. M.R. Thangamani, *Tourism: An Introduction* (Karur: Kongu, 2002), p. 392.
5. N. Rajalakshmi, *Tamil Nadu Economy* (Mumbai: Business Publication, INC, 1999) p. 207.

CHAPTER 5

Socio-economic Profile of Child Labour in Hotels

The present study endeavours to ascertain the variations among the child workers with respect to variables such as area-wise hotels and location-wise hotels (tourist place and non-tourist place hotels), age, religion, community, education, rural-urban background, size of family, family income, individual income, experience, types of job and changing the place of work.

Out of the total sample of 475 child workers taken for this study, 31.6 per cent (150) are from Tirunelveli District Headquarters, 18.0 per cent (85) are from Tenkasi town area, 12.6 per cent (60) from Ambasamudram town area, 9.5 per cent (45) from Nanguneri Taluk Headquarters, 7.4 per cent (35) from Palayamkottai Taluk Headquarters, 6.3 per cent (30) from Senkottai Taluk Headquarters, 7.4 per cent (35) from Sankarenkovil Taluk Headquarters, 4.2 per cent (20) from Sivagiri Taluk Headquarters and 3.2 per cent (15) from Rathapuram Taluk Headquarters.

HOTEL AREA-WISE DISTRIBUTION OF CHILDREN

It is important to understand the area-wise distribution of children in terms of those in hotels located in the Corporation limits, the Municipal limits and the Town Panchayat limits. Especially in the Corporation limits, hotel business is more flourishing and profitable as compared to Municipal and Town panchayat limits. Table 5.1 shows the distribution of children among the types of hotels and their area-wise location.

Table 5.1 (Fig. 5.1) disclose that out of 475 working children, nearly half (48.6%) work in hotels located in the Corporation limits, and over one-fourth (27.3%) are employed in hotels located in the Municipal limits. Over one-fifth (24.0%) work in hotels situated in Town Panchayat limits.

It is found that the working children prefer to work in big hotels for the reason that they get more facilities, salary and tips or *beta* than those in other hotels. In this regard, next to the big hotels they opt for similar hotels in the Municipal and Panchayat limits. Out of 231 children working in the Corporation limits, 44.1 per cent are in Type I hotels, 29.0 per cent in Type II hotels and over one-fourth (26.8 per cent) in Type III hotels (Table 5.1). Out of 130 hotels situated in the Municipal limit, Type I hotels absorb over a third of the children (39.2%), nearly one-third (32.3%) are absorbed by Type II hotels and over one-fourth (28.4%) of the children are in Type III hotels. There are 114 hotels within the Town Panchayat limits. Two-thirds of the children working in these hotels (66.6 per cent) work in Type I hotels, 10.5 per cent in Type II hotels, and over one-fifth (22.8 per cent) in Type III hotels. Of the three types of hotel, it is found that Type I hotels outnumber Types II and III hotels irrespective of the area in which they are located. The reason is that as compared to Type II and Type III hotels, Type I hotels involve less investment and less maintenance.

Table 5.1: Respondents by Area and types of hotel

Area-wise distribution of hotels	Types of hotel			Total
	Type I Hotel (Boarding only)	Type II Hotel (Boarding and Lodging)	Type III Hotel (Lodging with Canteen)	
Corporation Limit*	102 (44.1)	67 (29.0)	62 (26.8)	231 (48.6)
Municipal Limit**	51 (39.2)	42 (32.3)	37 (28.4)	130 (27.3)
Town Punchayat Limit***	76 (66.6)	12 (10.5)	26 (22.8)	114 (24.0)
Total	**229** **(48.2)**	**121** **(25.4)**	**125** **(26.3)**	**475** **(100)**

Note: * Tirunelveli Corporation limit includes the Taluk headquarters of Tirunelveli District, viz., Tirunelveli and Palayamkottai Taluk. A total of 37 big hotels of type I, II and III are located in this Taluk headquarters.

** Municipal limit includes three Taluk headquarters of Tirunelveli District, viz., Senkottai, Tenkasi, Sankarankovil Taluks. A total of 30 big hotels of type I, II and III are located in these three Taluk head-quarters.

*** Town Panchayat limit includes four Taluk headquarters of Tirunelveli District, viz, Ambasamudram, Nanguneri, Sivagiri, Rathapuram Taluks. A total of 28 big hotels of type I,II and III are located in these four Taluk headquarters.

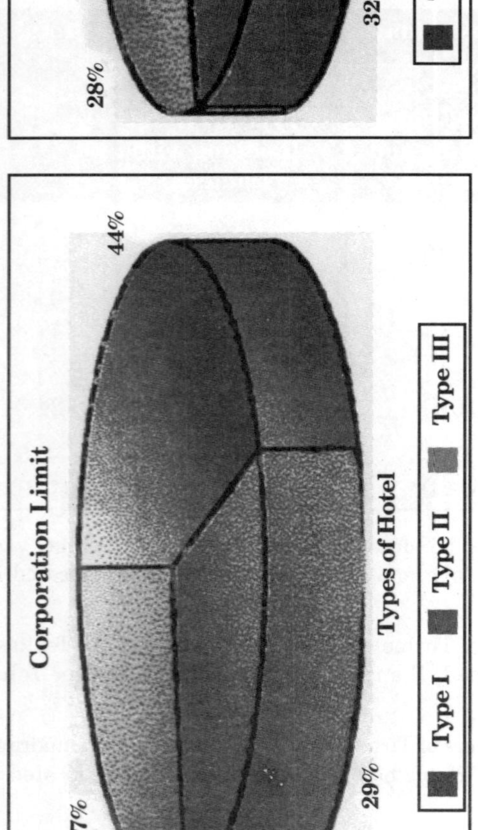

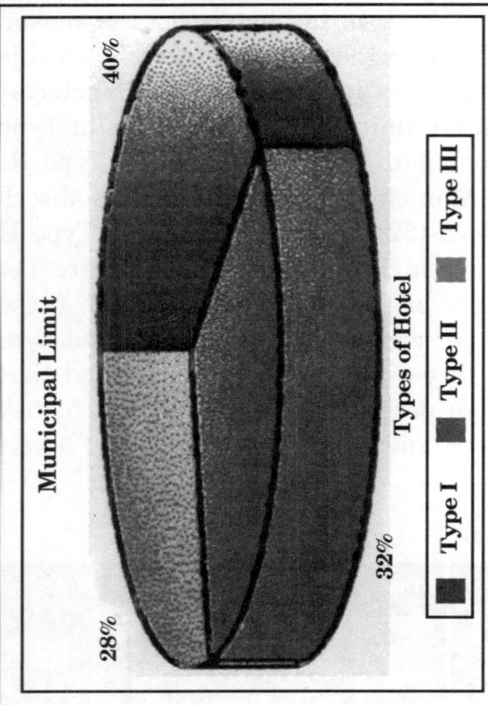

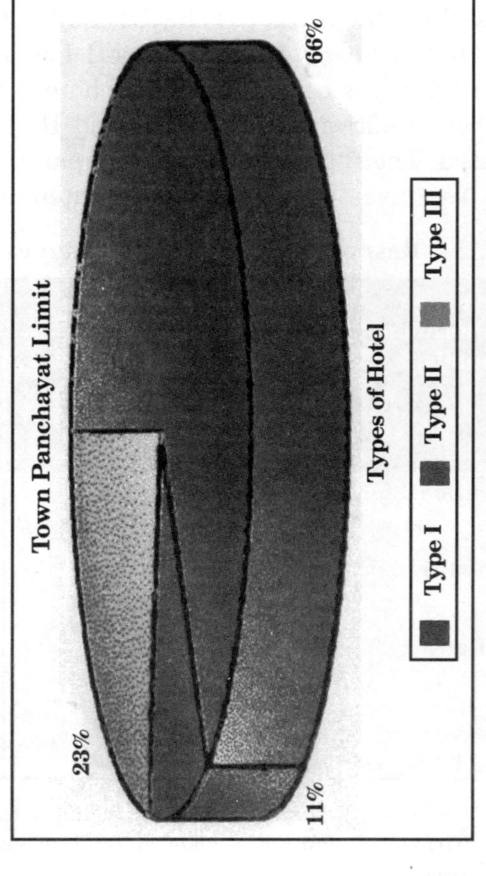

Fig. 5.1: Types of Hotels and Location of Hotels

HOTEL LOCATION-WISE DISTRIBUTION OF CHILDREN

It is also important to understand the location of the hotels in terms of tourist and non-tourist places. In tourist places, hotel business is more encouraging and profitable as compared to business in non-tourist places. Table 5.2 shows the distribution of the children according to the types of hotels and their location.

Table 5.2 shows that out of 475 children, over two-thirds (69.4%) work in hotels located in tourist centres, and nearly one-third (30.5%) work in hotels situated in non-tourist places. Thus, the proportion of children in the former type of hotels is more than thrice as much as of those in the latter type of hotels. Since the children in the former type of hotels get more facilities, salary and tips than those from the latter type of hotels, most of them desire to work in the former type of hotels.

Table 5.2: Respondents by location and Types of Hotel

Location of hotels	Types of hotel			Total
	Type I Hotel (Boarding only)	Type II Hotel (Boarding and Lodging)	Type III Hotel (Lodging with Canteen)	
Tourist Place*	184 (55.7)	100 (30.3)	46 (13.9)	330 (100)
Non-Tourist Place**	45 (31.0)	21 (14.4)	79 (54.4)	145 (100)
Total	**229 (48.2)**	**121 (25.4)**	**125 (26.3)**	**475 (100)**

Note: * Tourist centres include five Taluk headquarters of Tirunelveli District, viz., Tirunelveli, Playamkottai, Ambasamudhram, Sankarankovil and Tenkasi. A total of 66 big hotels of types I, II and III are located in these Taluk headquarters.

** The Non-Tourist Places include four taluk headquarters of Tirunelveli District, viz., Nanguneri, Sivagiri, Senkottai and Rathapuram. A total of 29 big hotels of type I, II and III are located in these Taluk headquarters.

AGE

Table 5.3 and Fig. 5.2 clearly show that these children are deprived of even primary schooling. It is also important to mention that parents are keen on pushing their children into work even at their tender age in order to supplement their family icome. It is clearly represented in Table 5.3.

It is found from the distribution of data in the table that 40.6 per cent of the respondents are in the age group of 10-12 years, and over one-fourth (26.5%) are in the age group of 8-10 years and one-third (32.8%) belong to the age group of 12-14 years. It is, thus, evident that more children in the age group of 10-12 years than those from other age groups are employed in hotels.

Nearly two-thirds (56.0 per cent) of the working children are found in the age group of 8-10 years in Type III hotels. This type of hotel are the entry point for most of the children. As regards the workload, working hours and wages paid, they are relatively low in lodges than in other types of hotels. In Type I hotels, children in the age group of 10-12 years are higher in proportion than in the other types. This may be explained in terms of the age and experience of the children. Children below 10 years of age gain knowledge in their jobs and develop their skills while working in lodges and afterwards, they switch over to Type II hotels. Nearly two-thirds (61.9%) of them in this type of hotels belong to the age group of 12-14 years, because they at this age acquire the required experience and skills to attend to the needs of the occupants of the hotel rooms, besides the usual work assigned to them. Therefore, they are rather busy always during the working time with only a brief interval for rest.

Table 5.3: Respondents by Age and Types of Hotel

Age Group (in yrs.)	Types of Hotel			Total
	Type I Hotel (Boarding only)	Type II Hotel (Boarding and Lodging)	Type III Hotel (Lodging with Canteen)	
8-10	50 (21.8)	6 (4.9)	70 (56.0)	126 (26.5)
10-12	115 (50.2)	40 (33.0)	38 (30.4)	193 (40.6)
12-14	64 (27.9)	75 (61.9)	17 (13.6)	156 (32.8)
Total	**229 (100)**	**121 (100)**	**125 (100)**	**475 (100)**

Median age of sample child workers as a whole : 11.15
Median age of sample child workers from Type I hotel : 11.12
Median age of sample child workers from Type II hotel : 12.39
Median age of sample child workers from Type III hotel : 8.00

$\chi^2 = 121.21$ df = 4 $P < 0.05$

Type II hotels are more profitable than the other types. The owners prefer to employ experienced and mentally matured children. On the other hand, the parents would rather send their children to this type of hotels keeping in mind future prospects like salary, security and food. Undoubtedly both the children of that age and their parents are keen on securing jobs in Type II hotels. Thus it is clear that a majority of the children in the age group of 12-14 years have advantages over those in other age groups in certain aspects. However, a considerable proportion of them belong to the age group of 10-12 years. This is substantiated by their Median Age (11.15 years).

On the whole, nearly three-fourths (73.4 per cent) of the children are in the age group of 10-14 years. This is, in one way or other, supported by I.S. Singh who discloses that over two-thirds of child workers belong to the age group of 12-14 years, and one-third are from the age group of 8-12 years.[1]

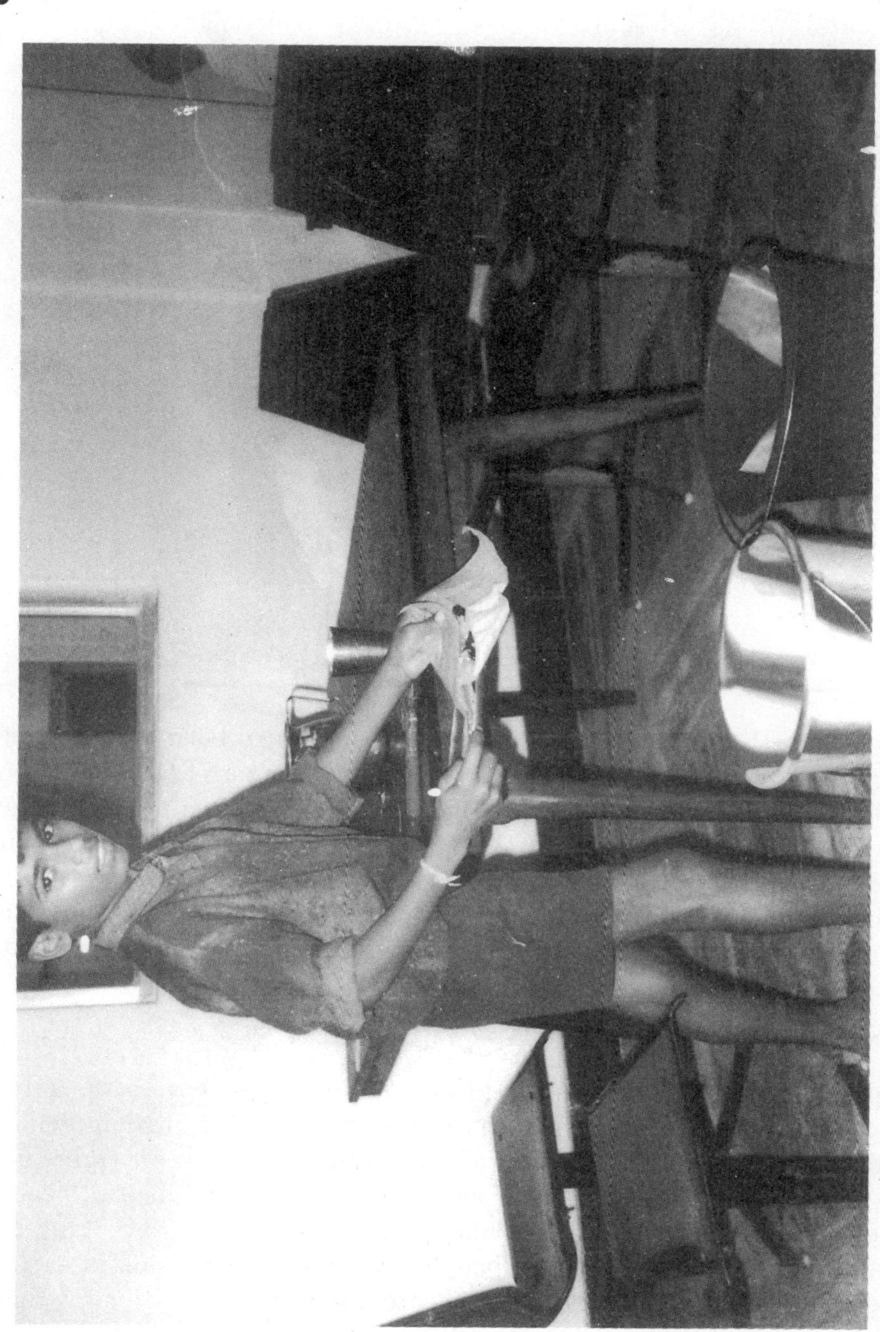

The Server-boy dutifully removing the plantain-leaf after being eaten from

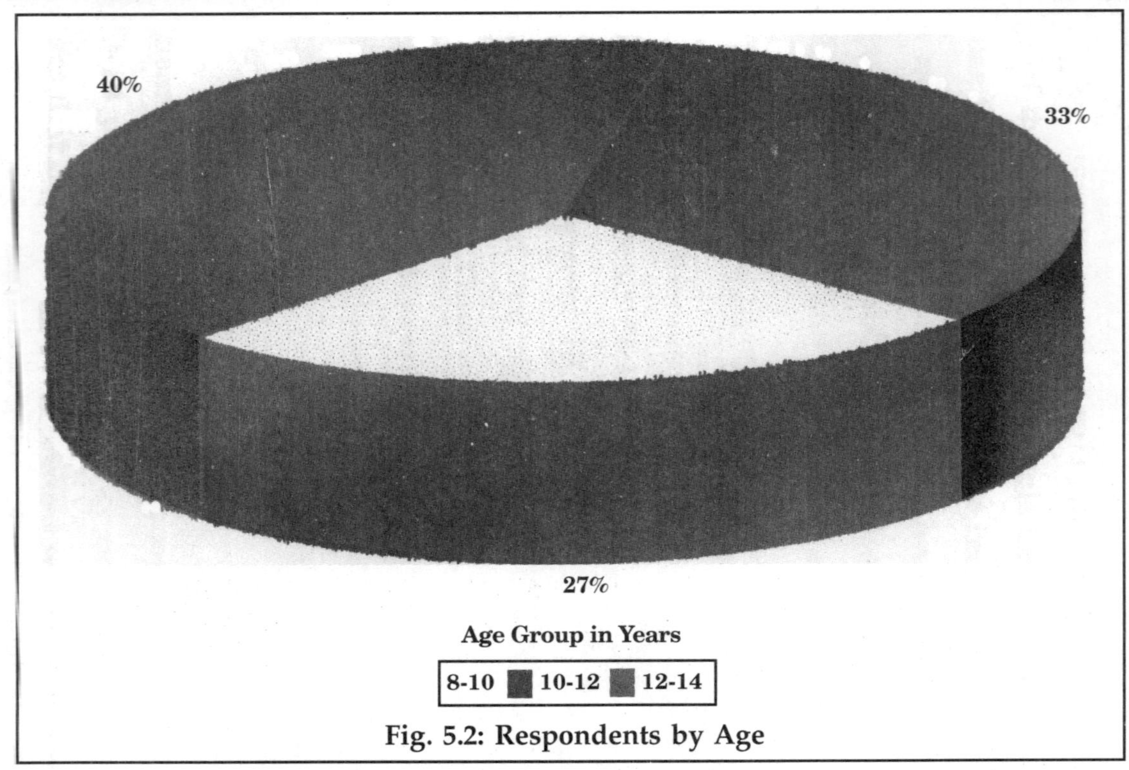

Fig. 5.2: Respondents by Age

Nearly one-fourth (23.4%) of the respondents are third-born children and nearly one-fifth (19%) of them are fourth-born children of their parents. Nearly one-fourth (23.8%) of them are fifth-born children and more or less the same proportion are second and sixth-born children of their parents. Less than five per cent of them are either first or seventh-born children. It is clearly understood from this that a majority (66.8%) of them are third, fourth and fifth-born children of their parents. It is found that these children are denied education after secondary level. They are forced to supplement their family income by securing jobs.

EDUCATION

The importance of education needs to be emphasized in the social milieu of any country and more so in the modern age of technology. Proper education creates in man the faculty of reasoning and the power of distinguishing between right and wrong. Education is widely regarded as a vital element in the socio-cultural, economic and political development of any country. It also plays a key role in satisfying the needs, aspirations and personal growth of the people. Without literacy, one is exposed to all kinds of danger in society: it is easy to get cheated, and one tends to go without access to information which is easy to get at for a literate person.

Despite the efforts taken by the government, illiteracy prevails in India. It forces the children to accept menial employment even during early childhood. Since education contributes to career orientation, it is important to understand the educational background of the children under study. Table 5.4 shows the distribution of children according to their educational status.

Table 5.4: Respondents by Educational Level and Types of Hotel

Educational Level	Types of Hotel			Total
	Type I Hotel (Boarding only)	Type II Hotel (Boarding and Lodging)	Type III Hotel (Lodging with Canteen)	
Semi-literates	129 (56.3)	35 (28.9)	93 (74.1)	257 (54.1)
Literates	100 (43.7)	86 (71.0)	32 (25.6)	218 (45.9)
Total	**229 (100)**	**121 (100)**	**125 (100)**	**475 (100)**

$\chi^2 = 52.08$ df = 2 $P < 0.05$

Note: Semi-literate refers to those who have completed Standard III and can hardly read and write, whereas literate refers to those who have completed Standard V and are capable of reading and writing.

It is found from Table 5.4 that, on the whole, a majority (54.1%) of the children are semi-literates and a large minority of them (45.9%) are literates. Nevertheless, there is a variation among them with regard to their educational level and their employment in types of hotel. For instance, a great majority of them (74.1%) working in Type III hotels are semi-literates. More or less the same proportion (71%) working in Type II hotels are literates. More or less a majority of them working in Type I hotels are semi-literates (56.3%) and literates are far fewer (43.7%). It is, therefore, concluded that there is a significant relationship between the educational level of the children and the types of hotels in which they are employed. This is proved by statistical analysis as well.

The trend may be explained in terms of the types of hotel in which the children are employed. Nearly three-fourths of the semi-literate children are employed in Type III hotels because they have to attend onlyto light work like cleaning the rooms, providing drinking water, supplying hot drinks from canteen, buying cosmetics and food from outside shops for the customers. For doing such work, they need not be literates, but need to be sincere. Moreover, their interaction with the customers is rather limited. On the other hand, in Type II hotels children have to be literates as they attend to foreigners and other educated and affluent persons who visit this type of hotel frequently. They also need communication skills and to be conversant with certain English words frequently used by the customers. That is perhaps the reason why nearly three-fourths of them employed in this type of hotels are literates. A similar situation prevails in Type

I hotels. Nearly a majority of the working children are literates who are able to satisfy the needs of the rich and educated customers who frequent the hotels.

RURAL-URBAN BACKGROUND

It is observed that almost all the respondents have migrated from different areas to the capital city either with their parents, relatives or with the employers. Table 5.5 shows the distribution of the children according to their rural-urban background.

Table 5.5: Respondents by Background and Types of Hotel

Background	Types of Hotel			Total
	Type I Hotel (Boarding only)	Type II Hotel (Boarding and Lodging)	Type III Hotel (Lodge with Canteen)	
Rural	181 (79.0)	93 (76.8)	88 (70.4)	362 (76.2)
Urban	48 (20.9)	28 (23.1)	37 (29.6)	113 (23.7)
Total	**229 (100)**	**121 (100)**	**125 (100)**	**475 (100)**

$\chi^2 = 3.37$ df =2 P >0.05

The data disclose that over three-fourths (76.2%) of the children have migrated from rural to urban areas. All types of hotel exhibit a similar trend with regard to the rural-urban migration of the children. The main causes for migration are poverty and non-availability of earning sources at their native places. As the city grows, so does the hotel industry. Most of the parents prefer hotel jobs for their children for obvious reasons like accommodation facility, security and food. Therefore, they send their children to towns and cities to secure jobs in hotels. However, Sumanta Banaraj finds different reasons for the migration of children such as lack of employment, monsoon failure and mechanization of agricultural work.[2] The proportion of urban children is considerably less, ranging from 20 to 30, in all three types of hotels.

As a result of the rural-urban migration of children, in each type of hotel, their proportion is very high. Obviously this trend is seen in the hotel industry all over Tamil Nadu. In order to confirm this the researcher had informal discussions with the parents of working children, hotel masters and supervisors from the sample areas. It is relevant here to present a statement given by a 52-year-old father of a child employed in a hotel:

> I am a coolie working in my village and also in neighbouring villages. I have two daughters and three sons. My second son is employed in a hotel at Tirunelveli Town and my two daughters are engaged in beedi-rolling. My first son is also a coolie and helps me in my work and another son is 3-years-old. There is very limited

chance for industrial employment in Tirunelveli district. Therefore, I have sent my second son to Tirunelveli Town to join a hotel as a worker with the help of a master cook in that hotel, who happens to be my village friend. In one way or other, I am happy about his job because he gets food three times a day, accommodation for his stay, and security. He could not have these advantages, if he were employed in some other organization. Moreover, I am regularly getting the monthly wages due to him. This helps me to provide at least two meals a day to my family members.

RELIGION

The data given in Table 5.6 disclose that an overwhelming majority (89.0 per cent) of the children are Hindus in all the hotels under review. Only 11 per cent are Muslims and Christians.

Table 5.6: Respondents by Religion and Types of Hotel

Religion	Types of Hotel			Total
	Type I Hotel (Boarding only)	Type II Hotel (Boarding with Lodging)	Type III Hotel (Lodging with Canteen)	
Hindu	200 (87.3)	109 (90.0)	114 (91.2)	423 (89.0)
Muslim	12 (5.2)	3 (2.4)	4 (3.2)	19 (4.0)
Christian	17 (7.4)	9 (7.4)	7 (5.6)	33 (6.9)
Total	**229 (100)**	**121 (100)**	**125 (100)**	**475 (100)**

$\chi^2 = 2.37$ df = 4 $P > 0.05$

It is reported that most of the Hindu children were already engaged in agricultural operations. Nevertheless, the failure of monsoon coupled with the necessity of supplementing their family income pushed them to enter hotels for employment. Only a limited number of Christian children are found in hotels because the local pastors and religious preachers patronize poor children in villages with the help of schools run by Christian Missionaries. In addition to this, some foreign Christian Missionaries have established educational institutions, hostels, etc. for poor Christian children. Thus, in this district, most of the Christian children are encouraged by the Christian Societies to pursue education.

A survey says that a large majority of Muslims happen to be natives of various towns in this district, and that a considerable number of them are full-time beedi workers. Some of them are engaged in mat-weaving and incense sticks manufacturing. However, a large number of them are economically backward.

It has been a traditional practice among the Muslims that they prefer home-based industries. Muslim children below the age of 14 years are predominantly from Melapalayam, Mukkudal, Kadayanallur, and Puliangudi and are engaged in *beedi*–rolling and related work. Muslims have large families unmindful of their poor economic condition. They are well-versed in preparing certain dishes like *briyani, parotta* and gravy. Their children find their way to hotels run by Muslims and prefer to do available work. Many small (**C** grade) hotels are run by Muslims in sub-urban and semi-urban areas.

COMMUNITIES

Caste continues to be an important criterion to determine the social status of people in India. Economic status and social status are closely linked with the caste structure. It impairs economic growth by creating caste barriers. There is a relationship between children's jobs in hotels and their community. This is shown in Table 5.7 and Fig. 5.3.

Table 5.7: Respondents by Community and Types of Hotel

Community	Types of hotel			Total
	Type I Hotel (Boarding only)	Type II Hotel (Boarding with Lodging)	Type III Hotel (Lodging with Canteen)	
ScheduledCaste	78 (34.0)	39 (32.2)	36 (28.8)	153 (32.2)
Most Backward Caste	75 (32.8)	32 (26.4)	39 (31.2)	146 (30.7)
Backward Caste	69 (30.1)	45 (32.2)	43 (34.4)	157 (33.0)
Forward Caste	7 (3.1)	5 (4.1)	7 (5.6)	19 (4.0)
Total	**229 (100)**	**121 (100)**	**125 (100)**	**475 (100)**

$\chi^2 = 4.33$ df = 6 $P > 0.05$

The data make it clear that nearly one-third (32.2%) of the working children belong to Scheduled Castes, Most Backward Castes (30.7%) and Backward Castes (33.0%). Only a negligible proportion (4.0%) belong to Forward Castes. It is also evident that the Most Backward Castes and Backward Castes supply more children to hotels (63.7%) than the Scheduled Castes.

It is a common practice among the Most Backward Castes and Backward castes that at times of economic crisis they do not mind doing menial jobs like cleaning, sweeping, loading and unloading in commercial centres or in other organisations. This is supported by the finding of G. Karunanithi in his study on *Child Labour in Beedi*

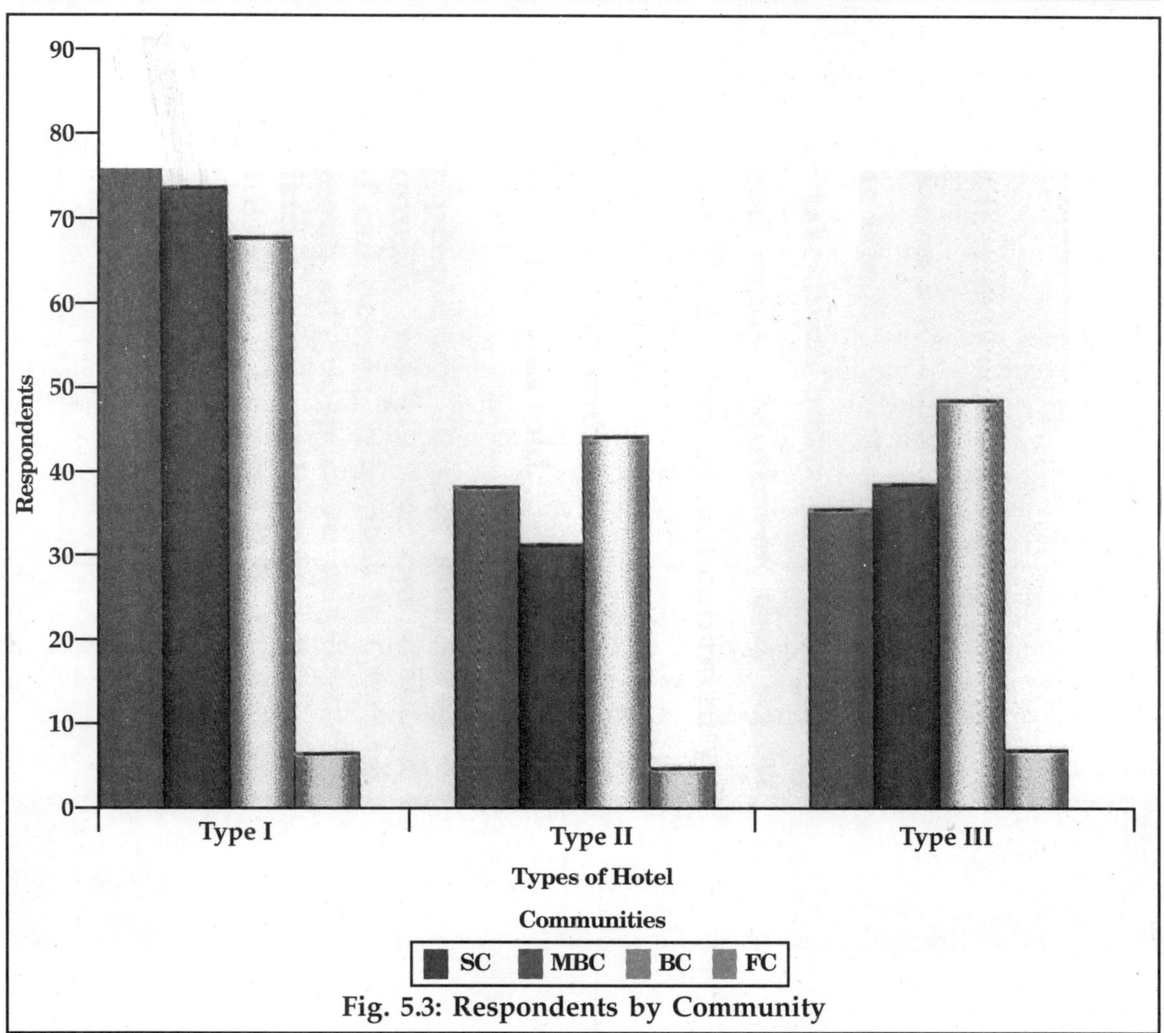

Fig. 5.3: Respondents by Community

Making that 86 per cent of the children engaged in *beedi* works come from Most Backward Castes and Backward Castes.[3] On the other hand, the Forward Caste people do not like such work even if they live in poverty because they are status conscious to a great extent.

It is important to mention that cleaning the dining tables, washing the plates, tumblers, spoons and other related jobs in hotels are considered menial jobs by caste Hindus. Even If such jobs get them attractive wages, they do not want to take them because, according to them, they are rather inferior to their social status. Moreover, they report that they would be criticized or blamed by their relatives and community for doing so.

In an in-depth interview with a middle aged Brahmin from one of the sample areas the researcher was told:

Generally my people are literate and some of them are well educated. Normally we educate our children up to graduate level. Most of our people migrated to Chennai and other cities in India in search of prospective employment. Of course in Tirunelveli District, beedi making is a predominant occupation, but we are not used to it because it is menial work. In a similar way, cleaning, washing and sweeping in hotels are menial jobs. Moreover, they are polluting jobs. Therefore, we never allow our boys to do such jobs. It is below our status to do such work.

There are about 150 Brahmin families here. Some of them are traditional agricultural families with several acres of fertile land. A limited number of heads of families are government employees. Most of the family members make their livelihood in the preparation of various pickles and raw sidedishes for lunch like *Papad, Vathal and Vadagam* (to be roasted in oil before eating). This is a dignified job done at home and the produce is sold in the market through middlemen.

TYPES OF JOB

Normally the types of job given to children in hotels include cleaning tables and vessels, sweeping, supplying water and assisting cooks in the kitchen. The types of job assigned to the sample children are shown in Table 5.8 and Fig. 5.4.

Table 5.8: Respondents by Types of Job and Types of Hotel

Types of Job	Types of Hotel			Total
	Type I Hotel (Boarding Only)	Type II Hotel (Boarding with Lodging)	Type III Hotel (Lodging with Canteen)	
Table Cleaner	77 (33.6)	36 (29.2)	42 (33.6)	155 (32.6)
Water Supplier	57 (24.9)	35 (28.9)	35 (28.0)	127 (26.7)
Tea Supplier/Room Boy	63 (27.5)	29 (23.9)	18 (14.4)	110 (23.2)
Vessels pickers/Cleaner	23 (10.0)	12 (9.9)	15 (12.0)	50 (10.5)
Kitchen Assistant	9 (3.9)	9 (7. 4)	15 (12.)	33 (6.9)
Total	**229 (100)**	**121 (100)**	**125 (100)**	**475 (100)**

$\chi^2 = 0.75$ df =8 P > 0.05

On the whole, one-third of the children (32.6 per cent) are asked to clean the tables. Over one-fourth (26.7 per cent) are assigned the job of supplying water and more or less the same proportion (23.2 per cent) are posted to supplying hot drinks and attending to the customers' needs. Only 10.5 per cent of them are given the job of cleaning the vessels and about 7 per cent of them are kitchen assistants helping the cooks in their work.

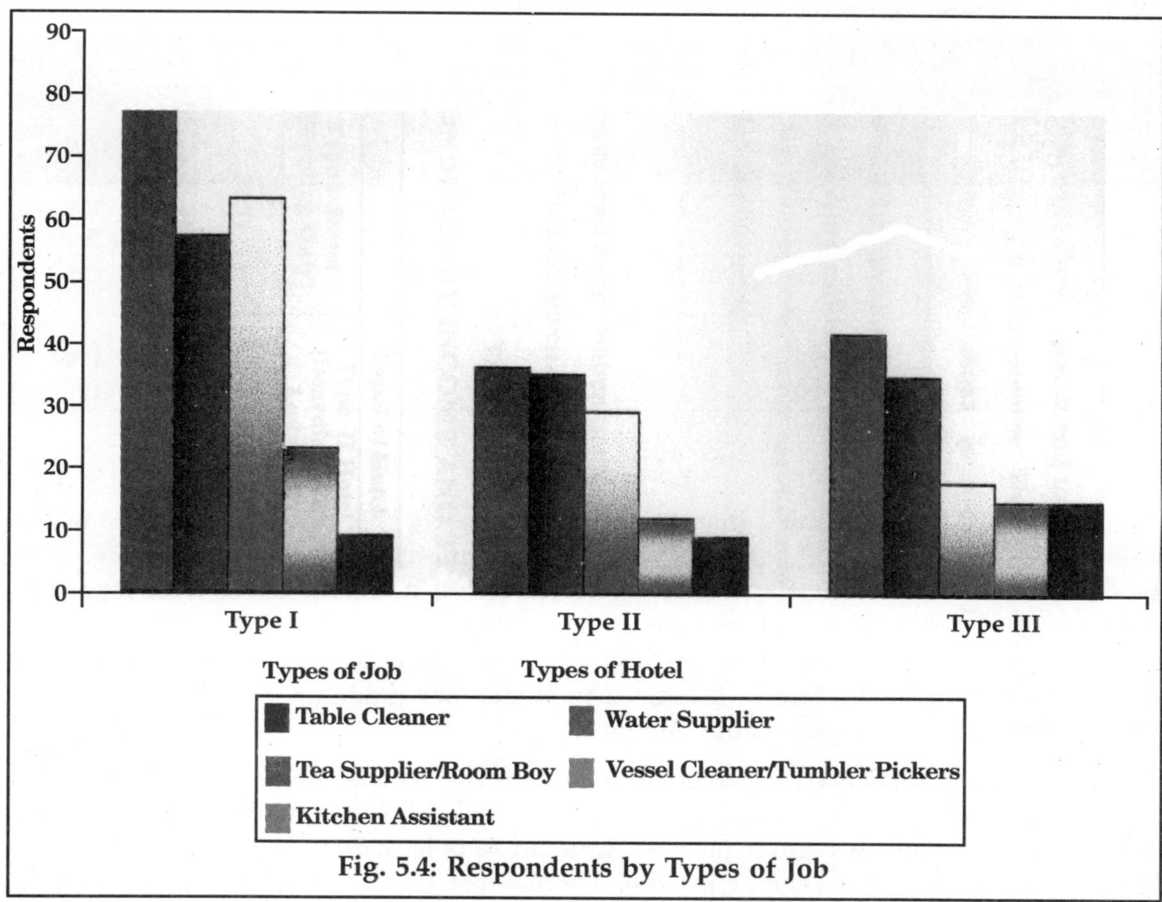

Fig. 5.4: Respondents by Types of Job

The work of Room Boys is rather different in the sense that it needs so much of care, sincerity and systemization. They have to clean the rooms as soon as the customers vacate, provide drinking water and change the pillow covers, bedspreds and bed-sheets. They have to respond to the calls of the customers immediately and attend to their needs like procuring for them cosmetics, cigarettes and eatables. They go out of the hotel premises often to buy things from shops in the neighbourhood. They are communicative, polite and responsible. With these qualities they are able to satisfy the customers and also maintain cordial relationship with the shop keepers. They get more exposed to society than their counterparts are. On the contrary, the children who render assistance in the kitchen hardly have contact with the outside world.

INCOME

The families of the children send the children out towork for the income that working generates for the families. The monthly earnings of the children are given in Table 5.9.

Table 5.9: Respondents by Income and Types of Hotel

Income (Rs.)	Types of Hotel			Total
	Type I Hotel (Boarding only)	Type II Hotel (Boarding with Lodging)	Type III Hotel (Lodging with Canteen)	
100-500	52 (22.7)	45 (37.1)	39 (31.2)	136 (28.6)
501-1000	177 (77.2)	76 (62.8)	86 (68.8)	336 (71.3)
Total	**229 (100)**	**121 (100)**	**125 (100)**	**475 (100)**

Mean Value = Rs.616.42.

χ^2 = 1.32 df = 2 P = > 0.05.

It is found from the table that on the whole, nearly three-fourths (71.36%) of the children earn Rs. 500-1,000 per month. But less than one-third (28.6%) get only up to Rs. 500 per month. All the three types of hotels reflect a similar trend with regard to the earning of the children. Their average monthly income is Rs. 684.80. This income would be a substantial addition to the family's income. In order to find the proportion of their contribution to the family income, the researcher made an attempt to find the monthly income of the respondents' families.

He found it difficult to collect data pertaining to the monthly income of the respondents' families because the family members who are primarly agricultural labourers do not make a regular income. Agriculture is basically a seasonal work and it does not provide a big or regular income. The nearest that the researcher could get to reliable statistics is given in Table 5.10 and Fig. 5.5.

Nearly two-thirds of the respondents' families earn Rs. 10,000-12,000 annually. Nearly one-third of them earn Rs. 12,000-14,000 annually. This shows that annual earnings of a majority ranges from Rs. 10,000-12,000. About 10 per cent of them earn Rs. 14,000-16,000. Their average annual income worked out to Rs. 12,018. This means that their average monthly income of is Rs. 1001.50.

When the average monthly income of the respondents is added to the average monthly income of their families, it works out to Rs. 1,686.30. If it is so, the children make a substantial contribution (40.56%). This clearly shows that the livelihood of their families partly depends on the earnings of the children.

Table 5.10: Respondents by Family Income and Types of Hotel

Family Income (Rs.)	Types of Hotel			Total
	Type I Hotel (Boarding only)	Type II Hotel (Boarding-Lodging)	Type III Hotel (Lodging with Canteen)	
10,000-12,000	131 (57.2)	75 (61.9)	76 (60.8)	282 (59.4)
12,000-14,000	75 (32.75)	36 (29.8)	33 (26.4)	144 (30.3)
14,000-16,000	23 (10.04)	10 (8.3)	16 (12.8)	49 (10.3)
Total	**229 (100)**	**121 (100)**	**125 (100)**	**475 (100)**

Mean Value = Rs. 12,018.

χ^2 = 2.7 df=4 P> 0.05

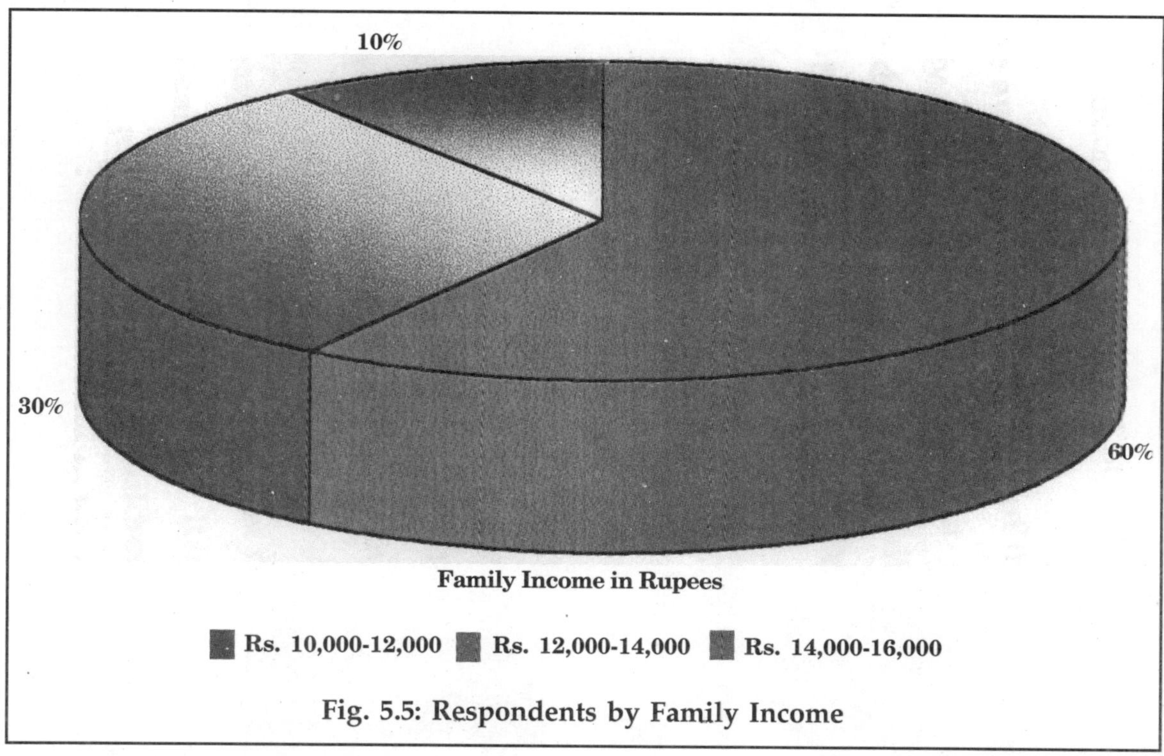

Fig. 5.5: Respondents by Family Income

However, it is evident that they live in poverty. According to a stipulation by the Government of India the families which earn an annual income of Rs. 12,500 are listed under poverty line.[4] The data show that of the 475 families of working chidren, 306

Boys too tender to slave for a bus stop vendor

(64.42%) make an annual income of Rs. 10,000-12,500. This means that nearly two-thirds of these families are below the poverty line. It is, therefore, concluded that a great majority of the children come from poverty-stricken families. A.N. Singh's findings also support this conclusion—that most of the child workers come from economically backward classes. It seems quite common in those classes that the parents send their children to work because they expect that every individual must contribute to his or her family's maintenance.[5]

In the sample hotels, the minimum wage paid is Rs. 100 in addition to three times food, tea and accommodation. The children below the age of 14 years earn a maximum of Rs. 1000. Yet it depends upon the age, experience and skills of the children. In the first instance, the parents send their children to Type III hotels, where the income is relatively low. They learn the skills of the job, and gain knowledge and experience. Within a period of three years, they try to move to Type I hotels mainly for higher income and better food. There they develop some additional skills over a period of time and try to move to Type II hotels for better prospects because this type of hotel is the best in terms of income, food and job security.

It is understood from the data that there is a significant relationship between the income of the children and the sources through which they secured the hotel jobs as shown in Table 5.11.

Table 5.11: Respondents by Sources of Recruitment and Monthly Income

Sources of recruitment	Monthly Income of Respondent (in Rs.)		Total
	100-500	501-1000	
Through middle management employees	18 (9.0)	182 (91.0)	200 (100)
Through brokers	118 (42.9)	157 (57.0)	275 (100)
Total	**136 (28.6)**	**339 (71.3)**	**475 (100)**

$\chi^2 = 65.0$ df = 1 $P < 0.05$

It is clear from the table that the proportion of children introduced by the owners themselves, managers, supervisors, and masters (91%), is nearly twice as much as the proportion of those introduced by the brokers (57%) with regard to their monthly earning of Rs. 501-1,000. It is obvious that the former category of children have an advantage over the latter category of children. The reason is that the former category of children are mostly taken care of by the employers and employees who themselves happen to be the introducers of these children. They recommend an increase in the monthly income of the children periodically. They feel that they are answerable to their parents who approach them at regular intervals. On the other hand, there is least support of employees to the children introduced by the brokers who promptly collect their brokerage and leave the children in the hotels, and they no take no more interested in them or their problems.

EXPERIENCE

The sample children have put in a maximum of 4 years' service in the hotels. This is represented in Table 5.12.

Table 5.12: Respondents by Experience in Hotel jobs and Types of Hotel

Experience in Hotel Job (in Years)	Types of Hotel			Total
	Type I Hotel (Boarding only)	Type II Hotel (Boarding with Lodging)	Type III Hotel (Lodging with Canteen)	
Less than 2	52 (22.7)	9 (7.4)	74 (59.2)	135 (28.4)
2-4 Years	177 (77.2)	112 (92.5)	51 (40.8)	340 (71.5)
Total	**229 (100)**	**121 (100)**	**125 (100)**	**475 (100)**

$\chi^2 = 8.79$ df $=2$ $P < 0.05$

The data in the above table disclose that nearly three-fourths of the children (71.5%) have 2-4 years of experience, and over one-fourth (28.4%) have less than two years. On the contrary, in Type II hotels, an overwhelming majority (92.5%) have more than two years of experience. In Type III hotels, nearly two-thirds have less than two years of experience. As referred to already, a majority of the beginners get employed in Type III hotels.

The children gain experience over the years and develop their skills in their job. The experienced child workers are in the age group of 12-16 years, whereas the beginners are in the age groups of 8-12 years. There are certain differences between the two age groups of children with respect to their job, behavior and expectations.

A manager from a Type I hotel at Tirunelveli Junction was interviewed elaborately in order to collect information regarding the behavior and experience of working children. He says:

> In this hotel you can see children from various caste groups, age groups and religious groups. Nine children are employed here. Five of them are in the age group of 8-12 years and the rest are between 12 and 14 years. They initially work here for two or three years. After that they leave the hotels for various reasons. Most of them hail from rural areas and a few of them are from urban centres. Sometimes we employ more working children of up to 12 or 15. It all

depends on the availability of children and the demands for labour from our side. Most of them have studied up to V Standard. Before assigning jobs to the new comers, we train them adequately in specific jobs through senior employees or a supervisor. The children below the age of 12 years are obedient, sincere, fast and committed to their work. About 50 per cent of the children in the age group of 12-14 years cope with their work, follow the schedule, guide their juniors and obey the manager and supervisor. They are very sincere and prompt in attending to outdoor work like transporting firewood, bringing grocery and vegetables from nearby shops. The other 50 per cent do not concentrate on their work.. So, we scold and beat them in order to extract more work from them. Generally, as a matter of fact, abusing and beating the children are common in this industry; otherwise, we cannot extract work from them.

Some children are neither interested in hotel jobs nor do they go back home. In such cases, we call upon their parents to either advise them to be attentive and sincere in their work or to take them back. Some of them are really active and sincere. Especially, those in the age group of 13-14 years are a bit careless and rather slow in their work. They are interested in observing the activities of the customers and their dress pattern. Sometimes, they stand at the entry for a while to see what is going on outside. Sometimes they doze off and start daydreaming. At other times, they crack jokes and gossip with co-workers during working hours. They are not as obedient as those in the age group of below 12 years. They imitate our behaviour and enjoy the fun. As they emulate adult co-workers, they become habituated to smoking, viewing blue films and drinking. If we beat them, they run away from here. Once they acquire adequate skills in hotel jobs and gain experience, they demand higher wages. If their expectations are not fulfilled, they simply switch over to some other hotels. They emulate the adult co-workers in their life.

Generally, it is found that the children join the hotels at the age of eight years. Especially, they join Type III hotels in the beginning for reasons explained already and in subsequent years, they start moving to other types of hotels.

CHANGING THE PLACE OF WORK

Child workers move from one hotel to another hotel in the same district or out of the district and within the State or out of the State. However, the sample workers have moved from one hotel to another within the district. This is shown in Table 5.13.

This Table shows that over two-thirds of the children (69.5%) have shifted twice from one hotel to another and less than 10 per cent of them have done so more than twice. However, less than one-fourth (22.9%) have not shifted their work place since the time of their joining.

Table 5.13: Respondents by Changing of Job and Types of Hotel

No.of moves from one hotel to another	Types of Hotel			Total
	Type I Hotel (Boarding only)	Type II Hotel (Boarding with Lodging)	Type III Hotel (Lodging with Canteen)	
Twice	177 (77.2)	92 (76.0)	61 (48.8)	330 (69.5)
More than twice	14 (6.1)	16 (13.2)	6 (4.8)	36 (7.5)
No shifting	38 (16.5)	13 (10.7)	58 (46.4)	109 (22.9)
Total	**229 (100)**	**121 (100)**	**125 (100)**	**475 (100)**

$\chi^2 = 59.36$, df = 4, P> 0.05.

Hotels are not always so lucrative to the children. Besides, they have to reckon with the problems caused by their masters, owners and adult co-workers. That is perhaps the reason why they want to move to other hotels, which would be a place of attraction for them for some time. While considering those who have shifted twice during their service, a majority (about 49%) belong to Type III hotels. But over three-fourths of them (77.2%), belong to Type I hotels. A similar proportion (76%) belong to Type II hotels. The reasons for shifting are heavy and long hours of work, oral and physical punishment, low wages, inadequate food, denial of leave, fewer fringe benefits, denial of certain facilities and the like.

The findings of M. Soundara Pandian support these. He points out that most of the children in hotel industry are found to have migrated from other districts of Tamil Nadu and from other States like Kerala, Karnataka and Andhra Pradesh. Mostly in one type or the other, they are found to have put in a minimum of one and a half years and a maximum of two year's service within the State or outside the State.[6]

FAMILY SIZE

It is important to study the size of the families of child workers because it has a bearing on their economic condition, which again has a falling effect upon their income and consumption. The distribution of child workers' families according to their size and the types of hotel in which the children are employed is explained in Table 5.14.

The average size of the family of working children is 5.38. Nearly a majority of the working children (47.7%) come from medium size families, and one-third (35.3%) belong to large families. Less than one-fifth of them hail from small families. One can witness a smilar trend in Types I, II, and III hotels.

Table 5.14: Respondents by Family Size and Types of Hotel

Family Size	Types of Hotel			Total
	Type I Hotel (Boarding only)	Type II Hotel (Boarding and Lodging)	Type III Hotel (Lodging with Canteen)	
Small (Up to 4)	43 (18.7)	16 (13.2)	21 (16.8)	80 (16.8)
Medium (4-6)	109 (47.5)	54 (44.6)	64 (51.2)	227 (47.7)
Large (Above 6)	77 (33.6)	51 (42.1)	40 (32.0)	168 (35.3)
Total	**229 (100)**	**121 (100)**	**125 (100)**	**475 (100)**

Median Value = 5.38

$\chi^2 = 4.18$ df = 4 $P > 0.05$

As a matter of fact, large families supply more child workers than small families do. Generally parents prefer to have more working hands to support them economically. We cannot brush aside the factors like low family income, low standard of living and lack of will. Ashok Mitra discloses in his study that the monetary help that the working children provide to their families and their capacity to help their parents in their old age are the two reasons for the employment of children in the age group of 5-14 in India.[7]

The socio-demographic profile of the working children presented in this chapter constitutes the base for studying them in terms of their working conditions, exploitation, health problems and unhealthy practices. The exploitation of child labour in the place of their employment is discussed in the next chapter.

Nearly one-fourth (23.4%) of the respondents are third-born children and nearly one-fifth (19%) of them are fourth-born children of their parents. Nearly one-fourth (23.8%) of them are fifth-born children and more or less the same proportion are second and sixth-born children of their parents. Less than five per cent of them are either first or seventh-born children. It is clearly understood from this that a majority (66.8%) of them are third, fourth and fifth-born children of their parents. [What is the relevance of this statistics? Would you advance any reason as to why there are so few first born and seventh born children in your sample? Could you say that the first born are not used for making money, for some reason like his duties to the family in the spiritual sphere or something like that? When you say that these children are denied education, do you imply that others in the families, not sent out to job in hotels are not involved in working and are sent to school]? It is found that these children are denied education after secondary level. They are forced to supplement their family income by securing jobs.

REFERENCES

1. I.S. Singh, *Child Labour*, (New Delhi: Oxford & IBH Publishing Co, Pvt. Ltd., 1992), pp. 16-17.
2. Sumanta Banarj, *Child Labour in India*, As Cited by Helan R. Sekar, Child Labour Legislation in India, (Noida: V.V. Giri National Labour Institute, 1997), p. 26.
3. G. Karunanithi, *Child Labour in Beedi Making in Tirunelveli District of Tamil Nadu* (Project Report Submitted to Ministry of Labour, Governement of India, 1996), pp. 36-42.
4. District Rural Development and Agricultural Office, Tirunelveli.
5. A.N. Singh, *Child Labour In India: Socio-Economic Perspectives* As Cited by Helen K. Sekar, Child Labour Legislation in India, *op.cit.*, p. 33.

6 M. Soundara Pandian, *A Study on Working Children in Hotel Industry in Chennai,* Proceedings of Workshop on Street children, (Department of Sociology, Gandhigram Rural Institute – Deemed University, 1999), p. 2.

7. Ashok Mitra, *India's Population: Aspects of Quality and Control*, As Cited by Helen R.Sekar, Child Labour Legislation in India, *op.cit*, p. 33.

CHAPTER 6

Children and Hotel Job

This chapter deals with the likes and dislikes of the working children towards their work in hotels and the reasons thereof. An attempt has been made to find the relationship between these aspects on the one hand and the variables like age, experience in hotel job and rural-urban background of the sample children on the other hand.

CHILDREN AND HOTEL JOBS

Children join hotels as table cleaners, water suppliers, tea and coffee-suppliers, room boys, vessel-cleaners/pickers and kitchen assistants irrespective of their rural-urban background, caste, class, religion and language. The owners give advertisements in local newspapers for two categories of children. One advertisement is for room boys and the other is for water boys without mentioning any specific age and salary in order to escape from the Acts concerned.

It is reported that some children run away from their homes in order to secure jobs in hotels. Some of them find these jobs with the help of the managers, supervisors and masters and others find them through brokers. It is easy especially for children below 14 years of age to get used to hotel jobs since they resemble their domestic work.

Children learn the jobs in hotels with the help of co-employees, senior workers or sometimes are trained by the managers, supervisors and masters. Several factors such as nature of work, hours of work, wage, physical condition, regular payment of wage and providing welfare measures influence their response to the jobs. Table 6.1 shows the number of children who like the job and the number of children who do not.

It is evident from the table that an overwhelming majority of the working children (85.2%) like hotel jobs, and only 14.7 per cent do not like them. In Types I and III hotels, more or less a similar proportion (92%) like the job. On the contrary, in Type II hotels, over two-thirds (66.9%) like the job, whereas one-third (33%) do not.

Table 6.1: Respondents According to Liking and Disliking the Job and Types of Hotel

Types of Hotel	Like the job	Do not like the job	Total
Type I Hotel (Boarding Only)	209 (91.2)	20 (8.7)	229 (100)
Type II Hotel (Boarding and Lodging)	81 (66.9)	40 (33.0)	121 (100)
Type III Hotel (Lodging with Canteen)	115 (92.0)	10 (8.0)	125 (100)
Total	**405 (85.2)**	**70 (14.7)**	**475 (100)**

$\chi^2 = 42.73$ df = 2 $P < 0.05$

I.S. Singh's study (1992) supports this finding. In his study, an overwhelming majority of the working children (90%) have reported that they are satisfied with the hotel jobs. Getting food thrice a day, getting free accommodation and attractive urban atmosphere make them like hotel jobs.[1] Similarly, C. S. Sanon's study (1998) discloses that nearly two-thirds of the working children like the hotel jobs. The urban life style, food thrice a day and free accommodation are the major attractions for the poor children.[2]

The data prove that before entering hotel jobs, the working children are very much interested in going to Type I and Type III hotels. But after two or three years, they enter Type II hotels. Presumably, the working children are physically and mentally matured, have gained work experience and begin to compare their wages and working hours with those of adult workers. This is perhaps why they prefer to join Type II hotels, which have the facility of boarding and lodging and therefore bring them more economic benefits. The present study discloses that the job brings them food thrice a day, and is a source of income.

It is evident from Table 6.2 that 405 working children like the job. Over two-thirds (69.1%) do the job primarily because it provides them with three meals a day. One-third of them like it because it is a source of income. In this study, a majority of the children come from rural families for various reasons like poverty, parents' unemployment, monsoon failure and large family. Therefore, most of them are happy to get three meals a day.

In Type I (25.71%) and Type III (17.14 per cent) hotels, a small number of children report that they do not like the job because of low wage and heavy work. In Type II hotels, a majority (57.14%) do not like the job because of low wage and heavy workload. In this type of hotels, they gain work experience, but the work is heavy and the wages are low.

These children seem to have more family obligations than their counterparts in other types of hotels. Over one-third (35.8%) from Type II hotels and over two-thirds (64.3%) from Type III hotels find the hotel job a rich source of income substantially increasing their family income. Parents also find their children's job a substantial source of income for the families. So, many parents send their children to hotels and collect an advance from the owners by pledging their children.

Table 6.2: Respondents by Reasons for Liking and Disliking Hotel Job and Types of Hotel

Types of Hotel	Reasons for Liking			Reasons for Disliking		
	Getting food thrice a day	Source of income	Total	Low wages	Heavy work	Total
Type I Hotel (Boarding only)	187 (89.4)	22 (10.5)	209 (100)	8 (44.4)	10 (55.5)	18 (100)
Type II Hotel (Boarding and Lodging)	52 (64.1)	29 (35.8)	81 (100)	9 (22.5)	31 (77.5)	40 (100)
Type III Hotel (Lodging with Canteen)	41 (35.6)	74 (64.3)	115 (100)	7 (58.3)	5 (41.6)	12 (100)
Total	**280 (69.1)**	**125 (30.8)**	**405 (100)**	**24 (34.2)**	**46 (65.7)**	**70 (100)**

Reasons for liking: $\chi^2 = 28.9$ df = 2 $P < 0.05$.

Reasons for Disliking: $\chi^2 = 6.34$ df = 2 $P < 0.05$.

While analyzing the relationship between the age of the children and their liking or dislike for the job, it is found that there is a significant relationship between these two variables.

Table 6.3: Respondents by Age and Liking or Disliking of Hotels Jobs

Age Group (in years)	Hotel job		Total
	Like the Job	Do not like the Job	
8-10	116 (92.0)	10 (7.9)	126 (100)
10-12	169 (87.5)	24 (12.4)	193 (100)
12-14	120 (76.9)	36 (23.0)	156 (100)
Total	**405 (85.2)**	**70 (14.7)**	**475 (100)**

$\chi^2 = 14.2$ df = 2 $P < 0.05$

The data presented in the table disclose that in the age group of 8-10 years, an overwhelming majority (92%) like the hotel job, and less than 10 per cent dislike it. In the age group of 10-12 years, an overwhelming majority (87.5%) likes the job, and only about 12 per cent of them dislike it. In the age group of 12-14 years, over three-fourths (76.9%) like the job, but nearly one-fourth (23.0%) dislike it.

This clearly shows that the children's acceptance of hotel job is inversely proportional to their age. The proportion of children who like hotel jobs decreases with the rise in the age. While entering hotels at the age of 8 or 9 or 10 years, they have hopes of a joyful life in the midst of several attractions within and outside the hotels. They start losing their hopes in course of time owing to work pressure and the punishments given them by the hotel owners, managers, masters and adult co-workers. At one point of time, they want to switch over to other hotels mainly for change and also to get more monetary benefits and other facilities.

It is observed that there is a relationship between the age of the children and the reasons given by them for liking or disliking the hotel jobs. This is clearly indicated in Table 6.4.

Table 6.4: Respondents by Age and Reasons for Liking and Disliking Hotel Jobs

Age Group (in years)	Reasons for Liking			Reasons for Disliking		
	Food thrice a day	Source of income	Total	Low wage	Heavy work	Total
8-10	101 (87.0)	15 (12.9)	116 (100)	5 (50.0)	5 (50)	10 (100)
10-12	126 (74.5)	43 (25.4)	169 (100)	9 (37.5)	15 (62.5)	24 (100)
12-14	53 (44.1)	67 (58.8)	120 (100)	10 (27.7)	26 (72.2)	36 (100)
Total	**280 (69.1)**	**125 (30.8)**	**405 (100)**	**24 (34.2)**	**46 (65.7)**	**70 (100)**

Reasons for liking the job : $\chi^2 = 53.9$ df = 2 $P < 0.05$.

Reasons for disliking the job : $\chi^2 = 1.86$ df = 2 $P < 0.05$.

It is clear from Table 6.4 that in the age group of 8-10 years, an overwhelming majority (87.0%) likes the hotel jobs because they get them food thrice a day. But 12.9 per cent of them like them because they are a constant source of income. Out of 10 children from this group who dislike the job, 50 per cent do so because of low wage and the other 50 per cent due to heavy workload. On the other hand, in the age group of 10-12 years, there is a decreasing trend in the proportion of children who like the job because of getting food thrice a day, whereas there is an increasing trend in the proportion of those who like the job as a source of income.

A similar trend is observed among those from the same age group, who do not like the job due to low wage and heavy workload. It is also important to note that a similar trend is found among those who are in the age group of 12-14 years.

It is evident from the analysis of data that there is a significant relationship between the age of the children and their reasons for their liking or disliking the hotel jobs. A majority of the children below 10 years of age (87%) like hotel jobs because they get them food thrice a day, 44.1 per cent from the older age group also like the job for the same reason. On the contrary, only 12.9 per cent of the children belonging to the age of 10 years like the jobs because they are a source of income, whereas 58.8 per cent of the children above 12 years like the job for that reason. A similar difference is found among those from the same age groups who attribute low wage and heavy workload as reasons for disliking the jobs.

A statement given by a child worker who is nine years old and is employed in a hotel in Tirunelveli Town is as follows:

> I joined this hotel with the help of my supervisor who hails from my native place. I have been working here for more than a year. I like this job as I get food thrice a day besides coffee or tea. Moreover, I have been provided with free accommodation. I take different varieties of tiffin and sweets. The manager, supervisor and master treat me kindly and politely. I enjoy the company of seven children working with me, as we are very informal and cordial to one another. We enjoy our job. If any one of us is absent, we will share his work and for that we are given extra money in the form of *beta*.
>
> I see films with my friends at least twice a week. I also see a few tele-serials, as we have access to a TV set at reception. I did not have this sort of entertainment in my village. I had to work with my parents for a pittance. Otherwise, my parents would force me to go for cattle grazing. They were unable to buy even a set of dress for me once a year. But here I am provided with colorful uniforms as and when I require.
>
> During rest times in the day and in the late evenings, I prefer to be with my co-workers from all age groups to while away the time gossiping or chatting. Especially, the jokes of adult co-workers are an entertainment for me. Therefore, I accompany the adult co-workers while shopping and seeing films. I did not have this sort of company and entertainment in my house. Moreover, the tasty food and varieties of food that I get thrice a day besides getting coffee and tea at regular intervals, is more pleasant for me than anything else. Therefore, I like the hotel job and wish to continue in the job.

However, after serving in hotels at least two-four years, the children want to get rid of the work due to reasons such as heavy workload, long hours of work and low wages. But the economic instability of their families forces them to continue to work. They think that it is an obligation on their part to support their families economically. Moreover,

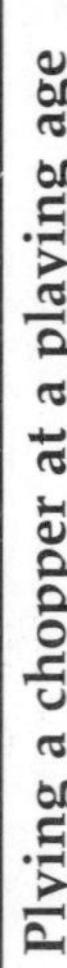

Plying a chopper at a playing age

their parents encourage them to stick to the hotel jobs so that they would be able to get an advance from the employers. In addition to this, they get monthly income regularly from the employers for the service of the children. So the children are in a dilemma whether to continue or to leave the job. A similar condition prevails among most of the children above 12 years of age. The following statement given by a 14 year old boy employed in a hotel in Tirunelveli Junction explains their problem:

> I have gained four years of experience in my hotel job. I was much interested in the job earlier because of the variety of food and the accommodation that I got.
>
> But at present I do not like this job, because I am given heavy and continuous work. In the beginning, I was given leave at least once in three months, but now it is denied. I work from 6 a.m. to 11 p.m. In spite of my hard work, I am paid less than Rs.700 per month. Instead, I am given various types of work at the same time. How can I do them? If I fail, I am scolded and beaten. I am also given extra work especially when a co-worker is absent. So I am planning to go over to Chennai or Mumbai. I want to get a job through some persons from my native place working in these cities. They told me that they do easy work and earn Rs. 50-100 per day.

The data show that there is a relationship between the children's liking or disliking the job and their experience in hotel job. This is represented in Table 6.5.

Table 6.5: Respondents by Experience and Liking or Disliking Hotel Jobs

Experience in hotel job (in years)	Hotel Job		Total
	Like the Job	Dislike the Job	
Below 2	125 (92.5)	10 (7.4)	135 (100)
2-4	280 (82.3)	60 (17.6)	340 (100)
Total	**405 (85.2)**	**70 (14.7)**	**475 (100)**

$\chi^2 = 7.95$ df = 1 $P < 0.05$.

It is evident from Table 6.5 that out of the 135 children with two years of experience, an overwhelming majority (92.5%) like the jobs, and only 7.4 per cent do not. But of the 340 children with 2-4 years of experience, nearly one-fifth (17.6 per cent) dislike the jobs against 82.3 per cent who like them. It is thus clear that the proportion of children who like the jobs decreases with the increase in age. Initially, the children like the job because they are beginners. But after working more than two years, they feel the heaviness of the job and realize that it is rather tough. After 2-4 years of experience, the children acquire skills in the jobs and also start comparing their wage, working hours, workload and the like with those of children working in various other places. As a result of this, they gradually lose interest in hotel jobs here and try to secure jobs in other places. It is important to find whether their experience exerts any influence on their reasons for their liking or disliking the job. This is represented in Table 6.6.

Table 6.6: Respondents by Experience and Reasons for Liking and Disliking Hotel Jobs

Experience in hotel job (in years)	Reasons for Liking			Reasons for Disliking		
	Food thrice a day	Source of income	Total	Low wage	Heavy workload	Total
Below 2	109 (87.2)	16 (12.8)	125 (100)	5 (50.0)	5 (50.0)	10 (100)
2-4	171 (61.0)	109 (38.9)	280 (100)	9 (31.6)	15 (68.3)	24 (100)
Total	**280 (69.1)**	**125 (30.8)**	**405 (100)**	**24 (34.2)**	**46 (65.7)**	**70 (100)**

Reasons for Liking: $\chi^2 = 27.5$ df = 1 $P < 0.05$.

Reasons for Disliking: $\chi^2 = 1.2$ df = 1 $P > 0.05$.

Table 6.6 and Fig. 6.1 reveal that out of the 125 children who liked the job and had less than two years experience, an overwhelming majority (87.2%) like the job because they get food thrice a day; 12.8 per cent of them like it for the reason that they have to support their family economically. Then out of the 10 children who dislike the job, half (50.0%) of them do so because of low wage. However, the same proportion (50.0%) dislikes it because of heavy workload.

Moreover, out of the 280 children with 2-4 years of experience, nearly two-thirds (61.0%) like the job because they get food thrice a day, whereas over one-third (38.9%) likes the jobs as they help them to support their families economically. On the other hand, out of the 60 children with the same years of experience, nearly one-third (31.6%) do not like the job because of low wage, whereas over two-thirds (68.3%) do so due to heavy workload.

It is reported that most of the parents send their children to this job at their early age to make them economic assets. Initially the children are attracted to hotel jobs primarily because of food supplied thrice a day, which the parents cannot provide them with. That is why a meager percentage (5%) of the children do not like the job because, according to them, it brings them low wages in spite of hard work.

It is evident from the analysis that there is a relationship between the age of the children and their liking or disliking for the job and also the reason for doing so. The proportion of children whose experience in hotel job is up to two years is nearly one and a half times higher than the proportion of those whose experience is 2-4 years in relation

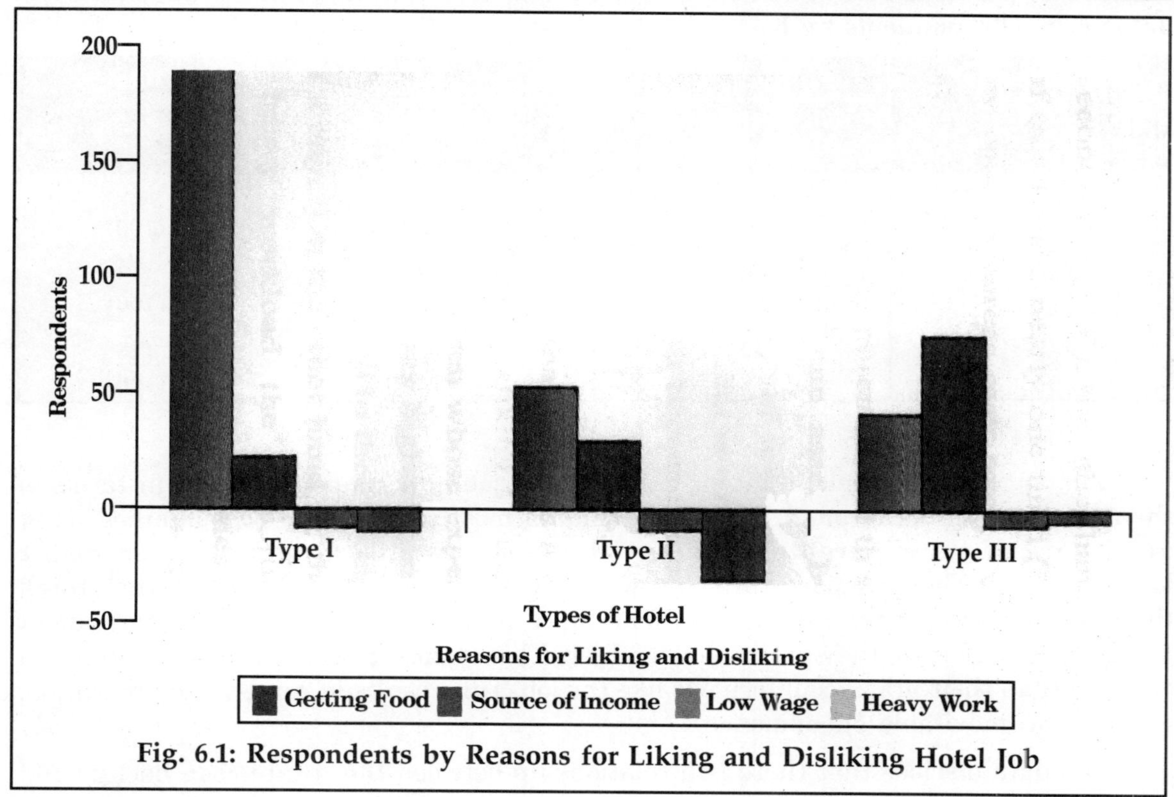

Fig. 6.1: Respondents by Reasons for Liking and Disliking Hotel Job

to their liking of hotel job because it gets them three meals a day. On the other hand, in the matter of disliking the job on account of heavy workload the proportion of children whose experience is 2-4 years is nearly one and a half times higher than those whose experience is up to two years. It is understood from this that the liking of the children whose job experience is up to two years turns negative gradually owing to their growing realization of their plight. However, workers with two to four years of experience feel their responsibility to the family much more than workers with up to two years of experience. Their proportion is three times higher. This shows that they become more responsible as they grow.

Like experience, the rural-urban background of the children is significantly related to their liking or disliking for hotel jobs. This is explained in Table 6.7.

It is evident from Table 6.7 that out of the 362 children from rural background an overwhelming majority (96.6%) like the hotel jobs, only 3.3 per cent do not like them. On the contrary, out of the 113 children from urban background, only a large minority (48.6%) like the job. More or less the same proportion (51.3%) does not like it.

Table 6.7: Respondents by Background and Liking or Disliking Hotel Jobs

Background	Hotel Job		Total
	No. of those who like the job	No. of those who Dislike the job	
Rural	350 (96.6)	12 (3.3)	362 (100)
Urban	55 (48.6)	58 (51.3)	113 (100)
Total	**405 (85.2)**	**70 (14.7)**	**475 (100)**

χ^2 =157.5 df = 1 P < 0.05

The variation in their liking or disliking the job is perhaps explained in terms of their rural-urban background. The rural children mostly come from poor families. They are aware of their parents' earnings, family expenditure and their economic backwardness. They compare rural life with urban life. As a result of this, they think that the hotel job is advantageous to them. Since they are unable to get any permanent job in the rural areas, they prefer the hotel job. This makes it very clear that more rural children than their urban counterparts like the job. This results in rural-urban migration, which is an inevitable phenomenon.

The data disclose that there is a relationship between the rural-urban background of the children and the reasons expressed by them for their liking and disliking the job. This is represented in Table 6.8.

Table 6.8: Respondents by Background and Reasons for Liking and Disliking Hotel Jobs

Background	Reasons for Liking			Reasons for Disliking		
	Food for thrice a day	Source of income	Total	Low wage	Heavy work	Total
Rural	262 (74.8)	88 (25.1)	350 (100)	5 (41.6)	7 (58.3)	12 (100)
Urban	18 (32.7)	37 (67.2)	55 (100)	39 (67.2)	19 (32.7)	58 (100)
Total	**280 (69.1)**	**125 (30.8)**	**405 (100)**	**44 (62.8)**	**26 (37.1)**	**70 (100)**

Reasons for Liking: χ^2 = 42.0 df = 1 P < 0.05.

Reasons for Disliking: χ^2 = 2.31 df = 1 P > 0.05.

It is evident from Table 6.8 that out of the 350 rural children who like the hotel job, three-fourths (74.8%) do so primarily because of getting food thrice a day, whereas one-fourth (25.1%) of them do so due to their obligation to support their family. On the

They watch their customers cat tasty varictics of food; for them rice all three times

other hand, heavy workload is the reason for disliking the job for a majority (58.3%) of the rural children. But low wage is the reason expressed by two-thirds (67.2%) of their urban counterparts for not liking the job.

It is clear from Table 6.8 that there is a significant variation in the reasons expressed by the rural and urban children for their liking and disliking the job. In other words, more rural children than their urban counterparts like the job because of the food they get. On the other hand, more urban children than their rural counterparts do not like the job because of low the wages. Thus, it is concluded that the rural children have more inclination to the food they get than their obligation of providing economic support to their families. It is also concluded that the urban children are more conscious about the wages they get than about their workload.

The first statement may perhaps be explained in terms of the access of rural children to food. In rural areas, the poor families prepare a simple meal once a day preferably in the evening and preserve a portion of it for the next day. Therefore, the children have access to one full meal at nighttime. They get a different variety of food only on festival occasions. But in many hotels they have access to varieties of tiffin items, meals and other dishes. [However, there are many hotels that cook a poor unvarying kind of food for the workers.] This is one reason why they are attracted to hotel jobs. But, unlike rural children, their urban counterparts taste such food items in hotels and other tiffin stalls on roadside. Therefore, they join hotels mainly to earn money rather than to get food. But it is hoped that is hotels they would gain access to varieties of tiffin items, meals and other dishes. This is perhaps one reason why they are attracted to hotel jobs. On the contrary, they get disappointed when they are given cheap rice food. In fact they get cheap rice food all three times a day against their expectation that they would be provides with varieties of testy food each times.

REFERENCES

1. I.S. Singh, *Child Labour*, (New Delhi: Oxford & IBH Publishing Co. Pvt. Ltd., 1992) pp. 66-67.
2. Chandragupt S. Sanon, *Working Children: A Sociological Analysis*, (New Delhi: APH Publishing Corporation, 1998), pp. 126-127.

CHAPTER 7

Working Conditions and Exploitation of Child Labour in Hotels

This chapter deals with the working conditions of child labour in hotels. The working conditions of child labour include duration of work, workload, extra work and wages. The fieldwork for this project shows that the children are exploited at seven levels. They are:

(i) long duration of work;

(ii) heavy workload;

(iii) extra work, i.e., personal work of employers and employees, besides the assigned work in the hotel;

(iv) low wage;

(v) punishment;

(vi) pledging of children; and

(vii) sexual abuse.

The exploitation of child labour has been analyzed by correlating it with other related variables.

CONCEPT OF EXPLOITATION

Generally the term "exploitation" is understood in two ways. It means, an extensive use of resources, natural or human. Secondly, a worker is said to be exploited if payment for work done is less than the value of that work. The latter meaning of exploitation was used by Karl Marx while explaining class conflict.

From the Marxian point of view, child labour is the product of capitalism and technologies it creates. Karl Marx considers the new technologies as an important factor that increases the demand for cheap, unskilled labour while decreasing the rate of profit that will lead the capitalists to exploitation the labourers. Children according to Marx, are part of the "industrial reserve army".[1]

Children are undoubtedly cheaper and easily available workers as compared to adult workers. They are hired not only because of their readiness to be paid lower wages but also because of their possibility to this sort of exploitation. The employers are keen on employing children to extract more for long hours and to pay them less than the value of their labours. There are other reasons:

(i) they are more flexible and they can be easily pressurized;

(ii) They are trouble-free since they cannot organize agitations through unions;

(iii) being minors, the membership of trade unions is not open to them;

(iv) They do not demand over-time, medical and other facilities which the industry is supposed to provide;

(v) employers find them more amenable to discipline, control; and

(vi) they can be coaxed, admonished, pulled up and punished for default without jeopardizing relationship.

Forcing the children by their parents and pulling them up by their employers would easily turn them in to labourers mostly in unorganized sectors. In such industries, they are at a greater risk of contracting diseases as their immunity level is far lower than that of adults. Occupational hazards lead to a large number of accidents and musculo-skeletal disorders more among as compared to their adult counterparts. A large number of these children are virtually confined to small rooms under inhuman environment and in most unhygienic surroundings. They are paid meager wages and are compelled to work in unsafe and unhealthy conditions. The hazardous conditions take their toll and they suffer mostly from respiratory problems.

A substantial portion of the workers are engaged in such unorganized sector. Their employment is characterized by job insecurity, irregular payments, and an absence of welfare measures. In India, children are exploited in large scale in the unorganized sectors such as un-incorporated enterprises and household industries (other than the organized ones) which are not regulated by any legislation and which do not maintain annual accounts or balance sheets.

Besides economic exploitation, another form of exploitation obviously found among the hotels is sexual abuse and exploitation. They are often subject to this sort of exploitation by adult co-workers and other hotel employees. It is a common practice prevailing mostly in hotels with boarding and lodging facilities. Since, this study includes this type of hotels as samples, it attempts to explain this practice with the help of available data and case studies.

The main reason for this exploitation is that the adult co-workers have to accommodate the children in a common room exclusively meant for hotel employees. The adult workers take the advantage of physical proximity to tempt the children in to homosexual activities.

Another form of exploitation observed at the level of children is that they are pledged to the hotel owners by their parents for an advance sum of money. Like pledged children employed in cottage industries especially in beedi making in Tamil Nadu, some children are pledged to the hotel owners at the time of employment by the parents entering in to a contract that the children should work in the hotels for a specific period compulsorily in order to compensate the advance. Therefore, the owners are keen on retaining the pledged children with the help of their managers and supervisors.

LONG DURATION OF WORK

In hotels, children normally work 12-14 hours a day. They are engaged in different types of work from early morning to late night. The number of hours of work depends upon a number of factors such as:

(i) type of hotel;

(ii) the situation of the hotel;

(iii) the availability of child workers;

(iv) the commands and orders of owners, masters and supervisors; and

(v) the nature of work.

Since no in-depth study on child labour in hotels has so far been undertaken in India, it is not possible to compare the findings of the present study with those of earlier ones. However, other studies on child labour in various sectors, mostly unorganized, have come to the conclusions that:

(i) the working hours of children are long;

(ii) adequate rest time is missing; and

(iii) weekly and other holidays are not given.

With a view to collecting factual information regarding the number of hours of work per day the child workers were interviewed. The information collected is presented in Table 7.1.

It is clear form Table 7.1 that out of the 475 working children, over one-third (38.4 per cent) worked 14 hours a day, and over one-fourth (28.4%) 13 hours a day. Almost one-third (32.8%) worked 12 hours a day. It is, thus, seen that normally the children in hotels work at least 12-14 hours a day. They start work at 5.30 a.m. and continue till 11.30. p.m. This shows that their working hours are relatively high as compared to the working hours of their counterparts in other sectors. But the Factory Act, 1948, and the

Catering Establishment Act, 1958, stipulates eight hours of work a day for adult workers. The hotel owners compel the children to work for longer hours, which is legally an offence. They want to retain the children on the premises so that they could extract the maximum amount of work from them. They prefer employing rural children.

Table 7.1: Respondents by duration of Working Hour and Types of Hotel

Types of hotel	Total working hours a day			Total
	≤12	13	14	
Type I Hotel (Board only)	55 (24.0)	69 (30.1)	105 (45.8)	229 (100)
Type II Hotel (Board and Lodging)	19 (15.7)	41 (33.8)	61 (50.4)	121 (100)
Type III Hotel (Lodge with Canteen)	82 (65.6)	25 (20.0)	18 (14.4)	125 (100)
Total	**156 (32.8)**	**135 (28.4)**	**184 (38.4)**	**475 (100)**

$c^2 = 87.96$ df=4 $P < 0.05$

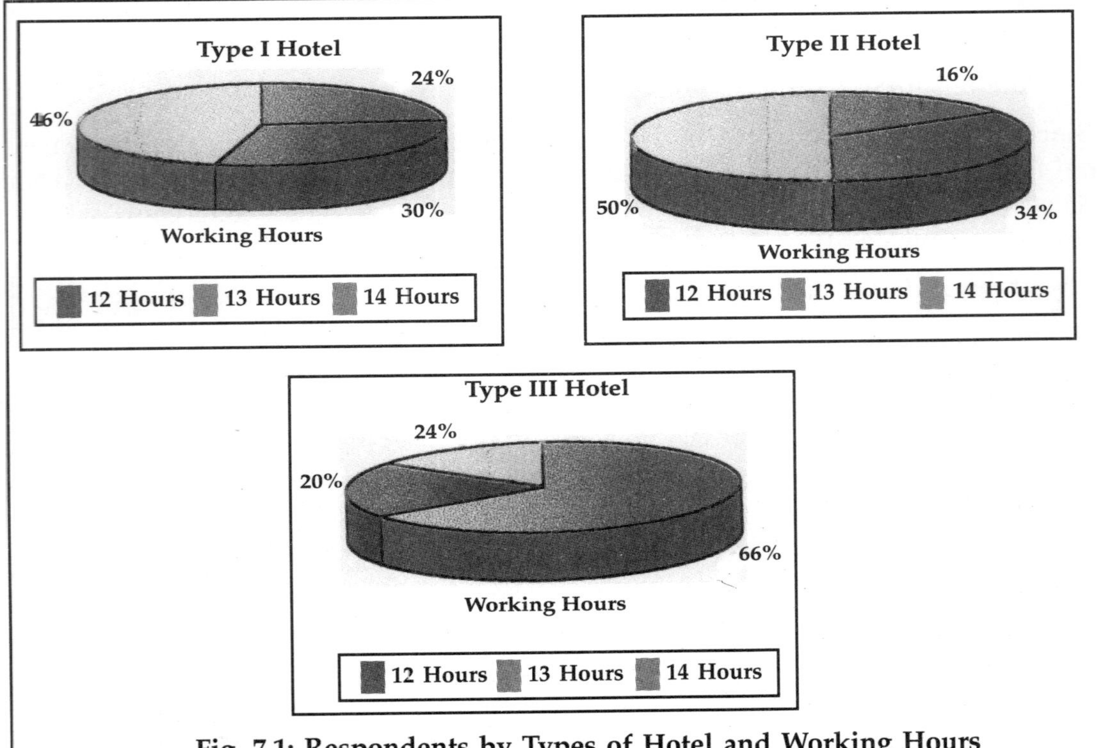

Fig. 7.1: Respondents by Types of Hotel and Working Hours

In Type III hotels, children work fewer hours than those in Types II and I hotels. The data disclose that two-thirds (65.6%) of them work up to 12 hours a day, one-fifth (20.0%) work up to 13 hours a day and less than 15 per cent (14.4%) work up to 14 hours a day (Table 7.1 and Fig. 7.1). In Type III hotels, their work, which is mostly outside the dining chamber, is to serve the lodgers by supplying drinks including liquor, tiffin, meals and the like. On the other hand, in Types I and II hotels, more or less half the children work 14 hours a day. A majority of the children in Type II hotels work 14 hours a day. These hotels are busy most of the day. As the employers want to cater to the customers to the maximum extent possible, they extract more work from the children by assigning them various types of work for 12-14 hours a day. In a study on child labour in hotels, Sushila Srivastva and Bhanumathi concluded that over two-thirds of the children in the catering sector of Madras city work 10-12 hours a day.[2]

It is important to mention that the children working in hotels situated in tourist places work more hours than their counterparts in hotels located in non-tourist places. This is shown in Table 7.2.

Table 7.2: Respondents by Location of Hotels and Duration of Work

Types of Place where hotels are located	Total working hours a day			Total
	≤12	13	14	
Tourist Centres	110 (33.3)	55 (16.6)	165 (50.0)	330 (100)
Non-Tourist Centres	46 (31.7)	80 (55.5)	19 (13.1)	145 (100)
Total	**156 (32.8)**	**135 (28.4)**	**184 (38.4)**	**475 (100)**

$\chi^2 = 87.7$ df=2 $P < 0.05$.

The distribution of data in Table 7.2 shows that a majority of the children (50%) in hotels situated in tourist centres work 14 hours a day. More or less the same proportion (55%) of their counterparts in hotels located in non-tourist centres work 13 hours a day. In this context, it is relevant to refer to a study on child labour by Geeta Lal who finds that 38 per cent of the children work 9-12 hours in hotels in tourist centres.[3] It is obvious that the children from the former type of hotels work more hours than those who work in the latter type of hotel. Thus the children from the former types of hotel are subject to more exploitation than their counterparts in the latter type of hotel.

There is a concomitant variation between the ages of the children and the duration of their work in the hotels. This is clearly presented in Table 7.3.

The bloom of Youth dissipated in drudgery!

The data in Table 7.3 show that the extent of exploitation of children in terms of extracting work differs with regard to their age. Out of 156 children in the age group of 12-14 years, nearly two-thirds (60.8%) work up to 14 hours a day. Out of the 193 children in the age group of 10-12 years, a majority (50.2%) work 14 hours a day. Out of the 126 children in the age group of 8-10 years, three-fourths (75.3%) work up to 12 hours a day.

Table 7.3: Respondents by Age and duration of Work

Age groups (in years)	Total working hours a day			Total
	≤12	13	14	
8-10	95 (75.3)	20 (15.6)	11 (9.9)	229 (100)
10-12	46 (23.8)	50 (25.9)	97 (50.2)	121 (100)
12-14	14 (9.9)	47 (30.1)	95 (60.8)	125 (100)
Total	**156** **(32.8)**	**135** **(28.4)**	**184** **(38.4)**	**475** **(100)**

$\chi^2 = 156.3$ df=4 $P < 0.05$.

It is obvious that there is a significant relationship between the age of the children and the duration of their work. In other words, the increase in the age of children results in increase in the duration of work. Children above ten years are far more subject to exploitation in terms of working hours than children between 8 and 10 years of age.

Since the variables age and experience travel in the same direction, the relationship between the age of children and the duration of their work in hotels is also applicable to the relationship between their work experience and their duration of work. This is represented in Table 7.4.

Table 7.4: Respondents by Experience and duration of Work

Experience (in years)	Total working hours a day			Total
	≤12	13	14	
Less than 2	96 (71.1)	25 (18.5)	14 (10.3)	135 (100)
2-4	60 (17.6)	110 (32.3)	170 (50.0)	340 (100)
Total	**156** **(32.8)**	**135** **(28.4)**	**184** **(38.4)**	**475** **(100)**

$\chi^2 = 128.03$ df=2 $P < 0.05$.

It is evident form the above table that the duration of work depends upon the experience in hotel jobs. A majority of them with 2-4 years of experience (50%) work for 14 hours a day. Above ten per cent with less than two years of experience also work for14 hours. The experience of the children is directly proportional to the duration of work.

The time taken by the children to complete the work depends on their workload. They have to work several hours if they have a heavy workload. This is exhibited in Table 7.5.

Table 7.5: Respondents by Heavy Work Load and duration of Work

Heavy work load	Total working hours a day			Total
	≤12	13	14	
Up to three types of work	128 (65.3)	53 (27.0)	15 (7.6)	196 (100)
More than three types of work	28 (10.0)	82 (29.3)	169 (60.5)	279 (100)
Total	**156 (32.8)**	**135 (28.4)**	**184 (38.7)**	**475 (100)**

$\chi^2 = 203.46$ df = 2 $P < 0.05$.

Note: Up to three type of work:

(i) Sweeping and washing the floors and tables;
(ii) Bringing in firewood; and
(iii) Carrying water.

More than three types of work:

(i) Sweeping and washing the floors and tables;
(ii) Bringing in firewood;
(iii) Carrying water; and
(iv) Supplying tea/coffee to the shopping centres.

Of 475 children, over one-third (41.2%) perform three types of work. A majority (58.7%) perform more than three types of work. Of the total children who do three types of work, nearly two-thirds (65.3%) work 12 hours a day. Of the total children who do more than three types of work, 60.5 per cent work 14 hours a day. Children attending to more than three types of work sweat for more hours than those who do three types of work. If there is an increase in the workload of children, they have to work longer hours.

It is already confirmed that the rural children have more workload than their urban counterparts. It is, therefore, a practice that the rural children work more hours than their urban counterparts. The data distributed in the Table 7.6 substantiate this view.

Table 7.6: **Respondents by Background and duration of Work**

Background	Total working hours a day			Total
	≤12	13	14	
Rural	96 (26.5)	103 (28.4)	163 (44.7)	362 (100)
Urban	60 (53.0)	32 (28.3)	21 (19.4)	113 (100)
Total	**156** **(32.8)**	**135** **(28.4)**	**184** **(38.4)**	**475** **(100)**

$\chi^2 = 33.8$ df=2 $P < 0.05$.

The data show that of 362 rural children, 44.7 per cent work 14 hours a day. Of 113 urban working children, a majority (53.0%) work for 12 hours a day. The reason is that the employers think that the rural children are strong and are able to withstand heavy workload. They do not hesitate to work for long duration and complete the assigned work. The employees think the urban children are not able to work hard and shoulder a heavy workload. If situations in a hotel warrant sharing a heavy workload, they run away and secure jobs in other hotels. These urbanites have gained experience in adapting themselves to the urban social environment. But it is also possible that urban children are unwilling to work hard. However, it is clear that they do not protest positively against too heavy work load but run away to other hotels.

It is also observed that employees discriminate between children introduced by the managers, supervisors and masters on the one hand and those introduced by brokers known to them directly or indirectly. The former category is given less workload. That is perhaps the reason why the children from the former category work for fewer hours than their counterparts in the latter category. If the employers or present employees are in one way or another responsible for recruiting the children of known parents, they show a concern for them while assigning them different types of work. On the other hand, they may not be so considerate to the children introduced by the brokers. This is clearly reflected in Table 7.7.

Table 7.4 show that of the total number of children introduced by hotel owners, managers, supervisors and masters, one-fourth (25%) have heavy workload working 14 hours a day. On the other hand, nearly a majority (48.7%) introduced by the brokers known to the hotel employers and employees have heavy work load, working 14 hours a day. It is inferred from this analysis that the heavy workload of children and long duration of their work depend upon the persons who introduce them to the hotel jobs.

Table 7.7: Respondents by Source of Recruitment and duration of Work

Recruitment	Total working hours a day			Total
	≤12	13	14	
Through middle management	101 (50.0)	49 (24.5)	50 (25.0)	200 (100)
Through brokers	55 (20.0)	86 (31.2)	134 (48.7)	275 (100)
Total	**156 (32.8)**	**135 (28.4)**	**184 (38.4)**	**475 (100)**

$\chi^2 = 51.29$ df=2 $P < 0.05$.

Note: Middle management includes Managers, Supervisors and Masters.

HEAVY WORKLOAD

When the children take jobs in hotels, the employers assign them one type of work– either table cleaning or vessel cleaning or water supplying or room service or kitchen assistance. But after a week or a month, depending upon the types of hotel and their location, the children are assigned more types of work. Table 7.8 and Fig. 7.2 explain the relationship between the heavy workload given the children and the types of hotel they work in.

Table 7.8: Respondents by Heavy Work Load and Types of Hotel

Types of Hotel	Heavy workload		Total
	Up to 3 types of work	More than 3 types of work	
Type I Hotel (Boarding only)	79 (34.4)	150 (65.5)	229 (100)
Type II Hotel (Boarding and Lodging)	30 (24.7)	91 (75.2)	121 (100)
Type III Hotel (Lodging with Canteen)	87 (69.6)	38 (30.4)	125 (100)
Total	**196 (41.2)**	**279 (58.7)**	**475 (100)**

$\chi^2 = 59.0$ df = 2 $P < 0.05$.

The data show that out of the 475 working children, 41.2 per cent do three types of work. But a majority of them (58.7%) do more than three types of work. Thus, the children are subject to exploitation in terms of extracting work making them work for more hours at a stretch.

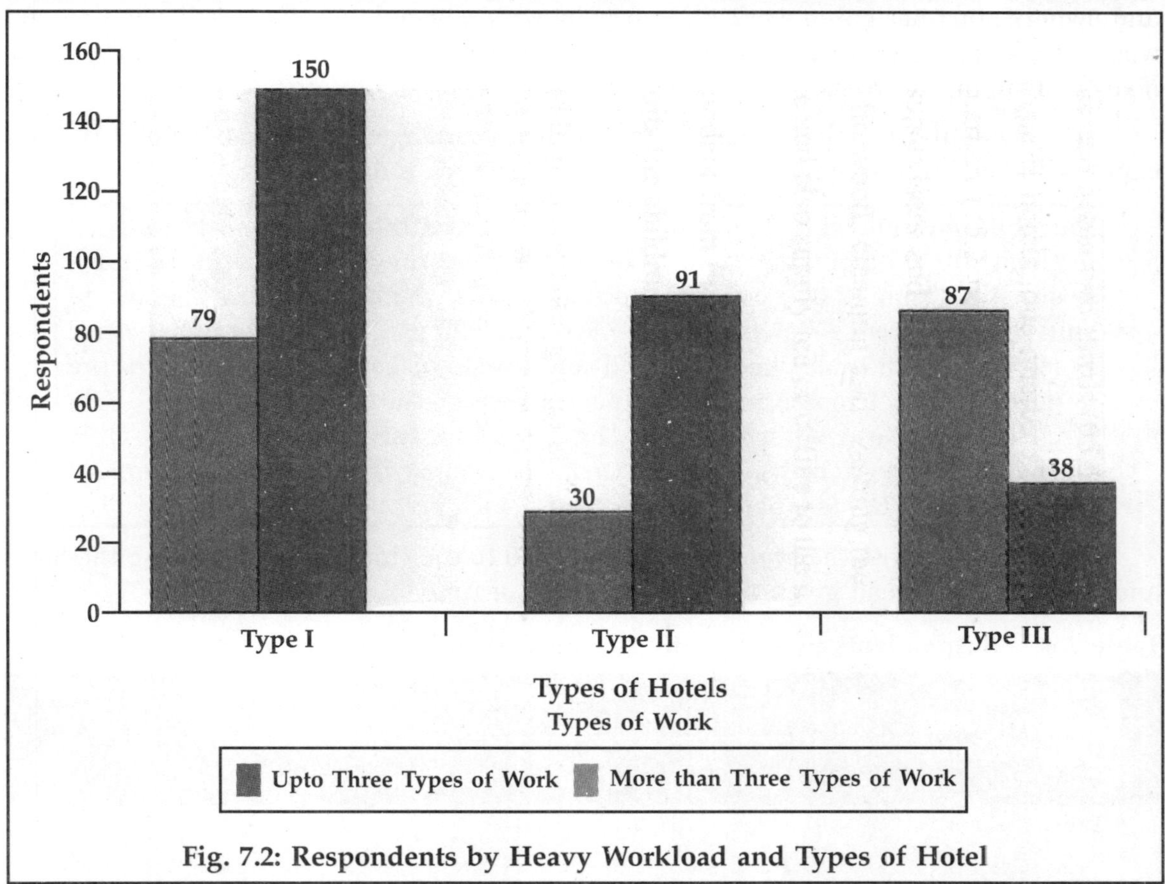

Fig. 7.2: Respondents by Heavy Workload and Types of Hotel

In Type III hotels, over two-thirds (69.6%) do three types of work, and nearly one-third (30.4%) do more than three types of work. Normally the workload is relatively low in Type III hotels because the children are mostly engaged in catering to the needs of the lodging customers. The attached canteen is very small in size and prepares limited items of tiffin and food according to the requirements of the customers. The children carry such items and tea or coffee to the customers as and when they require. In addition to this, they supply them drinking water regularly. They also supply tea or coffee to the nearby commercial and shopping complexes between 11.00 a.m. and 12.30 and 3.00 and 6.00 p.m.

But in Type I hotels, the workload is relatively heavier, because they are busy during business hours catering to the needs of the customers in terms of supplying varieties of tiffin and lunch from 6.00 a.m to 10.00 p.m. That is perhaps the reason why over one-third of the children (34.4%) do three types of work and about two-thirds (65.5%) do more than three types of work. In Type II hotels, one-quarter (24.7%) do three types of work and three-quarters (75.2%) do more than three types of work. The managers, supervisors and owners start assigning work like carrying water, bringing in firewood, cleaning and washing the floor and direct them to do room service and also supply tea or coffee to the nearby shopping centres.

It is evident from the discussion held with a manager of a Type II hotel that he exploits the children extracting about 14 hours of work a day.

> The children in our hotel get up at 5.30 a.m. and attend to the work assigned to them till 10.30 or 11.00 a.m. After a brief rest, they resume work as lunch is supplied from 12.00 noon. In addition to this, the children are directed to shift firewood from godown to kitchen. Around 2.30 p.m. they go for lunch. After lunch they clean tables and floor and continue to do so till 10.30 p.m. If there is garden or roof top service, they have to water the plants. At about 10.30 p.m. they take food. After that, they have to clean the entire dining chamber. Normally they go to bed only after 11.p.m. The salary that we pay them ranges from Rs.300 to Rs. 600 per month.

Table 7.9 presents the types of work assigned to the children while joining the hotel and the extra workload given to them in course of time.

Table 7.9: Respondents by Originally Assigned Work and Heavy Work Load

Type of work assigned at the time of joining	Heavy workload		Total
	Up to 3 types of work	More than 3 types of work	
Table Cleaner	58 (37.4)	97 (62.5)	155 (100)
Water Supplier	57 (44.8)	70 (55.1)	127 (100)
Tea Supplier/Room Boy	40 (36.3)	70 (63.6)	110 (100)
Vessels Cleaner	15 (30.0)	35 (70.0)	50 (100)
Kitchen Assistant	26 (78.7)	7 (21.2)	33 (100)
Total	**196 (41.2)**	**279 (58.7)**	**475 (100)**

$\chi^2 = 14.2$ df = 4 $P < 0.05$.

It is evident from Table 7.9 that of 155 table cleaners, over one-third (37.4%) do three types of work, whereas nearly two-thirds (62.5%) do more than three types of work. Of 127 water suppliers, 44.8 per cent do three types of work, whereas a majority (55.1%) do more than three types of work. Out of 110 tea suppliers, over one-third (36.3%) do

They wear dirty clothes; yet they mop the floor clean

three types of work, and nearly two-thirds (63.6%) do more than three types of work. Of 50 vessel cleaners, nearly one-third (30.0%) do three types of work, and over two-thirds (70.0 per cent) do more than three types of work. Out of 33 kitchen assistants, a great majority (78.7%) do three types of work, and over one-fifth (21.2%) perform more than three types of work.

In hotels, the owners, managers, supervisors and masters assign one type of work to the children in the beginning and later they assign more work to them. A boy of 13 engaged in a hotel job in Tenkasi town describes his pathetic condition as follows:

> I get up at 5.30 a.m. and get ready for work at 6.00 a.m. Within 30 minutes, I have to brush my teeth, wash my face and smear sacred ash on my forehead neatly. Otherwise my master would scold me and sometimes beat me.
>
> I collect the wastes and plates from the tables. I also clean the tables depending upon my shift. The cup of coffee given to me is not as tasty as that given to the customers. By 10.30 or 11.00 a.m. I complete my work and have breakfast. At that time, like other boys, I go to toilet after getting permission from my supervisor. If I do not do to so at that time, I may not get the time to go to the toilet.
>
> Sometimes, I rest between 11.00 and 11.30 a.m. depending on the situation. By 11.30 a.m. I start cleaning the floor with liquid wash or mop and arrange the tables neatly. I continue to do the assigned work till 2.30 p.m. After that, I take food, which is kept separately in the kitchen. The time that I spend to complete my lunch (normally 20-30 minutes) is a simple matter, but it is a serious matter for my supervisor. After lunchtime I clean the tables with acid and oil-soap.
>
> After that I have to get ready for the tiffin section after 3.00 p.m. and continue to work till 11.00 p.m. Sometimes, I relax for a while in the kitchen and sleep while standing or leaning against the wall. My supervisor gives me a slap to wake me up. He scolds me using filthy words. I normally do not take leave. The owner does not appoint substitutes for absentees. Therefore, the available workers have to share the work of the absentees. Sometimes, I have to go to buy vegetables, ration commodities and grocery for my masters. Before joining the hotel, I thought of only one type of work–either table cleaning or water supplying–but after some time, I have learnt to do all types of work.

It is found that there is a positive relationship between the age of the children on the one hand and the heavy workload assigned to them on the other hand. This is clearly shown in Table 7.10.

Table 7.10: Respondents by Age and Heavy Work Load

Age (in years)	Heavy workload		Total
	Three types of work	More than three types of work	
8-10	69 (54.7)	57 (45.2)	126 (100)
10-12	87 (45.0)	106 (54.9)	193 (100)
12-14	40 (25.6)	116 (74.3)	156 (100)
Total	**196 (41.2)**	**279 (58.7)**	**475 (100)**

$\chi^2 = 26.27$ df = 2 $P < 0.05$.

It is evident from Table 7.10 that the proportion of those doing more than three types of work increases with the increase in the age. Of the 126 children in the age group of 8-10 years, 45.2 per cent do more than three types of work; of 193 children in the age group of 10-12 years, 54.9 per cent do so. But of the156 children in the age group of 12-14 years, 74.3 per cent do so. This clearly shows that the age of the children is directly proportional to their heavy workload. It is, therefore, concluded that the children are assigned heavy or light work according to their age. Since there is a direct relationship between the age and experience of the children, it is understood that like their age, their experience also has a direct bearing on their workload. This is clearly presented in Table 7.11.

Table 7.11: Respondents by Experience and Heavy Work Load

Experience (in years)	Heavy Extra workload		Total
	Three types of work	More than three types of work	
Less than 2	96 (71.1)	39 (28.8)	135 (100)
2-4	100 (29.4)	240 (70.5)	340 (100)
Total	**196 (41.2)**	**279 (58.2)**	**475 (100)**

$\chi^2 = 69.2$ df = 1 $P < 0.05$.

Table 7.11 shows that out of 135 children with less than two years of experience, nearly three-fourths (71.1%) do three types of work, and over one-fourth (28.8%) do more than three types of work. On the other hand, of 340 children with 2-4 years of experience, over one-fourth (29.4%) do three types of work, and nearly three-fourths (70.5%) perform

His smile and the weight on his shoulder do not match

more than three types of work. It is thus evident that the workload assigned to the children depends on their work experience. In other words, their work experience has a direct bearing on their workload.

The owners, managers and supervisors believe that the more experienced children will do more than three types of work because they have acquired adequate skill in their work. Moreover, they are physically and mentally more mature to attend to different types of job than the beginners and semi-skilled workers.

It is found that there is a significant relationship between the rural and urban background of the children and their heavy workload. This is explained in Table 7.12.

Table 7.12: Respondents by Background and Heavy work Load

Background	Heavy workload		Total
	Three types of work	More than three types of work	
Rural	139 (38.3)	223 (61.6)	362 (100)
Urban	57 (50.4)	56 (49.5)	113 (100)
Total	**196 (41.2)**	**279 (58.2)**	**475 (100)**

$\chi^2 = 5.12$ df = 1 $P < 0.05$

It is clearly understood from the data distributed in Table 7.12 that more rural children (61.6%) attend to more than three types of work than their urban counterparts (49.5%). On the other hand, more urban children (50.4%) attend to three or fewer types of work than their rural counterparts (38.3%). It is, thus, evident that more rural children than their urban counterparts are assigned heavy workload. It is, therefore, concluded that more rural children than their urban counterparts are subjected to exploitation in terms of more work.

This trend may perhaps be explained in terms of the difference between the rural and urban background of the children. The rural children are more obedient and afraid of the owners and other employers than their urban counterparts. They are more happier about the food they get thrice a day than their urban counterparts. Therefore, the hotel management assigns more work to the rural children than to the urban children.

This is perhaps the reason why the owners prefer rural children to those from urban areas. This is well supported by the views expressed by the owner of a hotel situated at Tirunelveli Junction. His views are presented as follows:

> I have thirty years of experience in hotel business. I have seen hundreds of children and clearly understand their behavior. I find that the rural children are more obedient, sincere, truthful and hard working than their urban

counterparts are. Moreover, they do not often change the hotels in which they work. Unlike the urban children, they do not hesitate to attend to my personal and domestic work. They are more afraid of me than the urban children. That is the reason why I would like to employ more rural children than urban children.

The types of work assigned to the children are decided on the basis of the persons through whom they got the hotel job. Table 7.13 represents this.

Table 7.13: Respondents by Source of Recruitment and Heavy Workload

Source of Recruitment	Heavy workload		Total
	Three types of work	More than three types of work	
Through middle management employees	120 (60.0)	80 (40.0)	200 (100)
Through brokers	76 (27.6)	199 (72.3)	275 (100)
Total	**196 (41.2)**	**279 (58.2)**	**475 (100)**

$\chi^2 = 49.9$ df = 1 $P < 0.05$

It is a common practice in the hotels in Tirunelveli District as elsewhere that the managers, supervisors and masters recruit children of known parents. Sometimes they also take children of parents not known to them personally. They are more lenient to the children whose parents are known to them. They do not show such leniency to the children recruited through the brokers. This difference in the leniency shown by the middle management employees owes much to their personal relationship with the parents of the children.

The proportion of those who have secured hotel jobs through the middle management employees and who attend to more than three types of work is 40 per cent whereas the proportion of those who have joined the hotel jobs through brokers and who attend to more than three types of work is 72.3 per cent. It is thus evident that the children's personal relationship with the middle management employees plays a vital role in the allocation of work among the children. It is a common trend that most of the time the hotels located in tourist centres are crowded because of the increasing number of tourists every day during the season. This would result in an increase in the workload of the children. But it is not so in the hotels situated in non-tourist centres. This is represented in Table 7.14.

Table 7.14: Respondents by Location of Hotels and Heavy Work Load

Types of place where hotels are located	Heavy workload		Total
	Three types of work	More than three types of work	
Tourist Centre	98 (29.6)	232 (70.3)	330 (100)
Non-Tourist Centre	98 (67.5)	47 (32.4)	145 (100)
Total	**196 (41.2)**	**279 (58.7)**	**475 (100)**

$\chi^2 = 59.5$ df = 1 $P < 0.05$

Table 7.14 disclose that the proportion of children attending to more than three types of work in hotels situated in tourist centres is more than twice as much as the proportion of their counterparts with similar workload in hotels located in non-tourist places. It is evident that the children in the former type of hotels are subjected to more exploitation than those in the latter type of hotels. A 13-year-old boy whose duration of work is long in a hotel in a tourist centre explains his workload problem as follows:

> I work in a hotel located in a tourist place where there are three big waterfalls. In the hotel, the workload is heavy. There are 12 boys of my age doing different jobs. We start the work as early as 5.30 or 6.00 a.m. We complete the work after mid-night by 1.00 or 2.00 a.m. Our hotel is very popular in this area and it has board and lodging facilities and also has a wine shop. From June to February this tourist place is busy because of the season. During this time hundreds of tourists from far off places throng this place. In order to attract the tourists, the employers and employees of our hotel extract more work from us to maintain it clean in all respects. They stand at the dining chamber most of the time and observe our activities closely. If we are slow, they scold and beat us.
>
> When the hotels are crowded, the owner allows us group by group to have our tiffin and lunch within 15 minutes. We have to clean the tables and collect vessels as soon as the customers finish eating. Otherwise they shout at us and warn us using filthy language. Sometimes they mercilessly beat us.
>
> We have to clean the floor three or four times a day and wash it with acid every night after business hours. Every day we have to bring the firewood and grocery items to the kitchen from the godown. At times, the supervisor changes our work. For instance, I would be assigned to cleaning and washing for two weeks and afterwards to assist the masters in the kitchen. After that I would be given the work of supplying coffee or tea to the customers staying in the hotel rooms. Sometimes, I would be sent to attend the customers in the bar. It is rather difficult to work as room boy because I have to walk up and down to fetch the items required by the customers. Though I get more tips, I feel pain in my legs.

EXTRA WORK

In any industry exploitation of working children is observed in their workload, duration of work and wage. In hotels the children have to attend to the personal jobs of the owners, managers, supervisors, masters and adult co-workers. This is extra work for the children who are expected to do it without any return either in money or in kind. This is personal and domestic work of the employers and other employees.

The hotel owner has the power to recruit any new person or terminate his services. He provides the employees with food thrice a day and a monthly income. The manager, supervisor and masters supervise all sorts of work in the absence of the owner. Moreover, they arrange the purchase of vegetables, grocery items and other raw materials, gas and firewood. Every month, the manager or supervisor calculates the income and expenditure of the hotel, distributes their wages to the employees and clears the income tax, electricity and telephone bills.

Since the children work at the mercy of the owners, manager and supervisor, they make use of the children for their personal work. In any hotel, there is one head cook who is otherwise known as master, assisted by four or five assistant cooks. The hotel owner gives importance to the master because the quality and taste of the food items lies in his efficiency and talent. He also makes use of the children for his personal work. Since the children are in need of tea or coffee at least every two hours to stimulate themselves to attend to their work and tasty food thrice a day they have to depend on the master. Therefore, he gets his personal work done by the children.

In addition to this, the adult co-workers have a hold over the children. It is a common practice in hotels that the children are divided into three or four groups. Each senior adult co-worker is assigned to supervise a group of children. Therefore, the children show due respect to the adult co-workers. The adult co-workers promptly exploit the children using them for their personal work.

Nevertheless, the first exploiter of the children in this way is the hotel owner. The work includes supplying him with coffee or tea, carrying hot water for him, buying cigarettes and *pan-parag* for him and the like. He sends the children to attend to his domestic work such as getting provisions from ration shop, collecting gas cylinder, buying vegetables and grocery items, carrying drinking water from outside and carrying clothes to the launderer and fetching pressed dresses. In certain cases, the owners' family depends on hotel food. If it is so, in rotation, the children have to carry food for them thrice a day.

The second exploiter is the manager or the supervisor or the master. Most of them are away from their families because they are busy with hotel management. They take leave for a week once in six months. They live in houses close to the hotel. Since they live alone, they make use of the services of the children for their personal work. They send the children to buy things like cosmetics, *pan-parag*, liquor and cigarettes. They

Like professional coolies, they load and unload heavy firewood. Around them is darkness

also ask them to clean the house and bring drinking water from outside if there is no tap connection. The third exploiter is the adult co-worker who makes use of the services of the children to satisfy his personal needs. In this connection it is relevant to refer to the finding of Musafir Singh *et.al.* (1980) in their study. They point out that most of the working children attend to the personal work of the owners like washing their dress, pressing their legs, massaging their body, polishing their shoes, etc. In many cases, they have to attend to the domestic chores of their employers.[4]

Though the children have access to their owners and other employees, they are more obligated to the former than to the latter. The owner is the superior authority. It is up to him to retain an employee or send him out. The employees have to live up to their expectations. That is perhaps why they attend to the domestic work of their owners besides their work in the hotel. This is clearly shown in Table 7.15.

Table 7.15: Respondents by Service Rendered to Employers and Employees

Management persons	Personal and domestic work		Total
	Attending	Not Attending	
Owners	384 (80.8)	91 (19.1)	475 (100)
Middle management Employees	288 (60.6)	187 (39.3)	475 (100)
Adult co-workers	192 (40.4)	283 (59.8)	475 (100)

It is evident from the table that an overwhelming majority of the children (80.8%) attend to the domestic work of their owners. A majority (60.6%) do attend to the personal work of their managers, supervisors and masters. As they directly deal with the children, they have to oblige them. Otherwise, they deal with the children sternly and punish them unkindly. On the other hand, the adult co-workers move with the children in a friendly way. Therefore, the children prefer to be with them most of the time. The children confide their problems to them and seek their help and guidance. That is the reason why they are helpful to the co-workers.

Though the children are obedient to the employers and employees, they are not sincere and regular in attending to their personal work. Normally they do not force or compel the children in the age group of 12-14 years. Instead they force those in the age group of 8-12 years. So the proportion of the children of 8-10 years who attend to the personal and domestic work of their owners is relatively higher than the proportion of those 10-12 and 12-14 years. A similar trend is found in the case of other employees and adult co-workers. This shows that the elder children are aware of the fact that they have been exploited by the employers and employees. This is represented in Table 7.16 and Fig. 7.3.

His service extends beyond the hotel up to the owner's house on many an errand

Table 7.16: Respondents by Age and Rendering Service to Ownars and Employees

Age	Rendering service to employers & employees								
	Owners			Managers, Supervisors and Masters			Adult co-workers		
	Attending	Not Attending	Total	Attending	Not Attending	Total	Attending	Not Attending	Total
8-10	115 (91.2)	11 (8.7)	126 (100)	95 (75.3)	31 (24.6)	126 (100)	76 (60.3)	50 (39.6)	126 (100)
10-12	155 (80.3)	38 (19.6)	193 (100)	127 (65.8)	66 (34.1)	193 (100)	78 (40.4)	115 (59.5)	193 (100)
12-14	114 (73.0)	42 (26.9)	156 (100)	66 (34.1)	90 (57.6)	156 (100)	38 (24.3)	118 (75.6)	156 (100)
Total	**384 (80.8)**	**91 (19.1)**	**475 (100)**	**288 (60.6)**	**187 (39.3)**	**475 (100)**	**192 (40.4)**	**283 (59.5)**	**475 (100)**

(i) $\chi^2 = 14.92$ df = 2 $P < 0.05$.

(ii) $\chi^2 = 35.25$ df = 2 $P < 0.05$.

(iii) $\chi^2 = 37.2$ df = 2 $P < 0.05$.

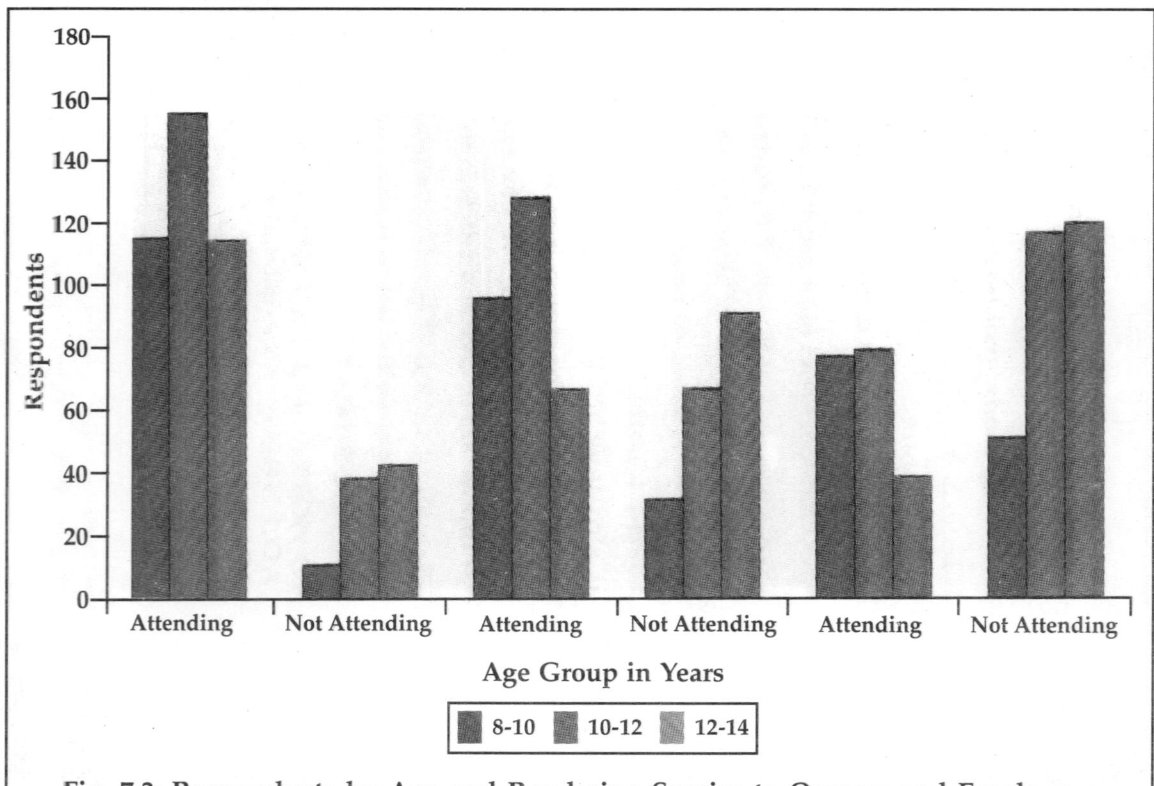

Fig. 7.3: Respondents by Age and Rendering Service to Owners and Employees

It is understood from the table and figure that there is a significant relationship between the age of the children and their services to the hotel owners and other employees. This shows that when the children grow, they realise that they have been exploited by the owners and other employees.

In a similar way, there is a relationship between the experience of the children and service rendered to the hotel owners and other employees. This is shown in Table 7.17.

Table 7.17: Respondents by Experience and Service Rendered to Hotel Employers and Employees

Experience (in years)	Rendering service to employers & employees								
	Owners			Managers, Supervisors and Masters			Adult co-workers		
	Attending	Not Attending	Total	Attending	Not Attending	Total	Attending	Not Attending	Total
Less than 2	122 (90.3)	44 (9.6)	135 (100)	108 (80.0)	27 (20.0)	135 (100)	82 (60.7)	53 (39.2)	135 (100)
2-4	262 (77.3)	78 (22.9)	340 (100)	180 (52.9)	160 (47.0)	340 (100)	110 (32.3)	230 (67.6)	340 (100)
Total	**384 (80.8)**	**91 (19.1)**	**475 (100)**	**288 (60.6)**	**187 (39.3)**	**475 (100)**	**192 (40.4)**	**283 (59.5)**	**475 (100)**

(i) $\chi^2 = 17.3$ df = 1 P < 0.05.

(ii) $\chi^2 = 29.5$ df = 1 P < 0.05.

(iii) $\chi^2 = 27.6$ df = 1 P < 0.05.

The data show that the increase in the age of children results in a decrease in the proportion of children who attend to domestic and personal work of the owners and other employees. It is also interesting to find that the proportion of children who attend to domestic and personal work decreases with respect to the position in occupational hierarchy in the hotel. For instance, the proportion of less experienced children who attend to the domestic and personal work of their owners (90.3%) is considerately higher them the proportion of those who attend to the personal work of the manger, supervisors and masters (80%) and the proportion of those who attend to similar work of adult co-workers (60.7%). It is thus clear that there is a significant relationship between the experience of the children and their services to the hotel owners and employees.

There is also a difference between the treatment of the children introduced by known persons [mostly the hotel employees] and of the children introduced by brokers who visit the hotels occasionally. The former group of children are taken care of by the employees become they secured the hotel jobs for them whereas the latter group of children have no guardians within the hotels. This leads to a variation in the response of the children with regard to attending to the domestic as well as personal work of the hotel owners and other employees. This is presented in Table 7.18.

Table 7.18: **Respondents by Sources of Recruitment and Service to Hotel Employers and Employees**

Recruitment	Rendering service to employers & employees								
	Owners			Managers, Supervisors and Masters			Adult Co-workers		
	Attending	Not Attending	Total	Attending	Not Attending	Total	Attending	Not Attending	Total
Through hotel employers and employees	131 (65.5)	69 (34.5)	200 (100)	99 (49.5)	101 (50.5)	200 (100)	70 (35.0)	130 (65.0)	200 (100)
Through brokers	253 (92.0)	22 (8.0)	275 (100)	189 (68.7)	86 (31.2)	275 (100)	122 (44.3)	153 (55.6)	275 (100)
Total	**384 (80.8)**	**91 (19.1)**	**475 (100)**	**288 (60.6)**	**187 (39.3)**	**475 (100)**	**192 (40.4)**	**283 (59.5)**	**475 (100)**

(i) $\chi^2 = 52.4$ df = 1 $P < 0.05$.

(ii) $\chi^2 = 18.6$ df = 1 $P < 0.05$.

(iii) $\chi^2 = 4.06$ df = 1 $P < 0.05$.

It is evident from the above table that the proportion of children introduced by the hotel employers and employees who attend to the domestic as well as personal work of owners (65.5%), other employees (49.5%) and adult co-workers (35%) is significantly lower than the proportion of those introduced by the brokers who do a similar service to those persons. It is, thus, obvious that more of the second category of children than the first category attend to personal and domestic work of their owners and other employees. This shows that the second category is subjected to more exploitation than their counterparts in the first category. It is thus clear that in the absence of someone in the hotel to look after them the children are exposed to exploitation.

LOW INCOME

The rate of payment depends upon various factors like the nature of the job and the skill acquired by the children. All the three types of hotels make monthly payment. Besides this payment, they provide the children with food and accommodation. The payment is made in three ways:

(i) the parents collect the income of their children at the end of the month;

(ii) the parents collect a small amount of money in advance at regular intervals instead of receiving the income of their children at the end of the month; (sometimes, the managers, supervisors and masters collect the advance of money and send it to the parents of children); and

(iii) the parents get an advance from the hotel owner (to the tune of Rs. 2,500-5,000) by pledging their children to them.

This amount is decided according to the skill of the children. Normally the income of the children depends on the duration of their work. In other words, more they work more the income they get. Thus there is a direct relationship between the duration of work and the income of the children as indicated in Table 7.19.

Table 7.19: Respondents by duration of Work and Monthly Income

Duration of work (in hours)	Monthly income of respondents (in Rs.)	Total Respondents
≤12	Up to 300	136 (28.6)
13	300-600	155 (32.63)
14	600-900	184 (38.73)
Total		**475 (100)**

It is evident from Table 7.19 that out of 475 working children, over one-third (32.8%) work for 12 hours a day and earn up to Rs. 300 per month, and over one-fourth (28.4%) work for 13 hours a day and earn Rs. 300-600 per month. Over one-third (38.4%) work 14 hours a day and earn Rs. 600-900 per month.

Though the monthly income of the children increases with the increase in the duration of their work, their income is unjustifiably low considering the duration of their work. The hotel management makes them work for long hours and pays them very little. This shows that the hotel management exploits them economically. It is observed that there is a significant relationship between the location of the hotels in which the children are employed and their monthly income. This is clearly exhibited in Table 7.20.

Table 7.20: Respondents by Jobs in Hotels Located in Tourist and Non-Tourist Centres and Monthly Income

Types of place where hotels are located	Monthly income of respondents (in Rs.)		Total
	100-500	501-1000	
Tourist Centre	86 (26.0)	244 (73.9)	330 (100)
Non-tourist Centre	50 (34.4)	95 (65.5)	145 (100)
Total	**136 (28.6)**	**339 (71.3)**	**475 (100)**

$\chi^2 = 38.4$ df =1 $P < 0.05$

It is clear from Table 7.20 that the proportion of children employed in the hotels located in tourist places (73.9%) is considerably higher than those employed in the hotels situated in non-tourist places (65.5%) within their monthly income of Rs. 501-1,000.

Since there is a great demand for workers in hotels in tourist places, the employers are prepared to pay them more than their counterparts in non-tourist places for the same duration of work. The children look for hotels paying more than what they get at present. That is perhaps why there is variation in the proportion of children from hotels located in tourist and non-tourist places with respect to their monthly income.

There is a significant difference between the income of the children and of their adult co-workers. It is observed that the suppliers who form the immediate higher category above the working children get Rs.1800 per month from the hotels located in tourist places and Rs.1,500 from the hotels situated in non-tourist places for 10 hours of work a day. The children who toil for 14 hours a day get Rs.600-900 per month. This is mainly due to the difference in age and experience between the two categories. Nevertheless, the children are assigned heavy workload and are subjected to physical punishment. Suppliers do not face such problems. In this context, it is relevant to refer to a finding of Musafir Singh *et.al.*, (1980) in their study. They point out that the children work for 12 to 16 hours in hotels in Mumbai, a popular tourist place, and get low wage. They feel that the hotel job is very heavy and continuous.[5]

It is noticed that the employers exploit the children by providing them with *beta*. For instance, if one or two children do not turn up for their work their work is allotted to other children. They have to attend to the allotted work besides their own work neatly and systematically. This results in a difficult situation in which the children have to shoulder heavy workload and assume more responsibilities. They are paid a *beta*, which, however, is rather low-around Rs.10 per day. For the meager sum of money, these children have to toil for hours together continuously. It is relevant to present here a case study:

> I am 13-year old and have been working in a hotel for three years. Many a times the boys employed in the hotel do not turn up to work. Sometimes, one or two boys run away due to the physical punishment given to them. In such circumstances, I am asked to attend to the work of those absentees besides doing the work assigned to me. It is very painful for me to shoulder a heavy workload. If I do not, I will be forced. For that I am given a *beta* of Rs. 5-10 per day. Every time I experience severe pain in my hip, legs and shoulders. Sometimes, I am unable to sleep in the night due to this problem. I have decided to leave the hotel as early as possible. But I cannot leave immediately as my father has already received an advance of Rs. 2000 from the hotel owner. I have to serve at least 2-3 years.

Sometimes, the children are put to work at tea stalls within the hotel complex. Their main work is to supply tea or coffee to the neighboring shopping centres at regular intervals. They are also compelled to supply at least an average of 100 cups of tea in the morning and the same number of cups of tea in the evening. This is understood from a case study:

They can't keep their hands or dress dry as they have to be always washing dishes

I have completed one year of service in this hotel. In the beginning I was cleaning the tables because the manager assigned that work to me. They then sent me to supply coffee and tea in the neighbouring shopping centres. The supervisor asked me to supply 100 cups coffee or tea every day. This is a target fixed for every day. If do not complete the target, I will not be made permanent. If I continue to be so, I will be sent out after some time. After supplying coffee or tea, I have to collect the money regularly and hand it over to the manager in the evening. He is keen on observing whether the money tallies for 100 cups of coffee or tea. Sometimes, the customers may not be able to pay for want of change. If it is so, the total amount will not be correct, and I will be physically punished by the managers. If I am unable to collect the money from the customers, that amount will be deducted from my monthly income. Moreover, my income will be fixed based on the completion of my target and the correct settlement of account every day.

The discussion in this section clearly shows that the children attend to the assigned work for about 14 hours a day. However, in the course of time, they are assigned to do three or more than three types of work simultaneously. Thus, they are made to shoulder heavy workload within a short period after joining the hotels. In addition to this, they have to attend to personal and domestic work of the employers and employees. In spite to their heavy workload and extra work, they are not paid justifiably.

PUNISHMENT

In hotels, it is a common practice to find that the owners, supervisors, managers, masters and adult co-workers punish the working children if they do not perform their work as expected. They are scolded, or punished physically. The following Table shows the proportion of children punished by the owners and the employees.

Table 7.21: Respondents by Punishment and Punishers

Punishers	Punishment		Total
	Yes	No	
Owners	396 (83.3)	79 (83.3)	475 (100)
Managers, Supervisors and Masters	240 (50.5)	235 (49.4)	475 (100)
Adult co-workers	190 (40.0)	285 (60.0)	475 (100)

It is evident from Table 7.21 that a great majority of the children (83.3%) are punished by the owners, a majority (50.5%) are punished by the managers, supervisors and masters and 40 per cent are punished by adult co-workers. It is thus clear that the owners punish the children more than the employees do.

They handle gas cylinders, which are of their size

In hotels, the punishment is of two types. One is oral and the other is physical. The data show that the types of punishment given to the children vary from person to person. This is presented in Table 7.22.

Table 7.22: Respondents by Types of Punishment and Punishers

Punishers	Types of Punishment		Total
	Oral	Physical	
Owners	249 (62.8)	147 (37.1)	396 (100)
Managers, Supervisors and Masters	83 (34.5)	157 (65.4)	240 (100)
Adult co-workers	124 (65.2)	66 (34.7)	190 (100)

In all types of hotels, nearly two-thirds of the owners and adult co-workers punish the children by scolding whereas one-third of them inflict corporal punishment. Since the owners are profit-oriented, they do not punish the children physically. They fear that the physical punishment would drive them out and as a result, they would have to recruit new children immediately in order to keep the work going. So they prefer to scold and try to correct them and retain them as far as possible. In a similar way, the adult co-workers punish them rarely because they are friendly and helpful to the children. On the contrary, nearly two-thirds of the managers and supervisors punish the children physically because they are keen on observing the performance of the children. When the children are lazy or slow in attending to the work and commit mistakes, the manager and supervisor punish them physically in order to correct them.

Out of 396 children punished by the owners, nearly two-thirds (62.8%) are punished orally. Over one-third (37.1%) are punished physically. Out of 240 children punished by managers, supervisors and masters, over one-third (34.5%) of the children are punished orally and nearly two-thirds (65.4%) are punished physically. Of 195 children punished by adult co-workers, about two-thirds (65.2%) are punished orally and over one-third (34.2%) are punished physically. Thus, the punishment given depends on the person who gives the punishment. In all types of hotel, most of the owners punish the children.

The managers and supervisors do not apply their minds to the question of why a particular boy does not do his job as they desire him to do it. They are only keen that for the moment the boy should be driven back to work. They seem to be confident that if one boy runs away, they would find others. They do not try to find the reasons for the boys running away with a view to solving the problems of the boys so that they would prefer to stay. Thus these middle order executives are not positive in their attitude even in their own interests. They seem to lack professional training. It may be suggested in this connection that professional training and at least a short exposure of these people to the theory of personnel management will do good all round.

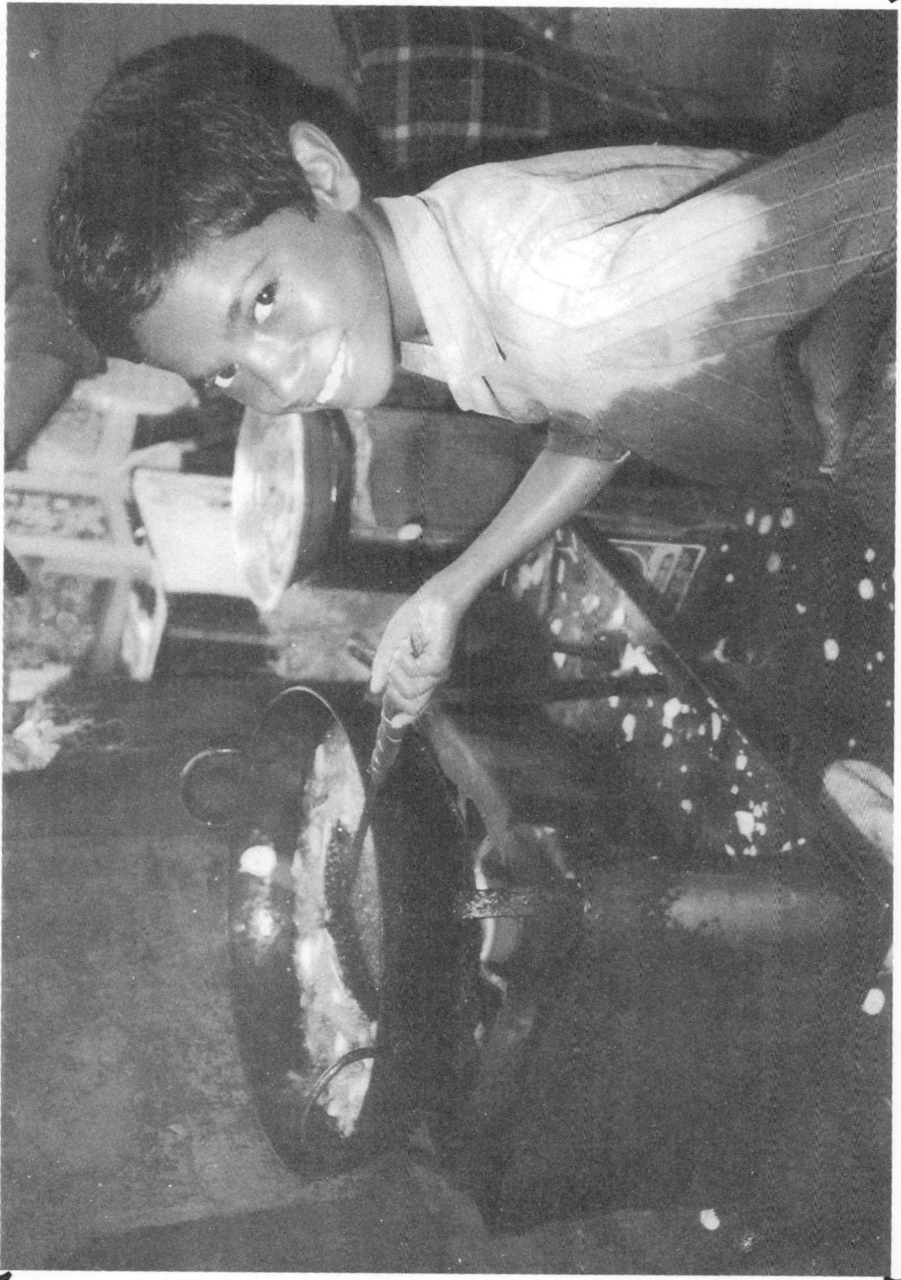

Too Young to be near sizzling oil-pan!

The managers and supervisors neither seriously look into the labour problem nor mind the children running away. When the children run away, the managers and supervisors promise the owners that they would bring some other children.

It is relevant to describe a few case studies which would very well explain the child abuse in the hotels. A boy of 14 engaged in a hotel job in the Junction area at Tirunelveli says:

> I studied up to IVth Std. I have two brothers and two sisters. I joined this job at the age of 10 and I have three and a half years' experience. I have also worked in hotels at Mumbai, Thiruvananthapuram and Chennai. My supervisor here has beaten me twice with firewood.
>
> My master often asks me to bring firewood by tri-cycle. The firewood is stored at a distance of two furlongs from the hotel. Once after bringing firewood I was resting at the staircase. My master scolded me using filthy words and beat me on my legs with firewood (showed the scar on the legs). However, the owner met all the medical expenses to treat the wounds on my legs. After two months, I left the job.
>
> When I was working in a hotel at Chennai, I was asked to clean all the 24 tables continuously because most of the boys were on leave for a few days for Diwali. As I was the only person attending to table cleaning, I became very tired and sat on a stool in the kitchen for a while. When the supervisor saw me, he hit my legs with an iron rod (a big scar is visible). Then I was admitted in a hospital. The owner met all medical expenses. Afterwards, I left the hotel and came to Tirunelveli.

Another 12-year old boy doing similar work in a hotel at Tirunelveli Town explains his plight as follows:

> Once my master asked me to attend to his domestic work, but I did not want to as his wife used to extract more work, sending me to ration shop, laundry shop, tailor-shop and market. I would not be given any tips for doing all this. So I did not want to go to his house. Angered the master poured hot tea dust on my right leg. I didn't expect this. I screamed in pain. (He showed his burnt leg). I had to rest for three days in the hotel itself. However, the owner met all expenses towards my medical treatment. But he did not permit me to rest longer than three days.

Chandragupt S. Sanon's study (1988) also describes the punishments given to children in hotels. According to him, it varies from scolding to beating in the presence of customers. The owners are keen on getting the profit, but they do not bother about the welfare of the working children. They know how to extract work from the children.[6]

It is found that there is a significant relation in the proportion of children with regard to their age and the punishment they get. This is represented in Table 7.23.

Table 7.23: Respondents by Age, Punishment and Punishers

Age Group (in years)	Owners			Managers, Supervisors and Masters			Adult Co-workers		
	Yes	No	Total	Yes	No	Total	Yes	No	Total
8-10	84 (66.6)	42 (33.3)	126 (100)	58 (46.0)	68 (53.9)	126 (100)	39 (30.9)	87 (69.0)	126 (100)
10-12	169 (87.5)	24 (12.4)	193 (100)	89 (46.1)	104 (53.8)	193 (100)	70 (36.2)	123 (63.7)	193 (100)
12-14	143 (91.6)	13 (8.3)	156 (100)	93 (59.6)	63 (40.3)	156 (100)	81 (51.9)	75 (48.0)	156 (100)
Total	**396 (83.3)**	**79 (16.4)**	**475 (100)**	**240 (50.5)**	**235 (49.5)**	**475 (100)**	**190 (40.0)**	**285 (60.0)**	**475 (100)**

Owners : $\chi^2 = 35.6$ df = 2 $P < 0.05$.

Managers, Supervisors & Masters : $\chi^2 = 7.30$ df = 2 $P < 0.05$.

Adult Co-workers : $\chi^2 = 14.3$ df = 2 $P < 0.05$.

Table 7.23 gives a picture of the children punished by three types of punishers. Out of 126 children in the age group of 8-10 years, two-thirds (66.6%) report that they were punished by the owners. 46 per cent were punished by the managers, supervisors and masters and one-third (31%) by adult co-workers. Out of 156 in the age group of 12-14, an overwhelming majority (91.6%) was punished by the owners, two-thirds by the managers, supervisors and masters and a majority (51.9%) by adult co-workers. The data show that fewer boys in the age group of 8-10 years were punished than in the age group of 10-12 years. Fewer children of 10-12 years were punished than children in the age group of 12-14 years. Thus, the number of children suffering punishment increases with the increase in their age. In other words, more of older children than younger are subjected to punishment.

There is significant variation in the proportion of children with regard to their age and types of punishment they suffer. This is represented in Table 7.24 and Fig. 7.4.

The data in Table 7.24 show a variation in the types of punishment. Out of 84 working children of 8-10 years punished by the owners, an over-whelming majority (83.3%) met with oral punishment. A lesser proportion (16.6%) suffered physical punishment. Out of 58 working children of the same age range punished by managers and supervisors, nearly three-fourths (72.4%) met with oral punishment and over one-fourth (27.5%) met with physical punishment. Out of 39 children of similar age punished by adult co-workers, 12.8 per cent underwent oral punishment and an overwhelming majority (82.1%) underwent physical punishment. Out of 143 children in the age group of 12-14 years punished by owners, over one-third (39.1%) was subjected to oral punishment and nearly two-thirds (60.8%) to physical punishment. Out of 93 children punished by the managers, supervisors and masters, nearly one-fourth (22.5%) were subjected to oral punishment and over three-fourths (77.4%) were subjected to physical punishment. Out of 81 children punished by adult co-workers, an overwhelming majority (91.3%) was subjected to oral punishment and 8.6 per cent to physical punishment.

Table 7.24: Respondents by Age, Types of Punishment and Punishers

Age Group (in years)	Owners			Managers, Supervisors and Masters			Adult Co-workers		
	Oral	Physical	Total	Oral	Physical	Total	Oral	Physical	Total
8-10	70 (83.3)	14 (16.6)	84 (100)	42 (72.4)	16 (27.5)	58 (100)	5 (12.8)	34 (82.1)	39 (100)
10-12	123 (72.7)	46 (27.2)	169 (100)	20 (22.4)	69 (77.5)	89 (100)	45 (64.2)	25 (35.7)	70 (100)
12-14	56 (39.1)	87 (60.8)	143 (100)	21 (22.5)	72 (77.4)	93 (100)	74 (91.3)	7 (8.6)	81 (100)
Total	**249 (62.8)**	**147 (37.1)**	**369 (100)**	**83 (34.5)**	**157 (65.4)**	**240 (100)**	**124 (65.2)**	**66 (34.7)**	**190 (100)**

Owners : $\chi^2 = 56.5$ df = 2 $P < 0.05$.

Managers, Supervisors & Masters : $\chi^2 = 48.3$ df = 2 $P < 0.05$.

Adult Co-workers : $\chi^2 = 71.7$ df = 2 $P < 0.05$.

The owners get the work done by scolding the younger children. If they punish them physically, the children may run away from the hotels, which in turn may affect the profit of the hotel. Hence, the owners resort to oral punishment. The owners feel that when the children grow older, they become disobedient, insincere and slow. So they have to be punish them physically. The same philosophy is followed by the hotel employees. The level of exploitation of the older ones is higher.

The proportion of higher age group children who undergo punishment is higher than the proportion of lower age group children punished by the employers and employees. A similar trend is reflected while analyzing the relationship between the experience of the children and the punishment they meet with during the work time. This is shown in Table 7.25.

While analyzing the data in terms of the experience of children, it is seen that more children with 2-4 years of experience than children with experience up to two years are punished by the employers and employees. The reason is that the children with experience up to two years are beginners and are very attentive and careful in their work. They want to gain experience in their work. They fear that they would be punished if they are inattentive or careless. On the other hand, children with more than two years of experience want to leave the hotels they are working in and to secure a similar kind of job in big hotels in cities so that they would get more salary, other allowances and attractive tips from the customers. That is perhaps the reason why they grow less attentive and careless in their work and for that they get punished.

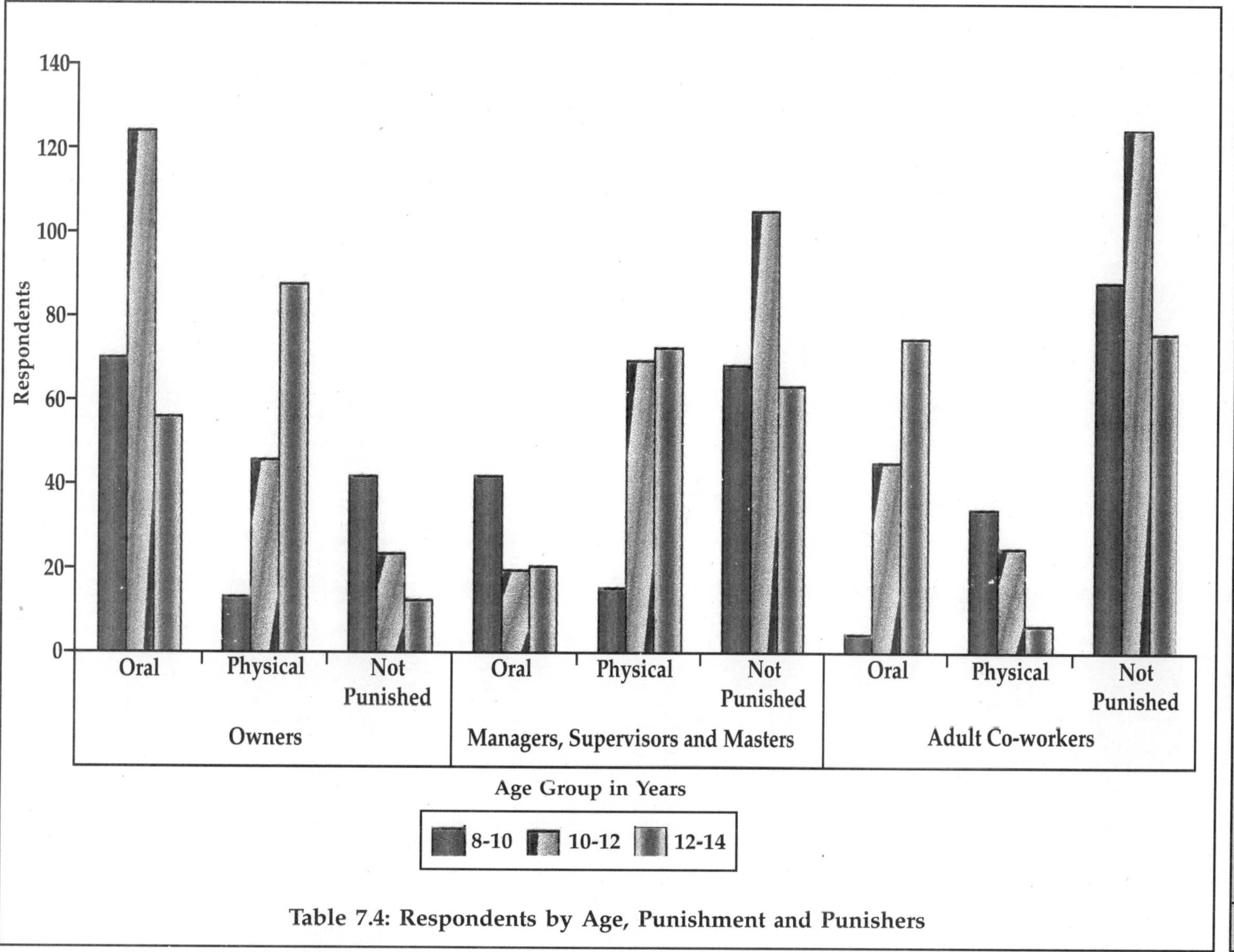

Table 7.4: Respondents by Age, Punishment and Punishers

Table 7.25: Respondents by Experience, Punishment and Punishers

Experience (in years)	Owners			Managers, Supervisors and Masters			Adult Co-workers		
	Yes	No	Total	Yes	No	Total	Yes	No	Total
Up to 2	65 (48.1)	70 (51.8)	135 (100)	48 (35.5)	87 (64.4)	135 (100)	41 (303)	94 (69.6)	135 (100)
2-4	331 (97.3)	9 (2.6)	340 (100)	192 (56.4)	148 (43.5)	340 (100)	149 (43.8)	191 (56.1)	340 (100)
Total	**396 (83.3)**	**79 (16.6)**	**475 (100)**	**240 (50.5)**	**235 (49.4)**	**475 (100)**	**190 (40.0)**	**285 (60.0)**	**475 (100)**

Owners : $\chi^2 = 169.0$ df = 1 P < 0.05.

Managers, Supervisors & Masters : $\chi^2 = 16.8$ df = 1 P < 0.05.

Adult Co-workers : $\chi^2 = 8.3$ df = 1 P < 0.05.

Out of 135 children with experience up to two years, nearly a majority (48.1%) are punished by the owners, over one-third (35.5%) are punished by the managers, supervisors and masters and a majority of them (30.3%) are punished by adult co-workers.

On the other hand, of 340 children with 2-4 years of experience, an overwhelming majority (97.3%) are punished by the owners, a majority (56.4%) are punished by the managers, supervisors and masters and over one-third (43.8 per cent) are punished by adult co-workers.

The proportion of children with more than two years of experience who undergo physical punishment by the employers and employees is significantly higher than the proportion of boys with less than two years of experience. However, the trend is reversed in the case of children who are punished physically by adult co-workers. This is exhibited in Table 7.26.

Table 7.26: Respondents by Experience, Types of Punishment and Punishers

Experience (in years)	Owners			Manager, Supervisor and Masters			Adult Co-workers		
	Oral	Physical	Total	Oral	Physical	Total	Oral	Physical	Total
Up to 2	56 (86.1)	9 (13.8)	65 (100)	30 (62.5)	18 (37.5)	48 (100)	20 (29.4)	48 (70.5)	68 (100)
2-4	193 (58.3)	138 (41.6)	331 (100)	53 (27.6)	139 (72.3)	192 (100)	104 (85.2)	18 (14.7)	122 (100)
Total	**249 (62.8)**	**147 (37.1)**	**396 (100)**	**83 (34.5)**	**157 (65.4)**	**240 (100)**	**124 (65.2)**	**66 (34.7)**	**190 (100)**

Owners : $\chi^2 = 17.8$ df = 1 P < 0.05.

Managers, Supervisors & Masters : $\chi^2 = 20.6$ df = 1 P < 0.05.

Adult Co-workers : $\chi^2 = 59.8$ df = 1 P < 0.05.

The reason for the significant difference in the proportion of children from the age groups of up to two years and 2-4 years who undergo physical punishment may be that the children with more than two years of experience are a bit careless in their work as they want to quit the present job and plan to secure a similar type of job in big hotels in cities for good salary and tips. On the other hand, adult co-workers might punish less experienced children corporally than those with more experience because the latter who are older would retaliate.

There is a variation in punishing the children with regard to their rural and urban background. This is represented in Table 7.27.

Table 7.27: Respondents by Background, Punishment and Punishers

Background	Owners			Manager, Supervisor and Masters			Adult Co-workers		
	Yes	No	Total	Yes	No	Total	Yes	No	Total
Rural	338 (93.3)	24 (6.6)	362 (100)	145 (40.6)	217 (59.9)	362 (100)	115 (31.7)	247 (68.2)	362 (100)
Urban	58 (51.2)	55 (48.6)	113 (100)	95 (84.4)	18 (15.9)	113 (100)	75 (66.3)	38 (33.6)	113 (100)
Total	**396 (83.3)**	**79 (16.6)**	**475 (100)**	**240 (50.5)**	**235 (49.4)**	**475 (100)**	**190 (40.0)**	**285 (60.0)**	**475 (100)**

Owners : $\chi^2 = 110.4$ df = 1 $P < 0.05$.

Managers, Supervisors and Masters : $\chi^2 = 66.76$ df = 1 $P < 0.05$.

Adult Co-workers : $\chi^2 = 42.78$ df = 1 $P < 0.05$.

It is understood from the table that a great majority (83.3 per cent) are punished by the owners, whereas 50.5 per cent are punished by the employees and 40.0 per cent by adult co-workers. More owners than employees punish the children. The owners are profit oriented and therefore they want to extract more work from the children in order to keep the tables, plates, spoons, floor and the like very clean and neat. Customers would be attracted by neatness and. hygienic atmosphere in the hotel. So they punish more the children who are careless and slow in work.

On the other hand, a lesser proportion of employees than owners punish the children. A majority of the employees have helped the children to get hotel jobs as the latter are, in one way or other, known to the former. Sometimes, both of them hail from the same village or town. So the employees take care of the children and help them when there are problems in the hotel.

While analyzing the data in terms of the rural-urban background of the children, it is found that an overwhelming majority of rural children (93.3%) are punished by the hotel owners. The reason is that the rural children are submissive and afraid of the hotel management. In order to extract more work from them the owners scold them. On the contrary, the proportion of the middle management employees (84.4%) and adult co-workers (66.3%) who punish the urban children, is more than twice as much as the proportion of those who punish the rural children. The reason is that most of the rural children in the hotels are introduced by these employees. Since they are morally responsible for safeguarding the interests of the rural children, a lower proportion of them punish those children.

It is observed that there is variation in the types of punishment with regard to the rural-urban background of the children. This is shown in Table 7.28 and Fig. 7.5.

Table 7.28: Respondents by Background, Types of Punishment and Punishers

Background	Owners				Manager, Supervisor and Masters				Adult Co-workers			
	Oral	Physical	No Punish-ment	Total	Oral	Physical	No Punish-ment	Total	Oral	Physical	No Punish-ment	Total
Rural	213 (58.8)	125 (34.5)	24 (6.62)	362 (100)	52 (14.36)	93 (25.6)	217 (59.9)	362 (100)	79 (21.8)	36 (9.9)	247 (68.2)	362 (100)
Urban	36 (31.8)	22 (19.5)	55 (48.6)	113 (100)	31 (27.4)	64 (56.6)	18 (15.9)	113 (100)	45 (39.8)	30 (26.5)	38 (33.6)	113 (100)
Total	**249 (52.4)**	**147 (39.9)**	**79 (16.6)**	**475 (100)**	**83 (17.47)**	**157 (33.0)**	**235 (49.4)**	**475 (100)**	**124 (26.1)**	**66 (13.8)**	**285 (60.0)**	**475 (100)**

Owners : $\chi^2 = 0.01$ df = 1 P > 0.05.

Managers, Supervisors & Masters : $\chi^2 = 0.24$ df = 1 P > 0.05.

Adult Co-workers : $\chi^2 = 1.22$ df = 1 P > 0.05.

It is evident from the data that more urban children than their rural counterparts are subject to punishment by the employees. The proportions of rural and urban children who are subjected to oral and physical punishment are more or less the same. The proportion of children who undergo oral punishment by the owners is significantly higher than the proportion of those who undergo physical punishment. On the contrary, the proportion of children who undergo physical punishment by the middle management employees and co-workers is significantly higher than the proportion of those who are subject to oral punishment.

There is a significant difference between the rural and urban children with regard to the types of punishment. The proportion of urban children who are subjected to physical punishment by the middle management employees and adult co-workers is significantly higher than the proportion of those who undergo oral punishment by the same category of employees. However, more or less the same proportion of rural children (38 1 per cent) and their urban counterparts (37.9%) undergo physical punishment by the owners. The reason is that normally the owners do not want to punish the children physically because they would run away from the hotels. In such circumstances, the owners find it difficult to manage the situation because, sometimes, they do not get skilled children to attend to cleaning and other work.

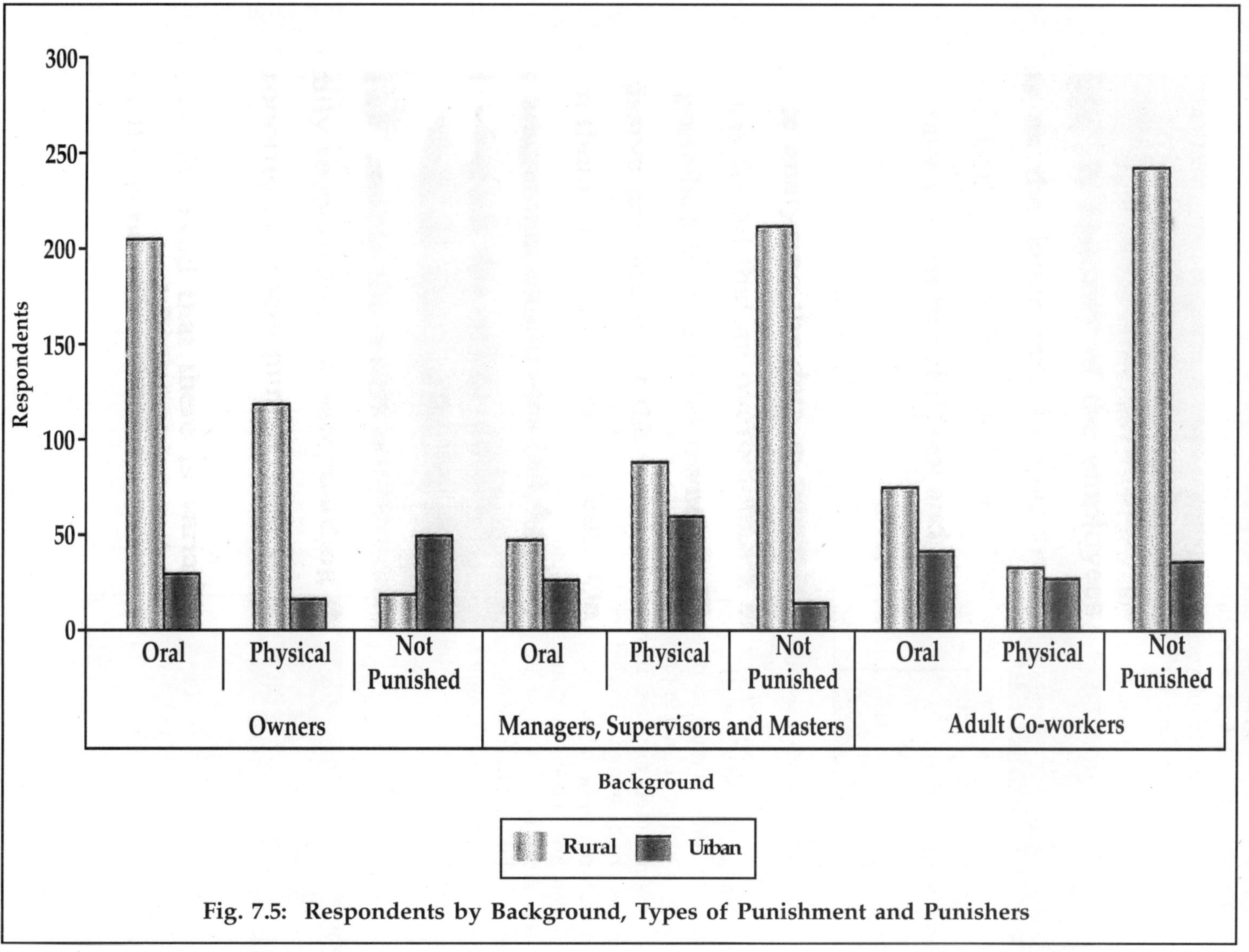

Fig. 7.5: Respondents by Background, Types of Punishment and Punishers

There is significant variation in the punishment of the children by the owners, middle management employees and adult co-workers with regard to the location of hotels. The distribution of data in Table 7.29 indicates this relationship.

Table 7.29: Respondents by Location of Hotel, Punishment and Punishers

Location of Hotels	Owners			Manager, Supervisor and Masters			Adult Co-workers		
	Yes	No	Total	Yes	No	Total	Yes	No	Total
Tourist Centre	301 (91.2)	29 (8.7)	330 (100)	178 (53.9)	152 (46.0)	330 (100)	139 (42.1)	191 (57.8)	330 (100)
Non Tourist Centre	95 (65.5)	50 (34.4)	145 (100)	62 (42.7)	83 (57.2)	145 (100)	51 (35.1)	94 (64.8)	145 (100)
Total	**396 (83.3)**	**79 (16.4)**	**475 (100)**	**240 (50.5)**	**235 (49.4)**	**475 (100)**	**190 (40.0)**	**285 (60.0)**	**475 (100)**

Owners : $\chi^2 = 47.8$ df = 1 $P < 0.05$.
Managers, Supervisors and Masters : $\chi^2 = 4.9$ df = 1 $P < 0.05$.
Adult Co-workers : $\chi^2 = 2.0$ df = 1 $P > 0.05$.

The data show that the proportion of children who undergo punishment from the owners, middle management employees and adult co-workers in hotels located in tourist places is higher than the proportion of those who are punished by the same category of persons in hotels situated in non-tourist places. The reason is that the hotels in tourist centres are busy and crowded most of the time. The owners and other employees expect the children to be active, careful and prompt in discharging their assigned work. If the children are not so, they are subjected to punishment. Thus, the children employed in hotels situated in tourist places work more than their counterparts in hotels in non-tourist places. There is significant variation in the types of punishment given to the children by the owners, middle management employees and adult co-workers with regard to the location of their hotels. The distribution of data in Table 7.30 indicates this relationship.

Table 7.30: Respondents by Location of Hotel Types of Punishment and Punishers

Location of Hotel	Owners			Managers, Supervisors and Masters			Adult Co-workers		
	Oral	Physical	Total	Oral	Physical	Total	Oral	Physical	Total
Tourist Centre	178 (59.1)	123 (40.8)	301 (100)	33 (18.5)	145 (81.4)	178 (100)	83 (59.7)	56 (40.2)	139 (100)
Non-Tourist Centre	71 (74.7)	24 (25.2)	95 (100)	50 (80.6)	12 (19.3)	62 (100)	41 (80.3)	10 (19.6)	51 (100)
Total	**249 (62.8)**	**147 (37.1)**	**396 (100)**	**83 (34.5)**	**157 (65.4)**	**240 (100)**	**124 (65.2)**	**66 (34.7)**	**190 (100)**

Owners : $\chi^2 = 7.43$ df = 1 $P < 0.05$.
Managers, Supervisors and Masters : $\chi^2 = 182.4$ df = 1 $P < 0.05$.
Adult Co-workers : $\chi^2 = 6.95$ df = 1 $P < 0.05$.

The study discloses that there is a significant variation in the physical punishment of the children by the employers and employees with regard to the location of the hotels in which they are employed. The proportion of children from the hotels located in tourist places who undergo physical punishment inflicted by the owners, middle managerial employees and adult co-workers is significantly higher than the proportion of their counterparts from the hotels located in non-tourist places who suffer similar punishment. As interpreted in the data in the previous Table, the hotels in tourist places are busy and crowded most of the time a day. Especially, the middle management employees punish more children (81.4%t) employed in the hotels located in tourist places. But the owners and the adult co-workers are similar in punishing physically the children (about 40%) employed in such hotels. The reason is that the former category of employees is keen on satisfying the customers by keeping the hotels clean. They punish the children physically when they are careless and slow.

It is inferred from this discussion that a majority of the children are subjected to oral as well as physical punishment. Sometimes, a small section of them meet with severe corporal punishment which ultimately leads them to running away from the hotels.

PLEDGING

It is found in some hotels under study that the parents pledged their children to get an advance from the owners. This system seems to be an easy way for the parents to get money in order to meet their family needs. While pledging their children, they get Rs. 2,500 to Rs. 5,000. This advance is decided based on the skill of a child in hotel job. A sum of Rs. 5000 is fixed for a skilled child, whereas a sum of Rs. 2500 is given for a beginner. Though this advance may be helpful to meet certain needs of the family, it is at the cost of the children who are forced to sacrifice their childhood without education, play and other activities. This study shows that more than one-third of the children are pledged to the employers.

It is clear form Table 7.31 that out of 475 working children, over one-third (36.6%) are pledged by their parents for an advance and the rest of them (63.4%) are not pledged. They were introduced to hotel jobs by various persons.

Table 7.31: Respondents by Pledging in Hotels

Sl. No.	Types of children	No. of Children	Per cent
1.	Pledged	174	36.6
2.	Not Pledged	301	63.4
	Total	**475**	**100**

The owners while offering the advance to the parents get their signatures on promissory notes or on stamped receipts. As a result of this, the children cannot leave the job or run away from the hotel. This is also a check on their part that they should not demand an increase in their wages. In this context, it is relevant to refer to a study on child labour by Chandragupt S. Sanon who finds that, in Allahabhad, some of the children became bonded workers in a hotel because their parents had received some money in advance from the employers.[7]

Normally, the parents receive an advance from the owners. The data show that 70.7 per cent of the children's parents directly collect an advance from the owners and for the rest of the children (29.3%) their introducers (managers, supervisors and masters) collect the advance on behalf of their parents. Later the parents collect it from them.

The managers, supervisors and masters are fraudulent because they do not give the actual advance mentioned to the parents. This is brought to light while crosschecking the information collected from the hotel owners, managers, supervisors and parents. Nevertheless, it must be acknowledged that in this regard a few employers are honest.

Sometimes, outside agents also introduce children to hotel jobs. But they are not dependable and frank. It is reported that an agent had taken two children from a village in a neighboring district promising them he would secure hotel jobs for them. The children went with him. At last he brought them to Tirunelveli Junction to put them in a hotel. On that day, there was tight police security in that area because of communal clashes. The agent became restless because of the fear that the police may enquire about the children. In order to escape from the police, he left the children in front of a hotel and quit the place immediately. Since the children were seen crying, a policeman came to know of the episode. He handed over the children to Saranalayam, a home for street children, run by a local NGO. Later, this NGO was able to find the village of the children, identify their parents and hand them over to their parents.[8]

The practice of sending children to hotel jobs through agents or hotel employees seems to have been in existence for a long time in Tirunelveli District. And children are sent to far away places in this quest. G. Karunanithi has pointed out in his unpublished but recent project report that some parents in a Harijan Colony of Pudupatti village in Tirunelveli District sent their boys to Bangalore and Mumbai through known persons to get employment in hotels.[9]

A study by Walter Fernandes concludes that the agents and contractors who supply labour to small factories, hotels, and tea stalls and provide domestic helpers to private families, go round villages in order to recruit them. As the rural parents are very poor, they fall a prey to the allurement of the middlemen. They send their children to cities hoping that their future would be better.[10]

It is obvious from Table 7.32 and Fig. 7.6 that out of 174 pledged children, the parents of 43.6 per cent have got up to Rs.2,500 whereas a majority of the parents (56.8%) have got Rs. 2500-5000.

Table 7.32: Respondents by Pledging for Money and Tenure of Work

Pledged for money (Rs.)	Tenure of work (in years)			Total
	1	1½	2	
Up to 2500	22 (28.9)	18 (23.6)	36 (47.3)	76 (100)
2500-5000	12 (12.2)	29 (29.5)	57 (58.1)	98 (100)
Total	**34 (19.5)**	**47 (17.0)**	**93 (53.4)**	**174 (100)**

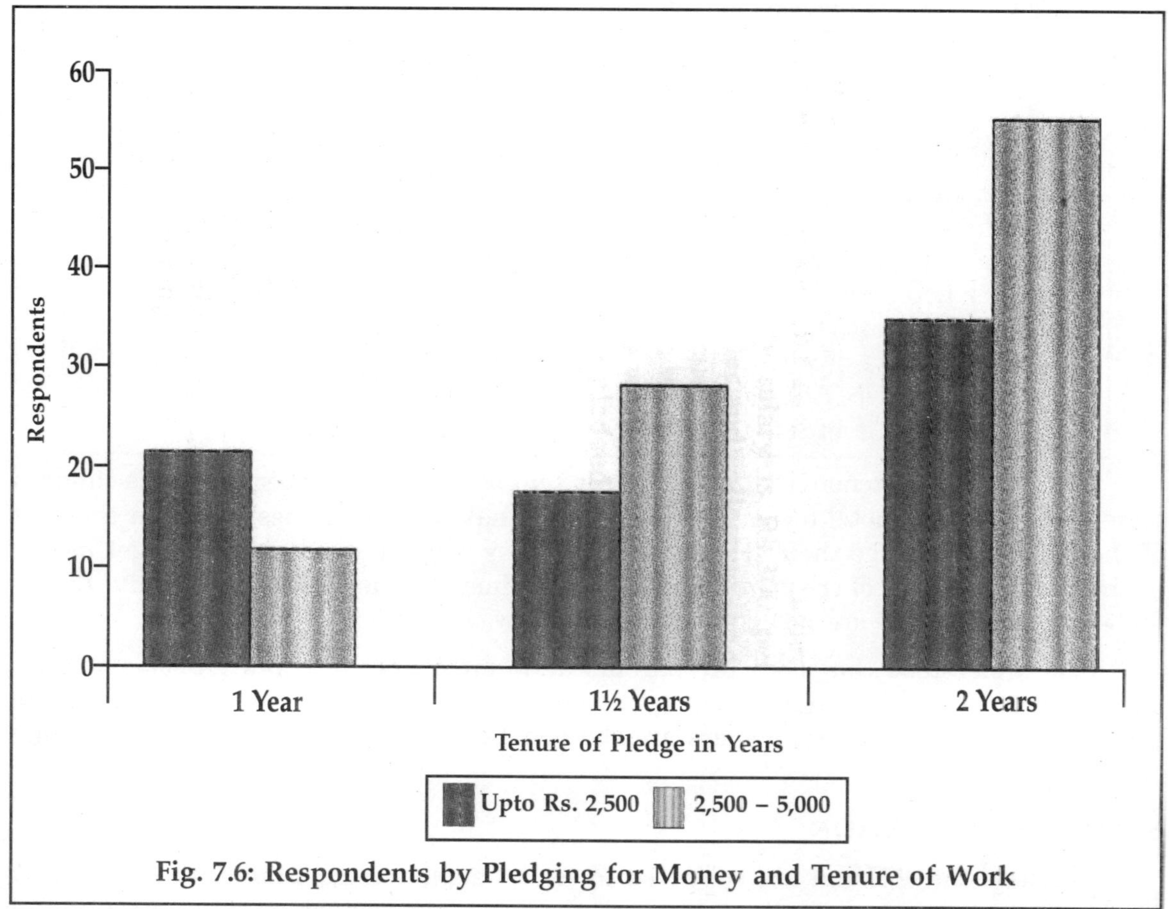

Fig. 7.6: Respondents by Pledging for Money and Tenure of Work

Of the total pledged children, one-fifth (19.5%) have agreed to work for a year; over one-fourth (27.0%) for one and half years and a majority (53.4 per cent) for two years.

A boy form Tenkasi town working in a hotel describes his pledged life as follows:

> I joined the hotel job at the age of 10 with the help of my cousin who happened to be a supplier in the same hotel. He took Rs.3,500 from the hotel owner and gave it to my father. For that I have to work for one year. My salary is Rs.300 per month. My work includes cleaning the tables and collecting the vessels. I do not feel unsafe in this hotel because seven persons (4 adults and 3 boys) from my native place are working here with me. However, I want to leave because of heavy workload and long duration of work. But I cannot do it, as I am a pledged worker here. Unless my father returns the advance, I will not be relieved from the job.

A father, who has pledged his son to a hotel owner, gives the following statement:

> I am a landless agricultural labourer. My wife is also an agricultural coolie. We have two sons and two daughters. The girls are engaged in beedi rolling. My sons work in a Hotel in Tirunelveli Town. My first son is 14 and the second son is 10. We belong to a Scheduled Caste. We couldn't meet our daily needs with a meager income. So I borrowed Rs. 5,000 from the hotel owner who belongs to a neighboring village, after pledging my first son to do cleaning job in his hotel. He is earning Rs.300 per month. My second son is also a cleaner in another hotel and is earning Rs.100 per month. I have taken an advance of Rs. 2000/- for him. They will have to work in the hotel for a minimum period of 15 months. Every week I meet my sons and collect the money which they get as tips and *beta*. After one and a half years, I want to extend the agreement and will get a sum of Rs. 10,000/ for our daughters' marriage.

It is distressing to note that about 37 per cent of the total number of sample children were pledged to the hotel owners. It is reported that there is no hesitation on the part of the parents to pledge their sons. This is the easy way for some parents to get money in thousands at times of crisis in their families. Primarily it is a violation of Child Rights for which the parents are not punished by the law.

It is understood that both the parents and employers are equally responsible for the pledging system in the hotels. It needs no explanation to conclude that the parents are the losers and the hotel owners are the beneficiaries who are keen on capitalizing on the opportunity.

SEXUAL EXPLOITATION

In hotels the children are subjected to sexual exploitation. A minority is forced by the hotel employees and adult co-workers to yield to homosexual activity. In the initial stage, they resist such compulsion. But in course of time, for obvious reasons, they subject themselves to such activity because they have no courage to antagonize their manager or supervisor or master or adult co-workers.

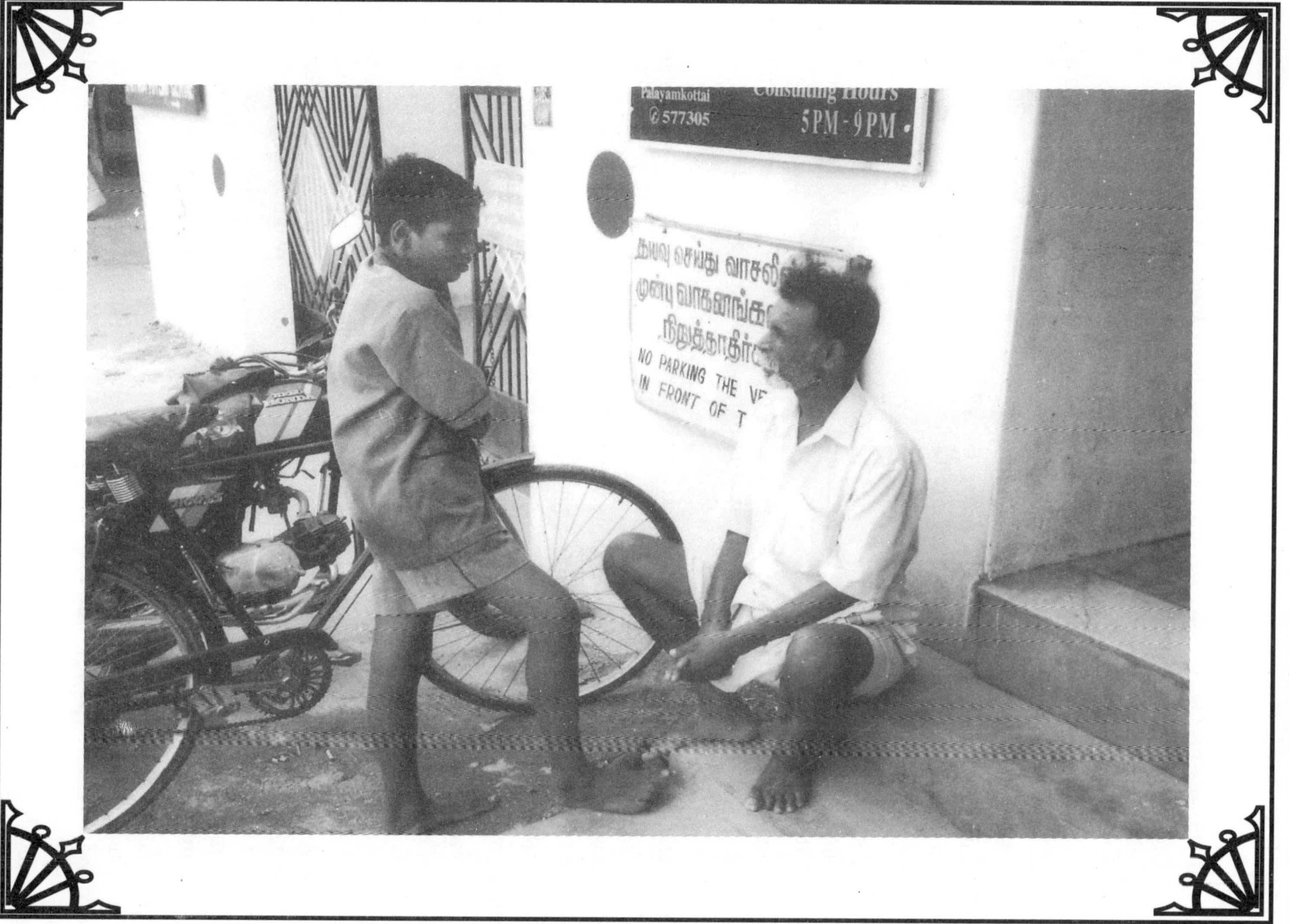

Parents come, collect advance from the owners and depart after a few words with their son's

CHILD SEXUAL ABUSE

Child Sexual Abuse has been defined as any kind of physical or mental violation of a child with sexual intent, usually by a person who is in possession of trust or power *vis-a-vis* the child. Child Sexual Abuse is also defined as any sexual behaviour directed at a person under 16, without informed consent. However, there is no uniformly accepted definition of child abuse.

The perpetrator can be any one who exploits the child's vulnerability to gain sexual gratification. It can also include activities which do not involve direct touching. Sexual exploitation takes different forms such as:

- Child labourers and young domestic workers are frequently used for the sexual gratification of employers and other adults.
- Children are sexually abused within the family, rape within a family has its own alarming numbers.
- With the advent of HIV/AIDS, there is and increased demand for younger child prostitutes.
- Children are used as attractions in sex tourism. Children are victims of a globally organized sex trade. In some countries this helps in bringing much-needed foreign exchange.
- Children are abused within the context of cultural or traditional practices such as Child-marriage.
- Children in institutions are vulnerable to sexual abuse from those who are supposed to take care of them.

Children in situations of conflicts, and displaced, migrant and refugee children are particularly vulnerable to all forms of sexual exploitation.[11]

It is found that 52 children (11%) have been approached by other employees for homosexual activity. Of them, the proportion of those who are approached by their masters (48.4%) is considerably higher than the proportion of those approached by the adult co-workers (36.5%and supervisors (15.3%). The reason is that the children mostly sleep with their masters (cooks) and adult co-workers in the same room. Moreover, the children have more respect for their masters than for their adult co-workers. Close to a majority of the children approached to engage in homosex were approached by their masters. Over one-third of the children are approached by the adult co-workers because the latter treat the former kindly. Often the former borrow pornographic and yellow books, hair-oil, soap, tooth paste from these elder workers and borrow money from them.

It is also found that of 52 children, 36 (69.2%) yielded to their masters, supervisors, and co-workers. However, a majority (58.33%) of them in Type II hotels (grade A), over-one third (36.11%) in Type I (grade B) hotels and 5.56 per cent in Type III hotels (grade B1), are used for homosex. Generally, they often remain silent about the abuse due to fear, guilt or shame.

Most of the hotel employees are away from their families and some of them are bachelors. Usually they sleep together in a common room. Many of them see blue films and read pornographic and yellow books. Many have sex with prostitutes, besides practising masturbation. These habits lead them to taking advantage of the chance for homosex with the innocent children who are more or less a captive group. Thus the children become victims to this practice.

In Tirunelveli District, especially in big hotels, there are 25-65 employees working. Most of them are away from their families. Quite a few of them are bachelors. Their recreation includes seeing films, playing cards, gossiping, loafing, and playing sex-related games. Some of the hotel employees collect cine-service sex albums and paste them on the walls and doors of common rooms in which they are staying. They also see blue films and read pornographic books. These activities tempt them sexually, but do not offer them guidance to live decently. Gradually this results in the kindling of their sexual urge. Consequently, they seek these children for homosex. Thus, homosexuality is slowly induced among the children. In turn, in their youth, they repeat what their predecessor practised.

During the fieldwork, the investigator had detailed discussions with five children working in hotels in Tirunelveli town. They reported that they had homosex with their master and supervisor. In this regard, it is relevant to present the statement of a 13-year-old boy in Tirunelveli town. He says:

> I joined this job with the help of my master. At present, I am cleaning tables and collecting plates. In the beginning, I worked as a kitchen assistant to my master. We slept in the kitchen or on the terrace. In the first instance, my master approached me for homosex during night time. I was a bit reluctant, but after sometime I started responding to his calls. Now both of us do it whenever we want to. He gives me Rs. 10-15 every month to see films. He treats me kindly. Sometimes, he is more affectionate to me than my parents are. Therefore, I want to be with him most of the time. However, I want to give up homosex because a friend of my age working with me is suffering from health problems due to homosex.

Another boy of 13 in a hotel situated in the junction area of Tirunelveli explains his habits and how they have affected him:

> An assistant cook of 27 is very close to me. His wife divorced him. He has the habit of homosex. Initially he repeatedly approached me for oral sex inspite of my reluctance. After sometime, I started responding to his calls. In course of time, I developed a taste for it. Now I find it difficult to give it up. At one stage, I left the hotel and started attending to customers in public toilets and isolated places late in the night. I could manage to collect Rs. 10-15 from a customer. After some months, I could not get customers. Therefore, I was starving for sometime and slept in the bus stand and the railway station. Due to hunger, I

sought the help of my hotel manager to join the same hotel. In fact, I had a tough time with him. He scolded and beat me for what I had done after leaving the hotel. However, I joined the hotel with great difficulty. Though I have given up homosex, sometimes I drink liquor as a relief from heavy workload and long duration of work.

A local Tamil eveninger published a news item on 24 February 2002 that children in hotels in Tirunelveli are forced by their masters into homosexual activity. A local NGO came to know about this and attempted to put an end to this practice with the help of the police. As a result of this, the NGO started a home to admit those children who had left hotels due to various atrocities done to them by the employees.[12]

Prakash Kothari has also pointed out in his study that some boys are employed in sleazy B and C grade hotels and lodging houses where, besides getting a hopelessly inadequate salary and leading a miserable life, they also face a sense of insecurity. In these circumstances, they are subjected to sexual abuse and sexual exploitation.[13]

The present study discloses that more children below 12 years of age are pressurized by other employees for homosexual activity This is represented in Table 7.33 and Fig. 7.7.

Table 7.33: Respondents by Age and Homosexual Activity

Age Group (in Years)	Approached for Homo sex		Total
	Yes	No	
8-10	18 (14.2)	108 (85.7)	126 (100)
10-12	26 (13.4)	167 (86.5)	193 (100)
12-14	8 (5.1)	148 (94.8)	156 (100)
Total	**52** **(10.9)**	**423** **(89.0)**	**475** **(100)**

$\chi^2 = 8.1$ df = 2 $P < 0.05$.

The data show that there is a significant relationship between the age of the children and their being sought for homosexual activity. The data prove that more children in the age group of 8-12 years than those in the age group of 12-14 are approached for homosex. Thus, the former group of children are more vulnerable to the sex hunger of their fellow employees.

Narrating his tale of woe to a kind soul

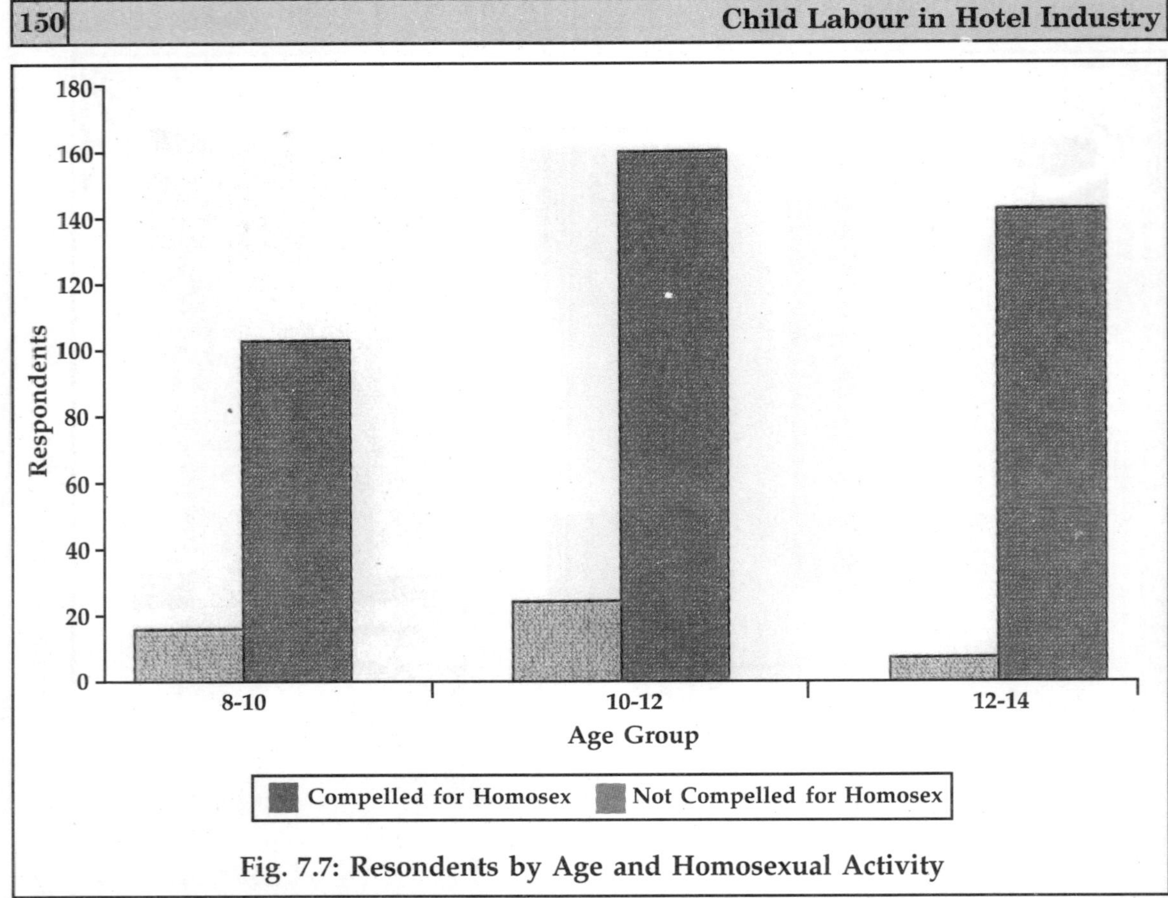

Fig. 7.7: Resondents by Age and Homosexual Activity

Table 7.34: Respondents by Age and Approach by Types of Employees for Homosex

Age group (in Yrs.)	Approached for homo sex			Response		
	Masters	Supervisors	Adult co-workers	Total	Yielded	Not Yielded
Up to 12	25 (56.82)	12 (27.27)	7 (15.91)	44 (84.62)	34 (77.27)	10 (22.73)
12-14	3 (37.50)	2 (25.00)	3 (37.50)	8 (15.38)	2 (25.00)	6 (75.00)
Total	**28 (53.85)**	**14 (26.92)**	**10 (19.23)**	**52 (100)**	**36 (69.2)**	**16 (30.7)**

Compelled for Homosex : $\chi^2 = 2.20$ df = 2 P > 0.05.

Yielded for Homosex : $\chi^2 = 8.42$ df = 1 P < 0.05.

It is clear from the Table that more masters than other employees approach the children in the age group of up to 12 years for homosex. But this variation is not significant with respect to other employees approaching the children for homosex.

It is found that there is relationship between the rural-urban background of the children and their response to the demand of employees for homosexual activity. This is exhibited in Table 7.35 and Fig. 7.8.

Table 7.35: Respondents by Background and Demand of Types of Employees for Homosex

Background	Solicited for homo sex by				Yielded		
	Masters	Supervisors	Adult co-workers	Total	Yes	No	Total
Rural	22 (55.0)	10 (25.0)	8 (20.0)	40 (84.62)	32 (80.0)	8 (20.0)	40 (100)
Urban	6 (50.0)	4 (33.3)	2 (16.6)	12 (23.08)	4 (33.3)	8 (66.6)	12 (100)
Total	**28 (53.8)**	**14 (26.9)**	**10 (19.2)**	**52 (100)**	**36 (69.2)**	**16 (30.7)**	**52 (100)**

Compelled for Homosex : $\chi^2 = 0.358$ df = 2 $P > 0.05$.

Yielded for Homosex : $\chi^2 = 9.394$ df = 1 $P < 0.05$.

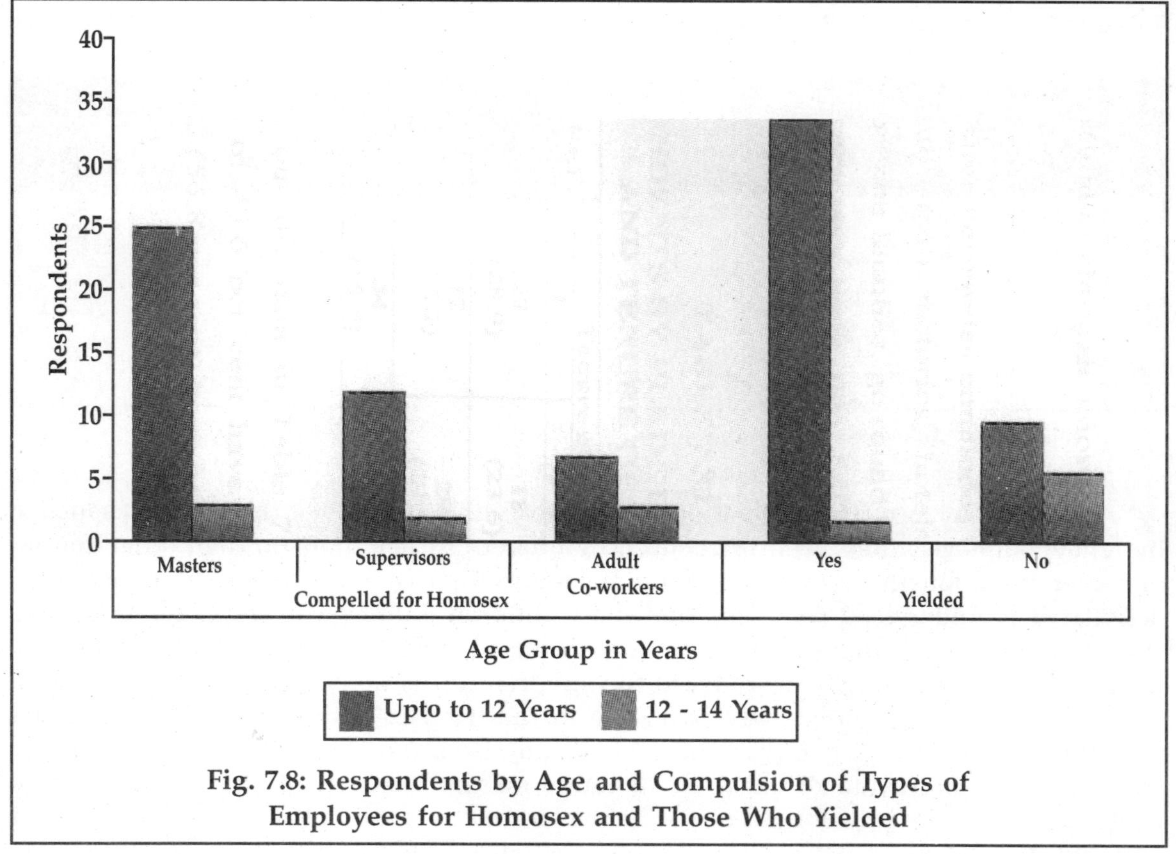

Fig. 7.8: Respondents by Age and Compulsion of Types of Employees for Homosex and Those Who Yielded

It is observed that over three-fourths (76.92%) of the children from rural areas are solicited by the employees for homosexual activity. Of them, an overwhelming majority (80%) has responded positively. On the other hand, only one-third (33.3%) of the children from urban areas are solicited by the employees. It is, therefore, inferred that more rural children than their urban counterparts are sought by employees for the homosexual activity. This leads to the conclusion that there is a significant relationship between the rural-urban background of the children and their response to the compulsion of employees for homosex. It is possible that the relative innocence of the rural children exposes them to this.

It is, thus, understood that more rural children than their urban counter- parts are sought for sex exploitation. Fewer urban children than rural children yield. The reason may be that the rural children are more innocent than the urban children. Moreover, they fear their masters, supervisors and adult co-workers because they depend on them for several things.

There is relationship between types of employees by whom the children secured employment in the hotels and the compulsion exerted on them by those employees for homosexual activity (Table 7.36).

Table 7.36: Respondents by Sources Recruitment and Compulsion of Types of Employee for Homosex

Recruitment	Approached for homosex				Yielded	
	Masters	Supervisors	Adult co-workers	Total	Yes	No
Through hotel employers and employees	2 (40.0)	1 (20.0)	3 (40.0)	6 (11.54)	3 (50.0)	3 (50.0)
Through brokers	26 (56.5)	13 (30.4)	7 (13.0)	46 (88.46)	35 (76.0)	11 (23.9)
Total	**28 (50.9)**	**14 (23.5)**	**10 (25.4)**	**52 (100)**	**38 (74.5)**	**13 (25.4)**

Compelled for Homosex : $\chi^2 = 4.371$ df = 2 $P > 0.05$.

Yielded for Homosex : $\chi^2 = 1.886$ df = 1 $P > 0.05$.

It is evident form the Table that an overwhelming majority of the children solicited by fellow employees had been introduced by brokers rather than through other routes, and over three-fourths of this sub-group yielded to their compulsion for the homosexual activity. It is understood from this that more children unknown to the hotel employees than the children introduced by them are subjected to sexual exploitation. The reason is obvious: the brokers who introduced the children to the hotels do not visit them even once in a while. Therefore, there is no one in the hotel to take care of them, whereas the other children are taken care of by the employees of the hotels. The data reveal that the sexual exploitation of children depends on the location of the hotels. Sexual exploitation is more pronounced in the hotels located in tourist places than in the hotels situated in non-tourist places. This is represented in Table 7.37.

Table 7.37: Respondents by Location of Hotels, Compulsion of Types of Employees for Homo Sex and Their Yielding to it

Location of hotel	Approached for homosex				Yielded		Total
	Masters	Supervisors	Adult co-workers	Total	Yes	No	
Tourist Place	23 (56.0)	11 (26.8)	7 (17.0)	41 (78.85)	29 (70.7)	12 (29.2)	41 (100)
Non Tourist Place	5 (45.4)	3 (27.2)	3 (27.2)	11 (21.15)	7 (63.6)	4 (36.3)	11 (100)
Total	**28 (54.9)**	**14 (27.5)**	**10 (17.6)**	**52 (100)**	**36 (69.2)**	**16 (30.7)**	**52 (100)**

Compelled for Homosex : $\chi^2 = 0.67$ df = 2 P > 0.05.

Yield for Homosex : $\chi^2 = 0.192$ df = 1 P > 0.05.

From the above table, it is evident that a great majority of the children who are forced into homosexual by fellow employees worked in hotels located in tourist places, while only one-fourth worked in hotels in non-tourist places. But while analyzing the relationship between the types of employees who exploit the children sexually and the location of hotels in which they are employed, it is found that there is no significant relationship between these two variables. Thus it is concluded that there is no significant variation among the types of employees with respect to the compulsive pressure they exert on the children for homosexual activity. Innocent children are induced in homosexual activity by the management employees and adult co-workers. This practice may spoil not only the health of the children but also their character in the years to come. The conventional thinking in India is that homosexuality is an evil practice and that it spoils the physical and mental health of the subjects. Homosexuality has not been either legally or socially accepted, as it is in many other countries especially in the west. So to a conventional person with social concerns, homosexuality is an evil in this situation. But one may leave aside the question of the legality of homosexual relationships–and the physical health side of the controversy, too–and yet see that the coercion in the matter can affect the mental health of the victims. The social stigma attached to the practice gives them a sense of sin and deviance, which may drive them into subterfuges and secrecy. This is a sociological problem in a society which is not permissive as most societies in the west and the developed world are.

REFERENCES

1. Joe Arimpoor, *Profile of the Child Worker;* Social Action, Vol. 44, (July-September 1994): p. 63.
2. Sushila Srivastava and R. Bhanumathi, *Child Workers in Farrming, Domestic and Catering Sectors*, Social Welfare, pp. 24-26.
3. Geeta Lal, *Child Labour in India—An over view*, Social Change, (September-December 1997): 3-4.

4. Musafir Singh, V.D. Kaura and S.A. Khan, *Working Children in Bombay—Study* (Delhi: National Institute of Public Co-operation and Child Development, 1980), p. 196.

5. Musafir Singh, Kaura, V.D.Khan, S.A, *Working Children in Bombay—A Study* op.cit, p. 196.

6. Chandragupt S. Sanon, *Working Children: A Sociological Analysis,* (New Delhi: APH Publishing Corporation,1998), op. cit., pp. 126-127.

7. *Ibid*. pp. 126-127.

8. *Nellaiyil Velai Vangi-t-taruvathaka Moondru Siruvarkal Kadathal,* Malai Murasu (19.03.2000), p. 1.

9. G. Karunanithi, *Report on Child Labour in Beedi Industry in Tirunelveli Kattabomman District of Tamil Nadu*, (New Delhi: Ministry of Labour, 1995), p. 106.

10. Walter Fernandes, Child Labour and the Processes of Exploitation, *Indian Journal of Social Work*, (April 1992): 183

11. *Convention on the Rights of Child*, India, First Periodic Report 2001, (New Delhi: Department of Women and Child Development, Ministry of Human Development, 2001), p. 391-392.

12. *Nellaiyel Sex Kodumaikku Alakum Siruvarkal*, Malai Murasu (24.02.2000), p. 4.

13. Prakash Kothari, *Sexual Exploitation of Working Children*, as cited by Walter Fernandes, *Child Labour and the Process of Exploitation*, *op. cit*., p. 183.

CHAPTER 8

Health Problems for Child Labour

The practice of child labour is economically unsound, psychologically disastrous and physically and morally dangerous and harmful to any society. There is a need to understand the health of children engaged in labour and their occupational diseases, which have a telling effect on their health.

The existing unhygienic working conditions in hotels are likely to cause various kinds of health problem among the children. In addition to this, the work that they do would itself cause health problems. These cannot be overlooked because certain occupations are detrimental to their health. Besides, the unhygienic working conditions obviously endanger the children's physical and mental health.

This chapter deals with the general hygiene of child workers in hotels, and their habits of personal hygiene like brushing their teeth, bathing, dressing, and types of food they eat, and the duration of sleep they are able to get. It also deals with the diseases prevalent among them and the types of medical treatment they get.

ORAL HYGIENE

The data disclose that out of the 475 children, a majority (52.4%) brush their teeth regularly. They are provided with low quality tooth powder. The data show that of 40.2 per cent of those from Type I hotels, an overwhelming majority (80.1%) from Type II hotels and nearly one-third (30.0%) from Type III hotels brush their teeth regularly.

However, in Types I and III hotels, the owners, managers and supervisors do not give due importance to the welfare and neatness of the children because their main aim is to extract more work from them. So a majority of the children (59.8%) in Type I hotels and over two-thirds (70.0%) in Type III hotels do not brush their teeth regularly. Nearly one-fourth of them use brick powder and cow-dung ash to brush their teeth. This practice would result in ulcers in the mouth and pain due to the inflammation of the gums.

In the case of certain Type II hotels, the situation is rather different. The customers from affluent families often visit this type of hotels because of their cleanliness and neatness. Therefore, the hotel management takes special care to maintain the standard in boarding and lodging. The management instructs the room boys and other employees to maintain a good standard in personal hygiene and neatness. The management pays an allowance for such things. So an overwhelming majority of the children (81%) brush their teeth regularly. Nevertheless, it is not so in all Type II hotels because the children do not always get such allowances.

During the data collection all the children reported that they brush their teeth regularly. But the adult co-workers say that the children do not do so. However, the children reason that they sleep late in the night after completing the work and get up early in the morning. If they do not do so, the employers scold them. As they have to get ready for work in the morning mostly by 6.00 a.m. they hurriedly brush their teeth and wash their face. Some children are lazy to brush their teeth neatly even if they have adequate time.

BATHING

Bathing is essential in human life. It not only reduces the body's heat but also cleans the body. Especially the manual workers need to bathe at least twice a day. This is applicable to the hotel workers too because they work at least 14 hours a day. Some of them work near the hearth and attend to various jobs in the kitchen which is not usually clean all the time, because they have to prepare tiffin in the morning and in the evening and meals in the noon. Therefore, the preparation of food items in the kitchen is continuous from starting till the closing of the dining section. That is why the kitchen is cleaned after 10.00 p.m. Since the children attend to various jobs in the kitchen besides cleaning the tables and washing the plates and other items, they have to bathe in the morning and late in the evening.

Out of the 475 children, one-third (30.2%) take bath regularly; 44.2 per cent twice a week and one-fourth (25.6%) once a week. While considering the hotel-wise distribution of children, it is found that in Types I and III hotels, about 25 per cent take bath daily and a majority (about 50%) do so twice a week, whereas over one-third (34.4%) in Type I hotels and nearly one-fourth (24.8%) in Type III hotels bathe once a week. In Type II hotels, nearly two-thirds (60.0%) bathe regularly. A majority of Type II hotels are located in tourist places and corporation areas because there is more scope here for better profits. Since the owners want to maintain the standard of their hotels, they keep them neat and clean, render kind service, and provide varieties of tiffin and food items and sweets to the customers to satisfy them.

A few hotel owners provide uniforms to the hotel employees, both adult and child. They also provide the employees with bathroom and toilet facilities. It is understood that though the hotel owners have a concern for their employees, they take these concerted efforts mainly to attract the customers in order to increase their revenue.

Another important point is that in Types I and III hotels, the employers and employees are keen on extracting work from the children and therefore give them less time for brushing their teeth, going to toilet and taking bath. Since they have to depend on only one bathroom, normally the priority to use it first goes to the masters and adult co-workers. The children are not able to go to toilet and take bath because they should get ready for their work by the prescribed time.

BATHROOM AND TOILET FACILITIES

According to the Catering Act, 1956, every hotel has to provide bathroom and toilet facilities to the hotel workers and customers. But most of the hotels provide only one toilet, which may be clean or unclean. Water facility may or may not be available. During the data collection, most of the working children complained that toilet facility is rather inadequate or worse. Therefore, they have to either go away from the hotel or jump into its backyard in order to respond to the calls of nature. Quite often they are forced to go out of the hotels in search of places to pass stools; or they do it somewhere in the place around the hotel, usually at the back of the hotels.

The children report that the hotel food causes dysentery and stomach ache. Consequently, they often relieve themselves at the empty space at the back of the hotels. After relieving themselves, they clean their anus with the help of a piece of paper or stone and afterwards they wash themselves at the time of taking bath.

Of the 475 children, nearly three-fourths use the open area at the back of the hotels. S. Vijayalakshmi's (1997) study in Sivakasi supports this finding. She finds that a majority of the children (73%) employed in unorganized sectors use open fields as toilets.[1]

It is reported that the working children have irregular toilet habits. They go to toilet only when they get free time. In case they feel like going to the toilet during working hours they have to get permission from the managers or supervisors. Sometimes the permission is denied. In such circumstances, they become restless and are not able to help the lapses in their work.

DRESSING

Out of the 475 children, over one-third (36%) change their dress regularly, whereas more or less a similar proportion (32%) do so once a week and the rest (32%) do so twice a week. Since most of them hail from villages and poor economic background, they own only two sets of dress and one towel. In Type II hotels, nearly two-thirds (60%) and in Type I hotels 40.1 per cent report that they change their dress regularly.

In Types I and II hotels, the owners provide a set of uniforms to the workers. In these hotels, the children should be in uniform during business hours. They wash the uniform only once or twice a month because their owners tell them that they are not entitled to any washing allowance. Therefore, the children in these hotels do not change their dress periodically.

The habit of wearing soiled uniform and changing it once or twice a week causes itching. While washing the vessels at regular intervals, their uniform gets wet. In a similar way, their uniform gets wet during hot summer due to sweating. The unclean dress and body coupled with sweating all over the day contribute very much to their health problems like scabies, itching and other skin diseases. The practice of exchanging the dresses among themselves is also an important contributing factor to such health problems.

FOOD

Out of the 475 children, 43.6 per cent say that they get adequate food while a majority (56.4 per cent) report they do not. Over one-third (35.5%) from Type II hotels and a majority (57.2%) from Type I hotels report that they are not provided with adequate food. But in Type III hotels, nearly three-fourths (74.4%) have the same complaint.

One may think that the children get various food items in the hotels. Discussing with them and observing them while taking food, the investigator came to know that in; many hotels they are not given the tiffin and other food items prepared for the customers. Instead, they are provided with rice (cooked) thrice a day. This practice is followed by most hotels irrespective of their type and location. Asked to explain this discrimination, they report that the food items prepared for the customers are costly because of their quality and taste. If they get such items regularly and adequately, the owners cannot get more profit, and they may even incur loss. A similar view is expressed by the managers and supervisors. However, these two categories of hotel employees have access to rich food items.

It is also important to mention that the food prepared thrice a day for the children, suppliers and masters (head cooks) is poor in quality because the hotel management supplies cheap rice, dall, oil, vegetables and other raw materials. In a similar way, cheap coffee powder, tea dust, palm sugar and diluted milk are supplied to them to prepare coffee in the morning and tea in the evening for themselves.

Sushila Srivastava and R. Bhanumathi (1990) find in their study that a high proportion of child workers in hotels (90%) were offered meals thrice daily.[2]

Most of the time the head cooks, assistant cooks and the adult co-workers set apart a large quantity of food for themselves after preparation. As a result of this, sometimes, the children do not get sufficient food. They have to content themselves with the available food.

The data show that a majority (56.42%) report that they get inadequate food.

Out of the 475 children, 40 per cent report that they take food in time, whereas a majority (60%) report that they do not. It is found that of those who do not take food in time, a majority (about 50%) belong to Types I and II hotels located in tourist places. The reason is that a row of customers visits those hotels continuously from morning to late evening. This forces the children attend to the assigned work continuously. Consequently, they are not able to take food in time.

SLEEPING

The hotels are kept open from 6.00 a.m. to 10.00 p.m. In accordance with this timing, the employees should get ready in time and work actively till the closing time. That is why they sleep only for 4-5 hours. The data show that out of the 475 children, over one-third (34.3%) sleep comfortably during night while the rest (65.7%) report that they do not sleep so long.

In Types I and II hotels, the workload is heavy, whereas it is less in Type III hotels. So in Type I hotels, nearly two-thirds (65%) and in Type II hotels, an overwhelming majority (82.7%) say that they do not have comfortable sleep at night. In Type III hotels, a majority (50.4%) have a similar problem. Of the 475 children, over one-third (39.7%) sleep after midnight and get up early in the morning. Consequently, they are very tired.

About 40 per cent state that they sleep in a single room, while one-fifth (20%) sleep in the storeroom. In most of the hotels, there is only one rest room allotted for the workers. In moderately big hotels, at least 25 workers occupy a fairly big room. All of them keep their luggage in the room and sleep there. Usually it is situated at the top floor of the hotel or near the kitchen. If it is situated near the kitchen, the workers are often subject to health problems. They have to reckon with the smoke from the kitchen. Some children sleep in the open terrace, portico, staircase, storeroom or kitchen because they do not want to sleep in an over-crowed room. Like adult co-workers, the children also sleep on thick wrappers obtained from nearby shops. Especially during winter, this does not protect them from the chill of the floor.

A study by Sushila Srivastava and R. Bhanumathi (1990) corroborates this. 64 per cent of the child workers in general had only a common room for stay and sleep and a common toilet with inadequate water facility.[3]

Those who sleep in the storeroom or kitchen do not sleep comfortably because the cooks start preparing the tiffin items from 3.30 a.m. As a result of this, they are not able to work actively during the daytime. However, due to heavy workload and long duration of work they develop body pain, headache, giddiness and other such problems.

Almost all the children complain that they sleep for only 4-5 hours in the night and that they do not sleep comfortably. A 14-year-old child worker in a hotel in Tirunelveli Junction describes his problems relating to sleep:

I have been working in the hotel for the last two years. I do not have comfortable sleep in the night, because we have been provided with only one rest room near the kitchen. The head cook, assistant cooks and suppliers occupy a major portion of the room. My co-workers and I sleep in a corner of the room. Normally we sleep after 11.30 p.m. We are not even provided with a mat, we sleep on the parcel wrappers and gunny bags. We do not sleep comfortably because the room is overcrowded with 30 members. As we lie down very close, we cannot turn freely on our sides. Besides, the snoring of cooks and other employers is a nuisance. At 3.30 a.m. the head cook wakes up his assistants to start preparing the tiffin items. Their shunting between the kitchen and the storeroom also disturbs my sleep.

The backyard of the hotel is used as open garbage ground where all the wastes are dumped. Mosquitoes from there disturb my sleep. Every morning I feel very tired due to disturbed sleep for a short period. So I feel sleepy while doing my work. Sometimes I sleep for a while with the support of a corner wall of the washing place. If the manager or supervisor happens to see me, he punishes me orally and physically. Many times I have experienced this problem.

DISEASE

The data show that out of the total sample of 475 children, nearly two-thirds (65.2%) report that they have diseases. Over one-third (34.7%) state that they have no diseases. In Type I hotels, out of the 229 children, nearly two-thirds (65.5%) have diseases. Of them, nearly one-fifth (18.6%) has an Amebiasis problem. More or less a similar proportion (19.3%) has scabies. Almost the same proportion (20%) has some skin disease. Altogether a majority (57.9%) complains of body and joint pain.

In Type II hotels, out of 121 children, nearly three-fourths (73.5%) report that they have diseases. Of them, nearly one-fourth (23.5%) has an Amebiasis problem, one-fifth (20.2%) has scabies and nearly one-fourth (22.4%), skin diseases. Altogether two-thirds (66.1%) complain of body pain and joint pain.

In Type III hotels, out of 125 children, a majority (56.8%) has diseases. Of them, nearly one-fourth (23.9%) has amebiasis problem, about 15 per cent have scabies and over one-fourth (25.3%), skin diseases. Altogether nearly three-fourths (74.1%) of them complain of body and joint pain.

The children are supplied with quality and costly food only when there is an unscheduled closure of hotels due to the sudden eruption of violence. Only then can the children eat varieties of food items and as much as available. Generally, they have problems of malnutrition. They take the food separately prepared for them and other employees, which is not a balanced diet. Thus vitamin deficiency and malnutrition affect their physical and mental development. Moreover, they are not able to take food in time owing to their busy schedule. That leads to ulcers in course of time. A 13-year-old boy in a hotel in a tourist place explains his health problem as follows:

> I am at present suffering from ulcer. After taking food, I get stomach ache. Often I have the problem of diarrohoea. Now I am taking Gelusil syrup and tablets. A month ago, I was admitted to a hospital with severe stomach ache. I was hospitalized for three days and afterwards I became all right. In addition to this, I have fever twice or thrice a year. Then I approach my head cook who normally treats me with local medicine.

Another boy of 12 working in a hotel located in a non-tourist place narrates his health problems as follows:

> There is a sore in my right knee which was caused by hot oil falling on it accidentally. It took one month to cure. However, I suffered a lot. After that I am very much careful while walking through the kitchen where the cooks put big pans containing boiling oil after preparing sweets and other food items. Earlier two other boys met with a similar accident. We make repeated requests to the cooks to keep the pans close to the walls, so that we can walk through the kitchen freely. But they never listen.

Vijayalakshmi's (1997) finding in her study of working children in hotels in Sivakasi supports this point. She says that over one-third of the children (36%) have met with similar kinds of accidents in the hotels.[4]

Generally, more children in Types I and II hotels are affected by diseases because they have heavy workload for long duration. Therefore, they get body and joint pain due to overworking for hours together. Since they do not take food in time, they lose appetite and develop ulcers.

In all types of hotel, the children sleep for 4-5 hours. They do not have sound and comfortable sleep due to disturbances within and outside the hotels. This disturbed and short sleep causes health problems such as giddiness, insomnia, narcolepsy and psychological problems.

The most common disease which is prevalent among the children is fungus because they are continuously engaged in washing and cleaning. It is painful and sometimes causes bleeding from the blisters mostly found in the gaps between fingers of hands and legs. In such a condition, they are unable to do any work. Since the marble (granite) floor, granite table, silver and glass vessels and washbasins are required to be cleaned and washed frequently, they use low quality soaps, bleaching powder, oil soaps, etc. provided by the owners. This causes itching in the hands and the toes.

Chandragupt S. Sanon's study (1998) supports this finding. He finds that during winter children's hands and feet develop cracks and at times there is bleeding from the cracks. This is because they are engaged in washing the utensils at regular intervals.[5]

Children, adult workers and masters crowd together amidst tattered mats, piled up boxes and hanging clothes

The analysis of data pertaining to the diseases of the children and their age discloses that there is a positive relationship between these two variables. This is clearly shown in Table 8.1.

Table 8.1: Respondents by Age and Presence of Disease

Age group (in yrs.)	Has a Disease at Present		Total
	Yes	No	
8-10	52 (41.2)	74 (58.7)	126 (100)
10-12	107 (55.4)	86 (44.5)	193 (100)
12-14	151 (96.7)	5 (3.2)	156 (100)
Total	**310 (65.2)**	**165 (34.7)**	**475 (100)**

$\chi2 = 108.6$ df = 2 $P < 0.05$.

In the age group of 8-10 years, out of 126 children, 41.2 per cent say that they suffer from some disease/s. In the age group of 10-12 years, a majority (55.4%) says so. Further, in the age group of 12-14 years, an overwhelming majority (96.7%) has diseases. Thus, it is evident that the proportion of children affected by diseases increases with the increase in their age. It is, therefore, concluded that a greater number of experienced children than beginners suffer from diseases.

This concomitant variation may perhaps be explained in terms of the work experience of the children. They contract several diseases if they continue to shoulder heavy workload for years together. In a long period of the children and their disease. This is presented in Table 8.2.

Table 8.2: Respondents by Experience and Conditions of Being Diseased

Experience (in Years)	Has a Disease at Present		Total
	Yes	No	
Less than 2	106 (40.7)	29 (48.8)	135 (100)
2-4	204 (75.0)	136 (27.3)	340 (100)
Total	**310 (65.2)**	**165 (34.7)**	**475 (100)**

$\chi2 = 14.5$ df = 1 $P < 0.05$.

The data in the table show that the proportion of children with experience of 2-4 years is nearly twice as much as those with experience of less than two years. It is therefore concluded that like age, the experience of the children has a direct bearing on their condition of being diseased. The same reasons, namely shouldering heavy workload for about 14 hours a day over years, sleeping only for 4-5 hours in the night, taking food at irregular intervals and being involved in unhealthy practices, hold good for explaining the significant relationship between these two variables.

The data show that like age and experience, the rural-urban backgrounds of the children have a bearing on their diseases. More rural children than their urban counterparts suffer from diseases. This is presented in Table 8.3.

Table 8.3: Respondents by Background and Condition of Being Diseased

Background	Has a Disease at Present		Total
	Yes	No	
Rural	252 (69.6)	110 (30.3)	362 (100)
Urban	58 (51.1)	55 (39.8)	113 (100)
Total	**310 (65.2)**	**165 (34.7)**	**475 (100)**

$\chi^2 = 12.55$ df = 1 $P < 0.05$.

The data disclose that the proportion of rural children (69.6%) is significantly higher than the proportion of their urban counterparts (51%) with regard to the condition of being diseased. It is, therefore, confirmed that the relationship between the rural-urban backgrounds of the children and their condition of being diseased is significant.

Generally, the hotel owners, managers, supervisors and masters prefer the rural children for cleaning the vessels and dumping the waste things in the backyard of the hotel because they are active and sincere in their work. Their hands and legs are wet throughout the working hours. In addition to this, the owners and other employees make use of their services for their personal and domestic work. Consequently, they confront heavy workloads and a long duration of work. That is perhaps why more rural children than their urban counterparts suffer from diseases.

On the other hand, unlike the rural children, the urban children are not active and sincere in their work in spite of repeated punishments given to them.

They think that it is not obligatory on their part to attend to the personal and domestic work of their hotel owners and other employees. Therefore most of them are reluctant to do so. It is observed that their workload is not heavy compared to that of the rural children. Moreover, they have a chance to visit their homes at least once a week because of proximity. Their parents also visit the hotels often to meet them. Therefore, it may be right to conclude that unlike the rural children, the urban children are not as much affected by diseases because of the less heavy work and parental care.

It is interesting to find that there is a relationship between the hotels situated in the tourist and non-tourist places on the one hand and the diseases of the working children on the other hand. This is explained in Table 8.4.

Table 8.4: Respondents by Location of Hotels and Diseases

Types of place where hotels are located	Has a Disease at Present		Total
	Yes	No	
Tourist Place	230 (70.0)	100 (30.0)	330 (100)
Non-Tourist Place	80 (55.1)	65 (44.8)	145 (100)
Total	**310 (65.2)**	**165 (34.7)**	**475 (100)**

$\chi^2 = 9.2$ df = 1 $P < 0.05$.

The data in the Table clearly show that the proportion of children in the hotels located in tourist places (70%) is significantly higher than that (55.1%) in the hotels situated in the non-tourist places. Generally, the workload of the children is relatively heavy in the former type of hotels compared to the workload of their counterparts in the latter type of hotels.

Moreover, the habits of smoking and drinking are more prevalent among the children employed in the former type of hotels than among those working in the latter type of hotels. In addition to this, in the former type of hotels, more than one-third of the children (34.5%) use *ganja* (intoxicant) and a majority (55.7%) use *pan-parag* and *beeda* (local intoxicants), which, in the long run, may lead to nervous weakness and oral cancer. That is perhaps why many of them are affected by diseases as compared to their counterparts in the latter type of hotels.

TREATMENT FOR DISEASE

Out of about two-thirds (65.2%) of children who suffer from diseases, nearly three-fourths (71.6%) take medical treatment in private hospitals, whereas over one-fourth (28.4 per cent) takes local treatment from their masters.

Hotel work is affected due to the ill health of the children. So the owners send the sick children immediately to private hospitals to get them treated so that they could resume work as early as possible. Some children prefer local treatment from their masters who treat them with indigenous medicine. Sometimes this sort of treatment is effective.

The discussion in this chapter addresses several health related aspects like oral hygiene, bathing, bathroom and toilet facilities, dressing, food, sleeping and diseases. Generally, the health status of the children is not satisfactory and needs to be promoted for sustenance over the years.

REFERENCES

1. S. Vijayalakshmi, *Working Conditions of Children Employed in Unorganized Sector in Sivakasi*, in Social Welfare, ed. A.S. Kohli, (Delhi: Anmol Publications, 1997), p. 34.

2. Sushila Srivastava and R. Bhanumathi, Child Workers in Farming, Domestic and Catering Sectors, *Social Welfare*, Vol. 41, (October 1990), p. 25.

3. Sushila Srivastava and R. Bhanumathi, *Child Workers in Farming, Domestic and Catering Sectors*, Social Welfare, *op.cit.*, p. 26.

4. S.Vijayalakshmi, *Working Conditions of Children Employed in Unorganinsed Sector: A Study in Sivakasi in Social Welfare*, ed. A.S. Kohli, op.cit., p. 24.

5. Chandragupt S. Sanon, *Working Children: A Sociological Analysis*, (New Delhi: APH Publishing Corporation, 1998), pp. 126-127.

CHAPTER 9

Unhealthy Practices among Child Labour

This chapter deals with the unhealthy practices found among the children employed in hotels and how they learn such practices.

But before going into the details, a statement has to be made regarding the difference between the attitude towards matters related to drinking and sex in India and in the advanced countries. The advanced styles of living influenced by the west believe in a life style that is not cramped by too much of a concern with drinking and sexual permissiveness. Drinking is a habit that is not generally frowned upon by such societies up to a certain limit; a person is branded a drunkard only when the drinking goes beyond this limit, becomes an addiction and begins to affect his/her health adversely. Otherwise, drinking is just a social matter, and it is part of conviviality. This is not part of the permissiveness of the "new" world but part of tradition - as creative literature reflecting the life styles of the past testify. The matter of drug addiction, indeed, is not so easily disposed of. Its history is tainted even from earlier times, and it is more easily accepted as addiction, bad.

But in India, in conventional or traditional society, drinking is considered wrong, a sin. It is not a question of degree, it is something absolute. It is only in recent times that the advanced layers of society have come to the westernized idea that some drinking is socially acceptable, part of good fellowship. Yet it is part of fashion, and yet not part of traditionally accepted behaviour. So drinking according to Indian standards is an evil practice which affects the physical health of the drinker and also his mental health. The person who drinks is a traitor to his family and a disturber of normal life. It may be that in a climate like India drinking is more harmful than it is in western countries. However, the younger generation is getting used to the idea of drinking as a normal course. But traditional life-represented not only in literary works but even widely canvassed political and social ideas-represents drinking as an evil practice. Gandhian ideals do not countenance drinking at any level. They represent Indian moral standards by and large. The political movement of the nationalist era spearheading the freedom movement of the country declared the anti-drink propaganda as part of its social agenda. There were agitations in front of shops that sold drinks. For quite a few years, the free governments of India help prohibition a national philosophy. When Prohibition was given up as a national policy, it was only for economic reasons and not on the basis of a revision of the guiding moral principles of the country. Non-drinking is not an ideal in this country but a norm. Drinking is an unpleasant deviation from the norm in the moral thinking of the country.

In the light of this controlling national attitude, this study also presents the habit of drinking as something bad. Considering the fact that the not too-well educated child and adolescent workers in the hotel industry are not likely to be controlled by ideas of moderation it is possible even for an objective sociologist to accept the idea of drinking as an evil practice. Considering the fact that these poor children are too ill paid to afford quality drinks, it is possible to concede that their health is dangerously exposed to diseases connected with drinking. Drink is for them an escape route, something that helps them forget their pains and their privations. That is the mental attitude that can easily push them over the verge of harmless and occasional indulgence and involve them in addiction and all its possible bad consequences. Several hundred lives of poor drinkers are lost every year in India to adulterated drinks. The adulteration is resorted to by the bootleggers and by illicit distillers and even by authorized sellers to satisfy the craving of their clientele for drinks with increasing potency. It is painful to note that women and very young males are among the victims. So in this study drinking is presented as a bad habit.

Similarly in the matter of sex, the Indian moral ideal is a one man-one woman relationship. The ideal is often broken, and bigamy is part of Indian tradition too, but the ideal remains. Though men violating the ideal of monogamy are not socially censured, they are not accepted as normal men. Society is capable of dealing harshly with women who violate the norm-ideal of man-woman relationship. So despite the change in terminology, labelling women conventionally called prostitutes as "sex-workers" and so on, the norm still holds good for the majority of Indians. Deviation from the norm is very slow in winning any amount of social acceptance. Homosexuality is widely accepted in the west, and it has even been accorded legal sanction in many countries. But in India it is not. Any traditional medicine-man's advertisement in the mass media represents all sexual deviation as evil and harmful-evil because harmful. The concept of single mother family is indeed catching attention in metropolitan cities and societies of the country, but it is not yet a practice as a matter of course.

Under such circumstances, the researcher reflects social norms in presenting in his study all deviation from the accepted sexual practices as bad habit and evil habit. In the light of such an attitude in society, it is easy to understand the absence of the idea of pornography and blue films as outlets for natural instincts. Sexual restraint is part of Indian ethos, and any deviation from that is unacceptable. So the deviant practices of the respondents of this study in these matters are presented as bad.

Children below the age of 14 years in the hotels do not have time to play, study, think, act on their own and share their joys and sorrows with others. As they are in frequent interaction with the owners, supervisors, masters, adult co-workers and customers, they imitate their way of life and contract the unhealthy practices. Through group discussions, case studies, observations and investigations, it is learnt that the children pick up some prominent unhealthy practices such as smoking, taking drugs, drinking liquor, reading pornographic and yellow books, watching blue films, masturbating and having sex with prostitutes.

The later part of the chapter deals with the employees who introduce the children to such practices and also describes how these practices affect them.

SMOKING

Smoking is injurious to health. Still a large section of the people smoke. In the hotels, the managers, supervisors, cooks, assistant cooks and adult co-workers smoke in the kitchens and in the rest rooms of the hotels. In turn, the working children start imitating them. The adult co-workers (servers) play a vital role in introducing the smoking habit. They send the children to buy *beedis* and cigarettes from nearby shops. When they smoke they tempt them to smoke for pleasure by supplying the *beedis* or cigarettes. However, in Type III hotels, the customers are mostly responsible for introducing this habit to the children. The children interact with the customers frequently to satisfy their needs.

It is found that there is variation between the types of hotel on the one hand and the smoking habit of children on the other hand. It is represented in Table 9.1.

Table 9.1: Respondents by Smoking Habits and Types of Hotel

Types of hotel	Smoking regularly	Smoking occasionally	Not smoking	Total
Type I (Boarding only)	102 (44.5)	82 (35.8)	45 (19.6)	229 (100)
Type II (Boarding and Lodging)	46 (38.0)	45 (37.1)	30 (24.7)	121 (100)
Type III (Lodging with Canteen)	46 (36.8)	29 (23.2)	50 (40.0)	125 (100)
Total	**193 (40.6)**	**157 (33.0)**	**125 (26.3)**	**475 (100)**

$\chi^2 = 19.1$ df = 4 P > 0.05.

Out of 475 children, a large majority (45.6%) has the habit of smoking regularly while one-third (33%) smoke occasionally. So, nearly three-fourths (73.6%) smoke. It is an unhealthy trend that a great majority of the children in the age group of 8-14 years smoke regularly or occasionally.

In Type I hotels, out of 229 children, 44.5 per cent are regular smokers while over one-third (35.8%) occasionally smoke. In Type II hotels, out of 121 children, a similar proportion of them are regular smokers (38%) and occasional smokers (37.1%). In Type III hotels, out of 125 children, over one-third (36.8%) are regular smokers, whereas nearly a quarter (23.2%) are occasional smokers.

The smoking habit affects the working children biologically in the sense that it causes cough, lung cancer, heart disease, loss of the sense of taste, cerebral hemorrhage and blindness. If they start smoking in their early childhood, it affects them quickly as they are already affected by nutritional anemia.

The smoking habit also affects the children economically in the sense that they spend at least Rs. 2.50-5.00 per day on this. If they get more *beta* or tips, they spend them on cigarettes or *beedis* instead of saving them.

In this context it is relevant to refer to a study on child labour in Bombay by Meenakshi et.al., (1985). They point out that working children in hotels smoke 1-10 beedis a day.[1]

It is understood from the data that there is significant relationship between the age of the children and their smoking habit. This is clearly presented in Table 9.2.

Table 9.2: Respondents by Age and Smoking Habits

Age group (in years)	Smoking regularly	Smoking occasionally	Not smoking	Total
8-10	10 (7.9)	35 (27.7)	81 (64.2)	126 (100)
10-12	77 (39.8)	90 (46.6)	26 (13.4)	193 (100)
12-14	106 (67.9)	32 (20.5)	18 (11.5)	156 (100)
Total	**193 (40.6)**	**157 (33.0)**	**125 (26.3)**	**475 (100)**

$\chi^2 = 175$ df = 4 $P < 0.05$.

It is clear from the data that out of 126 younger children, less than 10 per cent smoke regularly and over one-fourth (27.7%) smoke occasionally. Out of 193 children in the age group of 10-12 years, over one-third (39.8%) smokes regularly, while 46.6 percent smoke occasionally. Out of 156 children in the age group of 12-14 years, over two-thirds

(67.9%) smoke regularly while one-fifth (20.5%) smoke occasionally. This suggests that these children started smoking occasionally some time after joining the hotels and afterwards became regular smokers.

The children report that while beginning to smoke they were afraid of their owners, managers and supervisors. But in course of time they overcame the fear because smoking is common among the hotel employees. Nevertheless, it is found that the older children smoke more freely and regularly. The elder children get more *beta* and tips.

There is a significant relationship between the experience of the children and their smoking habit. This is represented in Table 9.3.

Table 9.3: Respondents by Experience and Smoking Habits

Experience (in years)	Smoking regularly	Smoking occasionally	Not smoking	Total
2	37 (27.4)	39 (28.8)	59 (43.7)	135 (100)
2-4	156 (45.8)	118 (34.7)	66 (19.4)	340 (100)
Total	**193 (40.6)**	**157 (33.0)**	**125 (26.3)**	**475 (100)**

$\chi^2 = 30.5$ df = 2 $P < 0.05$.

The data disclose that of 135 working children who have 2 years of experience, over one-fourth (27.4%) regularly smoke; over one-fourth (28.8%) smoke occasionally. In a sample of 340 working children who have 2-4 years of experience, 45.8 per cent smoke habitually and over one-third (34.7%) smoke occasionally. This clearly shows that the greater the experience of the children, the more certainly they smoke. It is obvious that the children become regular smokers only after serving a couple of years. It is inferred from this that the beginners may not smoke in their initial period.

In certain hotels, the management does not allow the children to smoke. In such hotels, if the management employees found the children smoking, they would beat them. In such circumstances, the children would run away from the hotels. On the other hand, in some hotels, the management employees encourage the children to smoke saying that it only energizes and stimulates them. Sometimes they supply beedis or cigarettes to the children.

It is found that there is a significant relationship between the background of the children and their smoking habit. This is clearly presented in Table 9.4.

Among 362 children who hail from rural areas, over one-third (34.2%) smoke regularly and more or less a similar proportion (37%) smoke occasionally. Among 113 children who hail from urban areas, about two-thirds (61%) have regular smoking habit while one-fifth (20.3%) smoke occasionally. It is evident that a higher proportion of urban children smoke habitually than their rural counterparts.

Table 9.4: Respondents by Background and Smoking Habits

Background	Smoking regularly	Smoking occasionally	Not smoking	Total
Rural	124 (34.2)	134 (37.0)	104 (28.7)	126 (100)
Urban	69 (61.0)	23 (20.3)	21 (18.5)	193 (100)
Total	**193 (40.6)**	**157 (33.0)**	**125 (26.3)**	**475 (100)**

$\chi^2 = 25.5$ df = 2 $P < 0.05$.

Generally, more urban child workers than their rural counterparts are exposed to various unhealthy practices. The anonymity of the urban areas is an important reason. It helps the children to contract such practices. Possibly that is why the working children in urban areas become regular smokers. On the contrary, the working children from rural areas are rather reluctant to smoke initially as they are afraid of their parents and their employers. The data show that over one-third of rural child workers smoke regularly (34.2%) and occasionally (37%). Nevertheless, there are more occasional smokers among the rural children than among the urban children. These children do not have any responsible counselors. They have to guide themselves. They either chose the wrong role models or cast about on their own. As urban society tends to be less restrictive and more permissive the children from urban areas pick up such habits easily.

There is a significant relationship between the location of the hotels and the smoking habit of the children. The distribution of data in Table 9.5 indicates this relationship.

Table 9.5: Respondents by Changing the Hotel and Smoking Habits

Changing the hotels	Smoking regularly	Smoking occasionally	Not smoking	Total
Twice	165 (50.0)	139 (42.1)	26 (7.8)	330 (100)
More than twice	23 (63.8)	6 (16.6)	7 (19.4)	36 (100)
Not changing	5 (4.5)	32 (11.0)	92 (84.4)	109 (100)
Total	**193 (40.6)**	**157 (33.0)**	**125 (26.3)**	**475 (100)**

$\chi^2 = 257.1$ df = 2 $P < 0.05$.

The data disclose that in the matter of regular smoking the proportion of children who changed the hotels more than twice during their service is higher than of those who changed the hotels twice during their service. It is evident that there is a significant relationship between the smoking habit of the children and the frequency of changing the hotels during their service. The reason is that the children who worked in different hotels situated in different places have interacted with various types of management employees and customers. Especially those who worked in hotels located in cities like Mumbai, Chennai and Bangalore might have followed certain unhealthy practices because of urban anonymity. Smoking has become a regular practice among the urban child workers. It is, therefore, confirmed that the children who changed the hotels more than twice are more regular smokers than those who changed the hotels twice.

It is observed that there is a significant relationship between the smoking habit of the children and the location of their hotels. This is presented in Table 9.6.

Table 9.6: Respondents by Location of Hotels and Smoking Habits

Location of hotels	Smoking regularly	Smoking occasionally	Not smoking	Total
Tourist place	153 (46.3)	110 (33.3)	67 (20.3)	126 (100)
Non-Tourist place	40 (27.5)	47 (32.4)	58 (40.0)	193 (100)
Total	**193 (40.6)**	**157 (33.0)**	**125 (26.3)**	**475 (100)**

$\chi^2 = 23.4$ df = 2 $P < 0.05$.

The data disclose that there is a variation in the frequency of smoking among the children with regard to the location of their hotels. More children (46.3%) in the hotels located in the tourist places than those in the hotels (27.5%) tourist places smoke regularly. The data also show that the proportion of the latter is twice as much as the proportion of the former with respect to non-smokers. It is inferred from this that fewer children employed in hotels located in non-tourist places are regular smokers.

The main reason for this variation is that the children working in hotels situated in tourist places are more exposed to such unhealthy practices than their counterparts in the hotels located in non-tourist places. It is more common to observe such practices in tourist places where various types of customers are entertained by wine shops, sex workers, gambling centres and the like. A majority of the customers are in need of liquor and women. Mostly the children employed in the hotels attend to their needs. As a result of frequent contacts with this sort of customer, the innocent children are tempted to drink and have sex with prostitutes. In course of time, they succumb to such unhealthy practices.

DRINKING HABITS

The consumption of alcohol by persons below the age of 18 years is illegal. Drinking affects the drinkers physically and mentally. In hotels with bars, customers are entertained by the employees. In other hotels, customers send room boys to buy liquor from nearby wine shops. While doing this job to satisfy the customers, the children are tempted to taste the liquor. They drink the small quantity of liquor left over by the customers. They become regular alcoholics in course of time.

The data show that of the total sample of 475, over two-thirds (67.5%) have the habit of drinking and about one-third (32.4%) do not. While analyzing the data in terms of the types of hotel and the proportion the children with the habit it is found that there is a significant relationship between the two variables as indicated in Table 9.7.

Table 9.7: Respondents by Types of Hotel and Frequency of Drinking

Types of hotel	Frequency of drinking			Total
	Monthly once	Monthly twice	Do not drink	
Type I (Boarding only)	116 (50.6)	69 (30.1)	44 (19.2)	229 (100)
Type II (Boarding and lodging)	10 (8.2)	49 (40.4)	62 (51.2)	121 (100)
Type III (Lodging with Canteen)	10(8.0) (53.6)	67 (38.4)	48 (100)	125
Total	**136 (28.6)**	**185 (38.9)**	**154 (32.4)**	**475 (100)**

$\chi^2 = 112.9$ df = 4 $P < 0.05$.

Out of 475 children, over one-fourth (28.6%) have the habit of drinking once a month while over one-third (38.9%) drink twice a month. In total, over two-thirds of them have the habit of drinking.

In the hotels surveyed, about 75 per cent of the employees (adult co-workers, masters and supervisors) consume liquor often. Especially those working in kitchens drink regularly in order to get rid of fatigue. They make use of the children to buy liquor from nearby wine shops. Sometimes they offer the children a small quantity of liquor.

In some hotels situated in tourist places, customers send the room boys to buy liquor. Sometimes, young customers prefer the company of the boys while drinking. Normally the beginners resist it. However, after some time they yield to the customers. In course of time, some children find it difficult to pass days without consuming alcohol.

In Type I hotels, out of 229 working children, a majority (50.6%) drink once a month, whereas 30.1 per cent drink twice a month. In Type II hotels, out of 121 working children, only 8.2 per cent have the habit of drinking once a month while 40.4 per cent of them drink twice a month. In Type III hotels, out of 125 working children, only eight per cent drink once a month while a majority (53.6%) drink twice a month.

It is evident from this analysis that in Types II and III hotels, the proportion of working children who consume liquor twice a month is high. The reason is probably that many of these hotel owners have wine shop licence and run the shops on the premises or nearby. The room boys buy liquor for the customers. For this they get more tips from the customers. In addition to this, they often get the liquor left over by the customers. Moreover, the children get more liquor than they require, especially at the time of parties or social gatherings held in Types II and III hotels.

The worst thing is that once the children start drinking they become addicted to it and go on increasing the quantity. It proves the proverb that *once a drinker always a drinker.* The habit of chronic drinking results in personal disorganization, which in turn leads to social disorganization. Undoubtedly, the drinking habit affects not only an individual's economy but also his family's economy.

Some working children run away from the hotels due to problems with the management. It is reported that a few of them join wine shops. They work for some months and afterwards return to the hotels. However, their experience in the wine shops turns them into regular drinkers. Therefore, after joining the hotels, they find ways to get liquor from the customers. If it is not available, they spend money to get it. They do not hesitate even to join their adult co-workers to drink in their company.

Within corporation limits and tourist places, hotel owners run wine shops near their hotels. Their wine shops remain open even during specific holidays such as Gandhi Jayanthi, Thiruvalluvar and Mahaveer Jayanthi. Liquor sale on these days is prohibited. However, during these days the owners supply liquor to the customers through the working children. It is reported that three of the sample children were arrested while carrying liquor bottles from the wine shops to the customers. They were in police custody for two days. Afterwards, the owners paid a penalty and got them released.

Besides supplying liquor to the customers in the hotel rooms, the children are given an additional and at the same time risky job of selling liquor in front of the hotel on certain specific holidays like Gandhi Jayanthi, Thiruvalluvar and Mahaveer Jayanthi. Since all other wine shops would be closed on those days as per the instruction of the Prohibition Enforcement Wing of the Police hotel owners arrange to sell liquor at a higher price through the children without opening their wine shops. When customers approach them to buy liquor bottles, the children collect an amount per bottle above the actual price. The children who are motivated by the extra income would readily come forward to do this job, in spite of the risk involved. Several children were arrested by the police during raids and kept in custody for a couple of weeks. However, their owners got them released after paying the penalty.

It is interesting to note that in Types II and III hotels, working children collect the empty liquor bottles from the rooms and sell them for Rs. 1-2 according to their size. They earn a sum of Rs. 10 to 50 at least twice a month. There is competition among them for doing so. Many of them spend the money on drinking, smoking and seeing films.

It is relevant to refer to a study on child labour by Walter Fernandes (1992). They find that the *dhabas* that are tea stalls during the day often become gambling dens at night. The child worker who might be serving tea during the day is often assigned to carry bottles of liquor and to peddle drugs for the clients during night. It is not surprising that many of these children themselves begin to drink and to use drugs at an early age. In other words, unscrupulous adults turn the child labour into criminals.[2] Chandragupt S. Sanon's (1998) study also supports the finding of the present study. He reports that 1.25 per cent of the working children in hotels at Allahabhad have the habit of drinking country liquor.[3]

It is found that there is a significant relationship between the age of the working children and the frequency of their drinking. This is clearly represented in Table 9.8.

Table 9.8: Respondents by Age and Frequency of Drinking

Age group (in years)	Frequency of drinking			Total
	Monthly once	Monthly twice	Do not drink	
8-10	33 (26.1)	18 (14.2)	75 (59.5)	126 (100)
10-12	56 (29.0)	88 (42.4)	49 (25.3)	193 (100)
12-14	49 (30.1)	79 (50.6)	30 (12.2)	125 (100)
Total	**136 (28.6)**	**185 (38.9)**	**154 (32.4)**	**475 (100)**

$\chi^2 = 67.47$ df = 4 $P < 0.05$.

It is clear from the Table that out of 126 working children in the age group of 8-10 years, over one-fourth (26.1%) have the habit of drinking once a month while 14.1 per cent drink twice a month. Out of 193 working children in the age group of 10-12 years, 29.0 per cent drink once a month, whereas 42.4 per cent do so twice a month. Out of 156 working children in the age group of 12-14 years, nearly a 30.1 per cent drink once a month while a majority (50.6%) do so twice a month.

It is evident from the analysis of data that the proportion of younger children is lower than the proportion of elder children with regard to their drinking once as well as twice a month. The reason is that the younger children fear their senior employees and parents. The elder children are not scared of these employees while drinking because of their long experience in the hotel job.

It is found that like age, bought of job the experience of the children is significantly related to the frequency of their drinking. This is clearly represented in Table 9.9.

Table 9.9: Respondents by Job Experience and Frequency of Drinking

Experience (in years)	Frequency of drinking			Total
	Monthly Once	Monthly twice	Do not drink	
2	42 (31.1)	21 (15.5)	72 (53.3)	135 (100)
2-4	94 (27.6)	164 (48.2)	82 (24.1)	340 (100)
Total	**136 (28.6)**	**185 (38.9)**	**154 (32.4)**	**475 (100)**

$\chi^2 = 52.28$ df = 2 $P < 0.05$.

While analyzing the relationship between frequency of drinking by the children and their experience in the hotel job, it is found that the two variables are related significantly. Out of 135 working children with two years of experience, nearly one-third (31.1%) of them have the habit of drink once a month, whereas 15.5 per cent do twice a month. Out of 340 working children with the experience of 2-4 years, over one-fourth (27.6%) drink once a month and nearly half (48.2%) of them do so twice a month. This clearly shows that the higher the experience of the children the higher their proportion with regard to drinking once or twice a month. The reason is that more experienced children get more tips from the customers and *beta* from their owners. Therefore they are free to spend their money on drinking.

The data show that the rural-urban background of the children influences the frequency of their drinking as indicated in Table 9.10.

Table 9.10: Respondents by Background and Frequency of Drinking

Background	Frequency of drinking			Total
	Monthly Once	Monthly twice	Do not drink	
Rural	88 (24.3)	129 (35.6)	145 (40.0)	362 (100)
Urban	48 (42.4)	56 (49.5)	9 (7.9)	113 (100)
Total	**136 (28.6)**	**185 (38.9)**	**154 (32.4)**	**475 (100)**

$\chi^2 = 50.4$ df = 2 $P < 0.05$.

It is observed from the Table that out of 362 rural children nearly one-fourth (24.3%) drink once a month, and over one-third (35.6%) drink twice a month. Out of 113 urban children, 42.4 per cent drink once a month, whereas 49.5 per cent do so twice a month. It is, thus, clear that the proportion of the urban children is more than the proportion of their rural counterparts in terms of drinking once or twice a month. This difference is perhaps explained in terms of their different cultural backgrounds, which play a vital role in shaping their personality. For instance, unlike the rural children, the urban children are exposed to several unhealthy practices to a greater extent because of urban anonymity.

It is found that there is a significant relationship between the frequency of changing the hotels and the frequency of drinking as represented in Table 9.11.

Table 9.11: Respondents by Changing the Hotel and Frequency of Drinking

Frequency of changing the hotels	Frequency of drinking			Total
	Monthly Once	Monthly twice	Do not drink	
Twice	103 (31.2)	150 (45.4)	77 (23.3)	330 (100)
More than twice	11 (30.0)	18 (50.0)	7 (19.4)	36 (100)
Not changing	22 (20.1)	17 (15.5)	70 (64.2)	109 (100)
Total	**136 (28.6)**	**185 (38.9)**	**154 (32.4)**	**475 (100)**

$\chi^2 = 23.7$ df = 2 $P < 0.05$.

The data disclose that out of 330 children who changed the hotels twice, nearly one-third (31.2%) drink once a month, whereas 45.4 per cent of them do so twice a month. Out of 36 respondents who changed the hotels more than twice, nearly one-third (30.5%) drink once a month, whereas a majority (50%) do so twice a month.

It is evident from the analysis that the frequency of drinking depends on frequency of changing the hotels. In other words, of the children who changed the hotels more than twice, the proportion of those who drink twice a month is higher than that of counterparts who changed the hotels twice. The more the frequency of changing the hotels, the more they get exposed to urban culture. It is important to note that previously these children worked in hotels situated in big cities such as Chennai, Bangalore, Mumbai and Trivandram.

The data confirms that the location of the hotels has a bearing on the frequency of drinking among the children. This is presented in Table 9.12.

The data in the Table disclose that out of 330 children working in hotels located in tourist places, nearly one-third (31.8%) drink once a month, whereas 42.7 per cent do so twice a month. Out of 145 children working in hotels situated in non-tourist places, over one-fifth (21.3%) drink once a month, whereas nearly one-third (30.3%) do so twice a month.

Table 9.12: Respondents by Location of Hotels and Frequency

Location of hotels	Frequency of drinking			Total
	Monthly once	Monthly twice	Do not drink	
Tourist place	105 (31.8)	141 (42.7)	84 (25.4)	330 (100)
Non-Tourist place	31 (21.3)	44 (30.3)	70 (48.2)	145 (100)
Total	**136 (28.6)**	**185 (38.9)**	**154 (32.4)**	**475 (100)**

$\chi^2 = 67.51$ df = 4 $P < 0.05$.

It is evident from the analysis that the proportion of children drinking liquor once as well as twice a month is more in hotels located in tourist places than the proportion of those doing so in hotels situated in non-tourist places. The former type of hotels have bar facility or easy access to nearby wine shops. The customers of these hotels mostly make use of the service of the children to buy liquor from those shops. Consequently, the children are slowly tempted to taste the liquor. In course of time, they drink the liquor left over by the customers. Sometimes, especially the young and friendly customers like the company of the children while drinking. In one way or another, the children get frequent chances to drink and ultimately this turns them into regular drinkers with the adult co-workers in the hotels.

Nevertheless, it is reported that they take a maximum of 100 ml. of liquor, which costs them Rs. 18-20. Most of the time they get it from the customers. If it is not possible, they are prepared to pay for it as they have developed the habit of drinking often.

A boy of 14 years explains his habit of drinking and its related problems as follows:

I am working as a room boy in a Type II hotel located at Courtallam, a popular tourist place in Tirunelveli District. Previously, I worked in a similar type of hotel at Chennai. While working there, I had the habit of drinking occasionally. Since the present hotel has bar facility, customers staying there are in need of alcohol especially during the nighttime. I am in charge of 10 rooms on the third floor of the hotel. The customers staying in these rooms depend on me to buy the required things. Most often I bring liquor for them from the bar or from the nearby wine shops.

Especially young customers are kind and friendly to me. They ask me to take the liquor left over by them. At least twice or thrice a week I would get 100 to 200 ml of liquor left over by the customers. This made me drink whenever I get liquor. Now, I am not able to stop it. If I am unable to get it for a week, I spend at least Rs. 18-20 to buy liquor for my use. Even if I do not have money, I am able to get a liquor bottle of 100 ml. from a well-known wine shop near the hotel promising the salesman that I would pay within a week.

Normally, I drink after 11.00 p.m. so that the other employees may not know it. Sometimes, I drink during daytime in order to get relief from the drudgery of my work. I was punished physically by my manager for spoiling the other children also. However, I did repeat the same thing on other occasions. As a result of this, I was sent out of the hotel. Then I joined the wine shop and worked for a couple of months. Afterwards, I was able to reenter the same hotel again with great difficulty on condition that I should not drink. Nevertheless, I continue to drink during nights without attracting the attention of other employees.

The discussion in this section shows facts relating to the drinking habits of the children working in different types of hotels. It is rather unfortunate to note that the children in the age group of 8-14 years have the habit of drinking once or twice a month. Some of them have turned habitual drinkers who consume liquor at regular intervals. It is important to note that unlike the children working in hotels, the children employed in other sectors including unorganized sectors do not have the habit of drinking. If at all a few of them drink, they do it occasionally. It is, therefore, concluded that the children in hotels get spoiled because of the kind of culture prevalent in the hotels.

USE OF DRUGS AND OTHER INTOXICANTS

Some of the children employed in hotels get accustomed to intoxicants such as *ganja*, *pan-parag* and *beeda*. Though they know that they are harmful to their health, they continue to take them regularly or occasionally. It is not initially the personal inclination of the children to take such intoxicants; it is understood that a great majority are motivated by the co-workers to take them for pleasure. It is found that there is variation among the children with respect to their habit of taking intoxicants as shown in Table 9.13.

Table 9.13: Respondents by Types of Hotel and Use of Drugs and Other Intoxicants

Types of Hotel	Use Of Drugs and other Intoxicants			Total
	Ganja	*Pan-parag* and *Beeda*	None of them	
Type I (Boarding only)	70 (30.5)	135 (58.9)	24 (10.4)	229 (100)
Type II (Boarding and Lodging)	60 (49.5)	50 (41.3)	11 (9.0)	121 (100)
Type III (Lodging with Canteen)	38 (30.4)	52 (41.6)	35 (28.0)	125 (100)
Total	**168 (35.3)**	**237 (49.8)**	**70 (14.7)**	**475 (100)**

$\chi^2 = 36.74$ df = 4 $P < 0.05$.

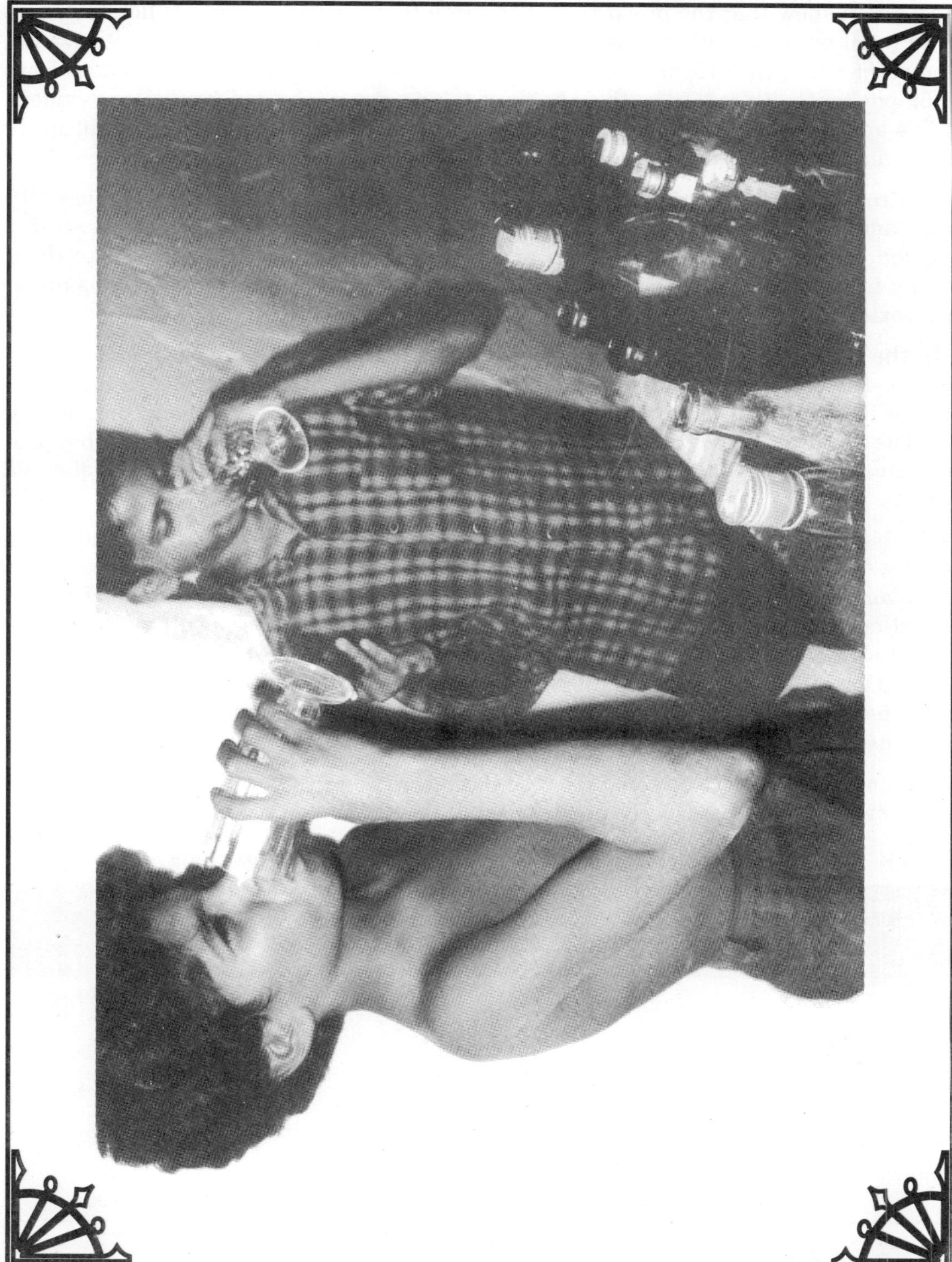

At a young age, they taste the lees of liquor left by others

The data show that the proportion of children from the three types of hotels ranges from 30 to 50 per cent with regard to their habit of taking *ganja* and other intoxicants. On the other hand, the proportion of children from the three types of hotels ranges from 41 to 59 per cent with regard to their habit of taking *pan-parag* and *beeda*. It is evident from this analysis that the proportion of children taking these intoxicants is significantly higher than the proportion of those taking *ganja*.

The reason is that the children cannot afford to pay much to get a small quantity of *ganja* and a required number of cigarettes because they smoke the cigarettes stuffed with *ganja*. Since the cost of *pan-parag* and *beeda* is rather moderate, they take them according to their need. Hence the variation among the children in terms of consuming such intoxicants.

In the hotels, the head-cooks and their assistants take *pan-parag, pan-masala and* other *pan*-related items. The habit of taking tobacco is also common among them. Whenever they are in need of such items, they send the children to buy them from nearby shops. The children taste those items out of curiosity and in course of time, they use them regularly. If they are not able to get them, they steal them from the bags of other employees.

The habit of chewing *pan-parag* and tobacco affects the children both mentally and physically. This habit results in mouth and lung cancer. Adult co-workers make them drink liquor and also use them as contact persons to visit prostitutes. Since they do not take food on time, they do not have a healthy appetite, which would ultimately cause ulcer and stomach problems. In this regard, it is relevant to refer to a study on child labour by Chandragupt S. Sanon (1998). He points out that in the hotels at Allahabhad, about 10 per cent of the working children smoke and chew tobacco. A similar proportion (10.02%) use *pan masala*.[4]

It is found that there is a significant relation between the age of the children and their use of drugs. This is clearly presented in Table 9.14.

Table 9.14: Respondents by Age and Use of Drugs and Other Intoxicants

Age Group (in Years)	Use of Drugs and Other Intoxicants			Total
	Ganja	*Pan-parag* and *Beeda*	None of them	
8-10	31 (24.6)	46 (36.5)	49 (38.8)	126 (100)
10-12	77 (39.8)	101 (52.3)	15 (7.7)	193 (100)
12-14	60 (38.4)	90 (57.6)	6 (3.8)	156 (100)
Total	**168 (35.3)**	**237 (49.8)**	**70 (14.7)**	**475 (100)**

$\chi^2 = 81.17$ df = 4 $P < 0.05$.

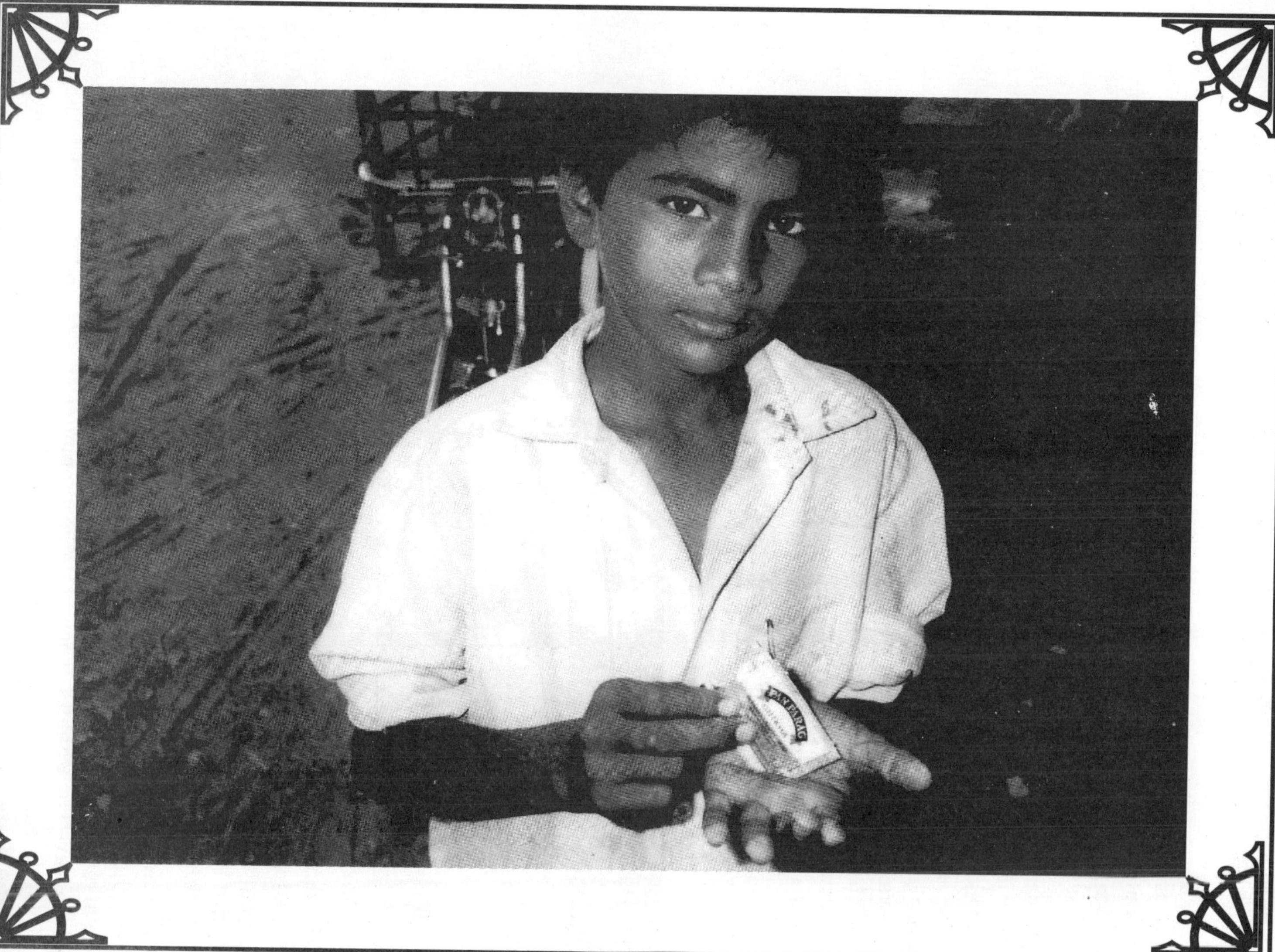

Mild intoxicants such as Pan-Parg would make him an addict for life

As shown in the Table, out of 126 working children in the age group of 8-10 years, nearly one-fourth (24.6%) use *ganja* while over one-third (36.5%) use *pan-parag* and *beeda*.

Out of 193 working children in the age group 10-12 years, 39.8 per cent have the habit of using *ganja,* whereas a majority (52.3%) of them use *pan-parag* and *beeda*. Among 156 working children in the age group 12-14 years, 38.4 per cent use *ganja* and a majority (57.6%) use *pan-parag* and *beeda*.

Ignorant children fall a prey to this sort of unhealthy practice, which they imitate from their owners, managers, supervisors, masters and adult co-workers. In order to get a new thrilling experience, the working children start smoking cigarettes filled with *ganja* and chew *beeda* and *pan-parag*. Both inside and outside the hotel, the habit of using *pan-parag* and chewing *beeda* is quite common among the working children. Mostly the adult co-workers provide them with these intoxicants and tempt them to use them. It is observed that this habit is more prevalent among the higher age group of children. The main reason is that they receive more tips and *beta* from which they could spend money to buy such intoxicants.

Like age, the work experience of the children has a direct bearing on their use of drug and other intoxicants in the hotels. This is represented in Table 9.15.

Table 9.15: Respondents by Experience and Use of Drugs and Other Intoxicants

Experience (in Years)	Use of drugs and other intoxicants			Total
	Ganja	*Pan-parag* and *Beeda*	None of them	
Less than 2	35 (25.4)	55 (40.7)	45 (33.3)	135 (100)
2-4	133 (39.1)	182 (53.5)	25 (7.3)	340 (100)
Total	**168 (35.3)**	**237 (49.8)**	**70 (14.7)**	**475 (100)**

$\chi^2 = 52.2$ df= 2 $P < 0.05$.

The data show that among the 135 working children who have 2 years of experience in hotel jobs, over one-fourth (25.9%) have the habit of using *ganja* while over 40.7 per cent use *pan-parag* and *beeda*. Out of 340 children who have gained 2-4 years of experience in hotel jobs, 39.1 per cent use *ganja*, and a majority (53.5%) have the habit of using *pan-parag* and *beeda*.

It is evident from this analysis of data that the greater the experience of the children, the more they use drugs and other intoxicants. The reason is that the children who have more experience have worked in various hotels, and also think they are mature enough to have such habits. They get a good amount of *beta* and tips which they spend thus. Usually *ganja, pan-parag* and *beed*, are available in certain shops in and around the bus stand area.

It is found that there is a significant variation among these children using intoxicants with respect to their rural-urban background. It is clearly represented in Table 9.16.

Table 9.16: Respondents by Background and Use of Drugs and Other Intoxicants

Background	Use of Drugs and other Intoxicants			Total
	Ganja	*Pan-parag* and *Beeda*	None of them	
Rural	124 (34.2)	174 (48.0)	64 (17.4)	362 (100)
Urban	44 (38.9)	63 (55.7)	6 (5.31)	113 (100)
Total	**168 (35.3)**	**237 (49.8)**	**70 (14.7)**	**475 (100)**

$\chi^2 = 10.37$ df = 2 $P < 0.05$.

The data in the table disclose that of 362 rural children, about one-third (34.2%) use *ganja* while 48.8 per cent use *pan-parag* and *beeda*. Among 113 urban children, 38.9 per cent have the habit of using *ganja,* whereas a majority (55.7%) have the habit of using *pan-parag* and *beeda*.

It is clear that the proportion of rural children is less than the proportion of the urban children with regard to the habit of using such intoxicants. The urban children easily fall a prey to such habits because they are common among the urban people.

The data show that there is a significant relationship between changing the hotels by the working children and their use of intoxicants. This is exhibited in Table 9.17.

Table 9.17: Respondents by Changing the Hotels and Use of Drugs and Other Intoxicants

Changing the hotels	Use of Drugs and other Intoxicants			Total
	Ganja	*Pan-parag* and *Beeda*	None of them	
Twice	135 (40.9)	178 (53.9)	17 (5.1)	330 (100)
More than twice	11 (30.5)	20 (55.5)	5 (13.8)	36 (100)
Not changing	22 (20.1)	39 (35.7)	48 (44.0)	109 (100)
Total	**168 (35.3)**	**237 (49.8)**	**70 (14.7)**	**475 (100)**

$\chi 2 = 99.9$ df = 4 $P < 0.05$.

It is clear from the distribution of data in the Table that out of 330 working children who changed the hotels twice during their service 40.9 per cent have the habit of using *ganja* while a majority (53.9%) use *pan-parag* and *beeda*.

Out of 36 working children who changed the hotels more than twice, nearly one-third (30.5%) have the habit of using *ganja*, whereas a majority (55.5%) use *pan-parag* and *beeda*. Out of 109 children who did not change the hotels, about one-fifth (20.1%) have the habit of using *ganja*, and over-one third (35.7%) use pan-*parag* and *beeda*.

It is obvious from the data that a higher proportion of children who changed the hotels use intoxicants rather than those who did not. The reason is that those who had worked in hotels in Chennai, Thiruvananthapuram, Bangalore and Mumbai. This is perhaps explained in terms of the influence of the urban life style on the children. In other words, their contact with the co-workers and customers leads them to such intoxicants.

It is found that there is a significant relationship between the location of hotels on the one hand and the use of *ganja* and other intoxicants by the children on the other hand. This is represented in Table 9.18.

Table 9.18: Respondents by Location of Hotels and Use of Drugs and Other Intoxicants

Location of hotels	Use of Drugs and other Intoxicants			Total
	Ganja	*Pan-parag* and *Beeda*	None of them	
Tourist places	114 (34.5)	184 (55.7)	32 (13.8)	330 (100)
Non-tourist places	48 (33.1)	59 (40.6)	38 (26.2)	145 (100)
Total	**168 (35.3)**	**237 (49.8)**	**70 (14.7)**	**475 (100)**

$\chi^2 = 23.46$ df = 2 $P < 0.05$.

The data in the table show that out of 330 children working in hotels located in tourist places, over one-third (34.5 per cent) have the habit of using *ganja,* and a majority (55.7%) have the habit of using *pan-parag* and *beeda*.

Out of 145 children working in non-tourist places about one-third (33.1%) use *ganja*, and 40.1 per cent have the habit of using *pan-parag* and *beeda*.

Generally tourists use drugs and other intoxicants because they seek pleasure and excitement. The children in the hotels use *ganja* and other intoxicants to forget their family problems and also to get relief from pain in joints. The intoxicants are easily available in tourist cebtres. The children working in hotels at tourist centers get more tips and *beta* which they spend on intoxicants. In the hotels located in non-tourist places, they do not get much tips and *beta,* and they cannot spend money on intoxicants.

Moreover, the drugs or intoxicants are not easily available in non-tourist places where fewer customers and children use them. The parents and relatives of the working children frequently visit the hotels in order to collect their salary, which means that the chances are rather limited for the children to buy such things. The drug sellers mostly haunt tourist spots. They use the children to establish a business link with the customers staying in the hotels. Initially the children use the drugs in an ambiguous and undecided state of mind. But in course of time, they become accustomed to them.

READING PORNOGRAPHIC AND YELLOW BOOKS

Inside the hotels, the children have no chance for recreation except reading pornographic literature and playing cards. They get such books from their adult co-workers. It is found that there is a significant relationship between the types of hotel on the one hand and the habit of the children reading pornographic and yellow books on the other hand. This is clearly represented in Table 9.19.

Table 9.19: Respondents by Types of Hotel and Habit of Reading Pornograpic and Yellow Books

Types of hotel	Habit of reading pornographic and yellow books		Total
	Yes	No	
Type I (Boarding only)	162 (70.7)	67 (29.2)	229 (100)
Type II (Boarding and Lodging)	98 (80.9)	23 (19.0)	121 (100)
Type III (Lodging with Canteen)	82 (65.6)	43 (34.4)	125 (100)
Total	**342 (72.0)**	**133 (28.0)**	**475 (100)**

χ^2 = 7.49 df = 2 P = < 0.05.

Out of 475 working children, nearly two-thirds (72.0%) read those books. They read them secretly during the night or on holidays. This pollutes their mind and induces them to homo-and other sexual activities. In Type I hotels, a great majority (70.7%) read such books. Similarly, in Type II hotels, an overwhelming majority (80.9%) do so. In Type III hotels, two-thirds (65.6%) have this habit.

In Types I and II hotels, the proportion of children reading such books is higher than the proportion of those who do so in Type III hotels. The reason is that the children in Type III hotels have no chance to read those books as their counterparts from other types of hotels have. It is relevant here to refer to a study on child labour by Prakash Kothari (1985). He says that the advertisements through television and films and posters and articles in magazines stimulate the sexual urge of a person but offer no guidance to him or her. The conflicting values among working children have noticeably increased in the last decade and brought to the surface a large number of problems that affect human sexual functioning.[5]

The data show that there is a significant relationship between the age of the working children and their habit of reading such books. This is clearly represented in Table 9.20.

Table 9.20: Respondents by Age and Habit of Reading Pornograpic and Yellow Books

Age group (in years)	Habit of reading pornographic and yellow books		Total
	Yes	No	
8-10	51 (40.4)	75 (59.5)	126 (100)
10-12	145 (75.1)	48 (24.8)	193 (100)
12-14	146 (93.5)	10 (6.4)	156 (100)
Total	**342 (72.0)**	**133 (28.0)**	**475 (100)**

χ^2 =207.9 df = 2 P = < 0.05.

It is understood from the Table that out of 126 working children in the age group of 8-10 years, 40.4 per cent read such books. Out of 193 children in the age group of 10-12 years, three-fourths (75.1%) have the habit. Out of 156 children in the age group of 12-14 years, an overwhelming majority (93.5%) has this habit. This shows that the higher the age of the children the higher their proportion with regard to reading such books.

The working children have easy access to such books. They borrow them from adult co-workers who in turn buy them from shops. Nevertheless, it is observed that the younger children are afraid of being caught reading those books. Unlike them, the elder children do not entertain any fear about senior employees scolding them for reading such books.

It is found that, like age, the experience of the children is significantly related to their habit of reading such books. This is clearly shown in Table 9.21.

It is clear that the experience of the children is a factor in their choosing to read pornographic books. In other words, the more the experience of the respondents the higher the number of children who read such books.

It is also found that the proportion of children with this habit from urban areas is significantly higher than the proportion of their rural counterparts. This is presented in Table 9.22.

Table 9.21: Respondents by Experience and Habit of Reading Pornograpic and Yellow Books

Experience (in years)	Habit of reading pornographic and yellow books		Total
	Yes	No	
Less than 2	70 (51.8)	65 (48.1)	135 (100)
2-4	272 (80.0)	68 (20.0)	340 (100)
Total	**342 (72.0)**	**133 (28.0)**	**475 (100)**

$\chi^2 = 37.8$ df = 1 P = < 0.05.

Table 9.22: Respondents by Background and Habit of Reading Pornograpic and Yellow Books

Background	Habit of reading pornographic and yellow books		Total
	Yes	No	
Rural	252 (69.6)	110 (30.4)	362 (100)
Urban	90 (79.6)	23 (20.3)	113 (100)
Total	**342 (72.0)**	**133 (28.0)**	**475 (100)**

$\chi^2 = 4.26$ df = 1 P = < 0.05.

It is clear from the data that out of 362 rural children; over two-thirds (69.6%) have the habit. Out of 113 urban children, over three-fourths (79.6%) have the habit. Therefore, the difference between the rural and urban children in this regard is confirmed. This is owing to their exposure to urban culture. They find easy access to such books kept by the adult co-workers. Sometimes they buy those books from shops according to their taste.

It is observed from Table 9.23 that there is a significant relationship between changing the hotels and their habits of reading pornographic and yellow books.

The data in Table 9.23 show that of 330 children who changed the hotels more than twice, a great majority (86.1%) read pornographic and yellow books. More or less a similar proportion of them who changed the hotels twice do so. It is, thus, concluded that the children's habit of reading such books is influenced by the frequency of their changing the hotels. Those who changed the hotels twice or more than twice are found to have worked in hotels in big cities. Their exposure to city life may have resulted in such an unhealthy habit.

Table 9.23: Respondents by Changing the Hotels and Habit of Reading Pornograpic and Yellow Books

Frequency of changing the hotels	Habit of reading pornographic and yellow books		Total
	Yes	No	
Twice	267 (80.0)	63 (20.0)	330 (100)
More than twice	31 (86.1)	5 (13.8)	36 (100)
Not changing	44 (40.0)	65 (60.0)	109 (100)
Total	**342** **(72.0)**	**133** **(28.0)**	**475** **(100)**

$\chi^2 = 70.43$ df = 2 P = < 0.05.

It is observed that the location of hotels where children are working has a bearing on their habit of reading pornographic and yellow books. This is clearly represented in Table 9.24.

Table 9.24: Respondents by Location of Hotels and Habit of Reading Pornograpic and Yellow Books

Location of hotels	Habit of reading pornographic and yellow books		Total
	Yes	No	
Tourist place	278 (84.2)	52 (15.7)	330 (100)
Non-Tourist place	64 (44.1)	81 (55.8)	145 (100)
Total	**342** **(72.0)**	**133** **(28.0)**	**475** **(100)**

$\chi^2 = 80.26$ df = 1 P = < 0.05.

The data in Table 9.24 disclose that out of 475 children working in hotels located in tourist places, a great majority (84.2%) read such books, whereas out of 145 children working in hotels located in non-tourist places, 44.1 per cent do so. This analysis of data shows that the hotels in tourist places influence the habit of the children in reading such books.

SEEING BLUE FILMS

In one or two theatres in Tirunelveli town, blue films are shown for a few minutes in the middle of regular films, especially after 11.00 p.m. The adult co-workers in the hotels prefer to go for second show at 10.00 p.m. mainly to see such films even if erotic scenes are shown only for a few minutes. Most of the time, the children join them as they are in need of their support while going to films. In the first instance, the children are taken by surprise to see such films. However, after some time, they want to see the blue films especially in the company of their peer group. Sometimes, they get chances to see those films on the television in their manager's room. As a matter of fact, the manager is able to get cassettes of blue films illegally from known sources in order to see them on television with the help of VCR. Sometimes, they allow a few children who attend to their personal work sincerely to see the films. It is reported that they see the blue films at least thrice or four times a year.

Table 9.25 shows the relationship between the children from three types of hotel and their habit of seeing blue films.

Table 9.25: Respondents by Types of Hotel and Seeing Blue Films

Types of hotel	Seeing blue films			Total
	Theatre	TV in manager's room	Not seeing	
Type I (Boarding only)	146 (63.7)	16 (6.9)	67 (29.2)	229 (100)
Type II (Boarding and lodging)	63 (52.0)	28 (23.1)	30 (24.7)	121 (100)
Type III (Lodging with Canteen)	45 (36.0)	30 (24.0)	50 (40.0)	125 (100)
Total	**254 (53.4)**	**74 (15.5)**	**147 (30.9)**	**475 (100)**

$\chi^2 = 37.6$ df = 4 $P < 0.05$.

It is clear from Table 9.25 that a great majority of the sample children see films. Indeed out of 475 children, over two-thirds (69%) see blue films. Of them, over a majority (53.4%) see those films in theatres, whereas only 15.5 per cent see them in their manager's room. This small proportion of employees consists of the manager, supervisor, master, a few suppliers and children in the hotels. Since the management employees are away from their families most of the time, they are in need of such entertainment. Therefore, they try to get blue film cassettes from known sources and see them secretly in the manager's room on television. But the children are not allowed to join them every time. Hence they join the adult co-workers to see those films in theaters. This might results in homosexual activities among them. Especially, the masters and adult co-workers make use of the children for this sort of activity.

In Type I hotels, out of 229 children, nearly two-thirds (63.7%) see those films in theatres, whereas only 6.9 per cent of them see them in their manager's room. In Type II hotels, out of 121 children, a majority (52%) sees them in theatres whereas nearly one-fourth (23.1%) sees them in the manager's room. In Type III hotels, out of 125 children, over one-third (36.0%) see them in theatres. At the same time, nearly one-fourth (24 per cent) of them see them in the manager's room itself.

Since there are more children in Types I and II hotels, the proportion of those who see the blue films is also high. But in Type III hotels, the children have fewer chances to see blue films because there are few employees available who may have time to interact with the children. Therefore, in the absence of close relationship with them, the children may not seek their support to go to films.

The children prefer to go with the adult workers to see films after 10.00 p.m. Occasionally children of the same age go together to such programmes. They are afraid of confronting the police in and around the bus stand. If the policemen happen to see them, they would enquire about them and sometimes take them to the police station under suspicion. Of the total 475 children, 18 (3.79%) report that when they were returning from the cinema theatre after mid-night, police men took them to the bus stand police station and kept them there till the next morning. Their manager came to the police station around 10.00 a.m. and got them released with the help of a known policeman. Therefore, they normally join the adult co-workers while going out in the late evening.

There seems to be a significant relationship between the age of children and their seeing blue films. This is clearly represented in Table 9.26.

Table 9.26: Respondents by Age and Seeing Blue Films

Age group (in years)	Seeing blue films			Total
	Theatre	TV in manager's room	Not seeing	
8-10	38 (30.1)	8 (6.3)	80 (63.4)	126 (100)
10-12	104 (53.8)	30 (15.5)	59 (30.5)	193 (100)
12-14	112 (71.7)	36 (23.0)	8 (5.1)	156 (100)
Total	**254 (53.4)**	**74 (15.5)**	**147 (30.9)**	**475 (100)**

$\chi^2 = 111.8$ df = 4 $P < 0.05$.

It is understood from the above table that out of 126 children in the age group of 8-10 years, nearly one-third (30%) see blue films in theatres, whereas only 6.3 per cent see them in their manager's room. Out of 193 working children in the age group of 10-12 years, over a majority (53.8%) see the films in theatres, whereas 15.5 per cent see them in their manager's room. Out of 156 children in the age group of 12-14 years, nearly two-thirds (71.7%) see such films in theatres, whereas over one-fifth (23%) see them in their manger's room.

It is thus evident that the age of the children influences their habit of seeing blue films. In a similar way, the proportion of those who see those films through the television in their manager's room increases with the increase in their age. After seeing these films, the children discuss them with one another during the small break in the morning as well as in the evening.

Like age, their experience influences their habit of seeing blue films. This is clearly represented in Table 9.27.

Table 9.27: Respondents by Experience and Seeing Blue Films

Experience (in years)	Seeing blue films			Total
	Theatre	TV in manager's room	Not seeing	
2	62 (45.9)	14 (10.3)	59 (43.7)	135 (100)
2-4	192 (56.4)	60 (17.6)	88 (25.8)	340 (100)
Total	**254 (53.4)**	**74 (15.5)**	**147 (30.9)**	**475 (100)**

$\chi^2 = 15.05$ df = 2 $P < 0.05$.

The data given in Table 9.27 explain that out of 135 children with two years of experience, a large minority (45.9%) sees the blue films in theatre, whereas 10.3 per cent see them in their manager's room. Out of 340 children with experience of 2-4 years, a majority (56.4%) see blue films in theatres, whereas 17.6 per cent do so in their manager's room.

It is, thus, clear that the proportion of children seeing those films depends on their experience in the hotel jobs. The reason is that more experienced children might have worked in various hotels and established cordial relationship with different types of adult co-workers. So about three-fourths of them see the blue films in theaters with the help of adult co-workers. On the whole, it is positive to conclude that the proportion of less experienced children is significantly associated with the lower proportion of those seeing blue films.

Table 9.28 indicates, there is a relationship between the rural–urban background of the children and their seeing blue films.

The data given in Table 9.28 disclose that out of 362 rural children 46.6 per cent see blue films in theatres, and 14.0 per cent do so in their manager's room. Out of 113 urban children, three-fourths (75.2%) see such films in theatres, and one-fifth (20.3%) see them in their manager's room.

It is evident from the analysis that the rural-urban background of the children influences their habit of seeing blue films. The urban oriented children have more exposure to unhealthy practices than their rural counterparts. This can be explained in terms of the differences between their rural and urban backgrounds. The rural children's fear of their hotel owners, employees and parents prevents them from seeing such films. On the other hand, it is not surprising that the urban children fall prey to this practice mainly owing to their contact with peer groups which plays a vital role in encouraging them to see blue films.

Table 9.28: Respondents by Background and Seeing Blue Flims

Background	Seeing blue films			Total
	Theatre	TV in manager's room	Not seeing	
Rural	169 (46.6)	51 (14.0)	142 (39.2)	362 (100)
Urban	85 (75.2)	23 (20.3)	5 (4.4)	113 (100)
Total	**254 (53.4)**	**74 (15.5)**	**147 (30.9)**	**475 (100)**

$\chi^2 = 48.7$ df = 2 $P < 0.05$.

The data disclose that there is a significant relationship between changing the hotels by the children and their habit of seeing blue films. This is represented in Table 9.29.

Table 9.29: Respondents by Changing Hotels and Seeing Blue Films

Frequency of changing the hotels	Seeing blue films			Total
	Theatre	TV in manager's room	Not seeing	
Twice	182 (55.1)	62 (18.7)	86 (26.0)	330 (100)
More than twice	25 (69.4)	6 (16.6)	5 (13.8)	36 (100)
Not changing	47 (43.1)	6 (5.5)	56 (51.3)	109 (100)
Total	**254 (53.4)**	**74 (15.5)**	**147 (30.9)**	**475 (100)**

$\chi^2 = 13.09$ df = 4 $P < 0.05$.

The above table shows that out of 330 children who changed the hotels twice, a majority (51.1%) sees blue films in theatres, whereas 18.7 per cent see them in their manager's room. Out of 36 children who changed the hotels twice, over two-thirds (69.4%) see blue films in theatres, whereas 16.6 per cent do so in their manager's room. Out of 109 children who did not change hotels, 43.1 per cent see those films in theatres. On the other hand, less than five per cent of them see them in the manager's room.

It is evident from this analysis that the proportion of children who see blue films in theatres increases with the increase in the frequency their changing the hotels. It is thus confirmed by statistical analysis that the habit of seeing blue films varies with the frequency of changing the hotels. In other words, the frequency of changing the hotels by the children influences them to see the films.

There is a significant association between the location of the hotels and children seeing the blue films as clearly indicated in Table 9.30.

Table 9.30: Respondents by Location of Hotels and Seeing Blue Films

Location of hotels	Seeing blue films			Total
	Theatre	TV in manager's room	Not seeing	
Tourist place	188 (56.9)	66 (20.0)	76 (23.0)	330 (100)
Non-Tourist place	66 (45.5)	8 (5.5)	71 (78.9)	145 (100)
Total	**254 (53.4)**	**74 (15.5)**	**147 (30.9)**	**475 (100)**

$\chi^2 = 37.7$ df = 2 $P < 0.05$.

The distribution of data given in Table 9.30 shows that out of 330 children from the hotels located in tourist places, a majority (56.9%) sees blue films in theatres. On the other hand, one-fifth (20%) do so in their manager's room. Out of 145 children from hotels situated in non-tourist places, 45.5 per cent see blue films in theatres, whereas only 5.5 per cent do so in their manager's room. Thus the proportion of children seeing blue films is higher in hotels located in tourist places than the proportion of their counterparts from hotels situated in non-tourist places. It is, thus, concluded that the location of the hotels has a bearing on the children's habit of seeing blue films.

It is important to mention here that the theatres which show blue films are many in tourist places. The children working in such hotels receive more *beta* and tips than their counterparts from the hotels located in non-tourist places. Therefore, the children from the former type of hotels can afford to pay for seeing such films.

It is important to mention that the children collect information often from their masters and other cooks on blue films currently being shown in theaters. Most of the time, they do not want to miss such films even if they have a heavy workload. Generally, three or more boys would go collectively to see the films. So on such occasions their sleeping time would be reduced to four or less than four hours. The fatigue due to workload and inadequate sleep result in dullness, headaches, and sometimes giddiness.

The habit of seeing blue films among the children spoils their childhood, pollutes their mind, and jeopardizes their soul and body. They spend so much time every month on blue films. When they do not have money, they don't hesitate to borrow money from other employees. Ultimately seeing the blue films tells on their health. This habit also leads to frequent homosexual as well as heterosexual activity affecting them with psychological problems. They are affected by Sexually Transmitted Diseases and AIDS.

MASTURBATION

In the hotels, most of the adult co-workers are away from their families for months together. They remain in the hotels without any recreation except going to films. Some of them read pornographic and yellow books and gossip with other workers. They also have the habit of masturbation. In course of time, they introduce this practice to the working children. For instance, the adult co-workers play with them teasing them and touching their genitalia while sleeping in the night. This manual stimulation of their sex organs drives them to masturbate in the toilet or bathroom.

The present study discloses that there is a significant relationship between the types of hotel and the habit of masturbation among the children as shown in Table 9.31.

Table 9.31: Respondents by Types of Hotel and the Habit of Masturbation Among the Children

Types of hotel	Habit of masturbation		Total
	Yes	No	
Type I (Boarding only)	36 (15.7)	193 (84.2)	229 (100)
Type II (Boarding and Lodging)	26 (21.4)	95 (78.5)	121 (100)
Type III (Lodging with Canteen)	13 (10.0)	112 (89.6)	125 (100)
Total	**75 (15.7)**	**400 (84.2)**	**475 (100)**

$\chi^2 = 6.0$ df = 2 $P < 0.05$.

The data given in Table 9.31 show that out of 475 children, 15.7 per cent masturbate. In Type I hotels, out of 229 working children, 15.7 per cent are prone to masturbation. Of 121 children in Type II hotels, over one-fifth (21.4%) have this habit and of 125 children in Type III hotels, 10 per cent are used to this. It is, thus, evident from the analysis that the proportion of children from Types I & II hotels is considerably higher than the proportion of their counterparts from Type III hotels with regard to the habit of masturbation. The reason is that the children from the former type of hotels often interact with several adult co-workers and other employees, but those from the latter type of hotels do not have chances to do so because these hotels that have lodging facilities with small canteens employ only a limited number of children as room boys and accommodate only a few adults as managers or supervisors.

It is understood from the data that more children from the age group of 12-14 years than those from the age group of 8-10 and 10-12 years masturbate. It is found that there is a significant relationship between the age of the children and their habit of masturbation. This is explained in Table 9.32.

Table 9.32: Respondents by Age and Habit of Masturbation

Age group (in years)	Habit of masturbation		Total
	Yes	No	
8-10	5 (3.9)	121 (96.0)	126 (100)
10-12	28 (15.5)	165 (85.4)	193 (100)
12-14	42 (26.9)	114 (73.0)	156 (100)
Total	**75 (15.7)**	**400 (84.2)**	**475 (100)**

$\chi^2 = 27.8$ df = 2 $P < 0.05$.

It is clear from Table 9.32 that out of 126 children in the age group of 8-10 years, only 3.9 per cent have the habit. Of 193 children in the age group of 10-12 years, 15.5 per cent have the habit and out of 156 children in the age group of 12-14 years, over one-fourth (26.9%) has this habit.

This shows that the proportion of those who have the habit of masturbation increases with increase in age. It has been proved by a statistical test that there is a concomitant variation between the ages of the children on the one hand and their habit of masturbating on the other hand because both the variables travel in the same direction.

In a similar way, their experience is an important factor influencing their habit of masturbation. This is indicated in Table 9.33.

Table 9.33: Respondents by Experience and Habit of Masturbation

Experience (in years)	Habit of masturbation		Total
	Yes	No	
Less than 2	15 (11.1)	120 (88.8)	135 (100)
2-4	60 (17.6)	280 (82.3)	340 (100)
Total	**75 (15.7)**	**400 (84.2)**	**475 (100)**

$\chi^2 = 2.9$ df = 1 $P > 0.05$.

The data given in Table 9.33 show that out of 135 children with less than two years of experience, 11.1 per cent have the habit of masturbation while of 340 children with 2-4 years of experience, 17.6 per cent have this habit. It is thus clear that an increase in the period of their experience results in an increase in the proportion of their getting into this habit. The reason for this concomitant variation is that the age and work experience of the children go together as the latter depends on the former. Nevertheless, this may not hold good for all the children who have this habit. It is reported that a limited number of children in the age of 12-14 years have less than two years of work experience because they joined the hotels after completing 12 years of age.

Like age and experience, the rural-urban background of the children has a bearing on their habit of masturbation as exhibited in Table 9.34.

Table 9.34: Respondents by Background and Habit of Masturbation

Background	Habit of masturbation		Total
	Yes	No	
Rural	35 (10.0)	327 (90.3)	362 (100)
Urban	40 (35.3)	73 (64.6)	113 (100)
Total	**75 (15.7)**	**400 (84.2)**	**475 (100)**

$\chi^2 = 37.9$ df = 1 $P < 0.05$.

The data in the above table clearly present the relationship between the rural-urban background of the children and their habit of masturbation. It is observed that the proportion of urban children is more than twice as much as the proportion of their rural counterparts in relation to their habit of masturbation. This may perhaps be explained in the following terms. The urban children are more exposed to such unhealthy practices than their rural counterparts are. The former type of children are subjected to several attractions. So they feel free to do whatever they want to do because of urban anonymity. On the other hand, the latter type of children carry their traditional moorings wherever they work. Nevertheless, they are subjected to certain changes due to external pressure or situational factors. But it seems that unlike urban children, many rural children have not gone to the extent of accepting several changes taking place in the life of those employed in hotels.

It is common to find that the children who change the hotels several times due to various reasons are more prone to those unhealthy practices than those who do not do so. It is also found that most of the former category of children worked in hotels in Chennai, Bangaluru, Thiruvananthapuram and Mumbai for a few years and afterwards came back to their native districts in search of employment in the hotels located within their districts. Many of them, after joining these hotels, found that they were not suitable physically and mentally to the work culture in the hotels. Therefore, they changed the hotels. Some of them might have been sent out of the hotels due to various reasons.

Normally they smoke, drink and have sexual contact with the sex workers. They are rather reluctant to follow the instructions of the hotel management employees and are careless in the work assigned to them. They are mainly responsible for introducing the innocent children to these unhealthy practices. That is why a majority of them have those habits which are harmful to their health. Table 9.35 shows that their proportion is significantly higher than the proportion of other children with respect to the habit of masturbation.

Table 9.35: Respondents by Changing Hotels and Habit of Masturbation

Frequency of changing the hotels	Habit of masturbation		Total
	Yes	No	
Twice	52 (15.7)	278 (84.2)	330 (100)
More than twice	17 (47.2)	19 (52.7)	36 (100)
Not changing	6 (5.5)	103 (94.4)	109 (100)
Total	**75 (15.7)**	**400 (84.2)**	**475 (100)**

$\chi^2 = 35.9$ df = 2 $P < 0.05$.

It is evident from Table 9.35 that the proportion of children who changed the hotels more than twice is thrice as much as the proportion of those who did so twice during their service with respect to the habit of masturbation. It is, therefore, concluded that the children who changed the hotels several times are prone to those habits as they have got exposed already to such habits while working in the hotels located in big cities. On the other hand, the children who never changed the hotels or changed only twice do not have such exposure and therefore a lower proportion of them have this habit.

The location of the hotels is also an important factor which has a bearing on the habit of masturbation among the children as shown in Table 9.36.

It is observed from the data that the proportion of the children from the hotels located at tourist places is more than twice as much as the proportion of those from the hotels situated at non-tourist places with regard to their habit of masturbation. This may be due to the reason that the chances of seeing blue films, reading pornographic books and practicing homosexual activities with the adult workers are more in tourist centres than in non-tourist places. These attractions stimulate them.

Table 9.36: Respondents by Location of Hotels and Habit of Masturbation

Location of hotels	Habit of masturbation		Total
	Yes	No	
Tourist place	65 (20.0)	265 (80.0)	330 (100)
Non-Tourist place	10 (6.8)	135 (93.1)	145 (100)
Total	**75 (15.7)**	**400 (84.2)**	**475 (100)**

$\chi^2 = 12$ df = 1 $P < 0.05$.

On the whole, it is found that the proportion of those who have the habit of masturbation increases with age and experience. This increase also depends on their urban background, frequency of changing the hotels and the location of the hotels.

CONTACT WITH SEX-WORKERS

The hotel is one of the recreational centres in urban areas. Hotel owners obtain permission from the Government to run a bar, swimming pool, theatre and club. But the Tamil Nadu Government has banned certain items meant for recreation. However, some hotels have them illegally. For instance, illegal sex with sex-workers is prohibited in hotels with lodging facility. But it is in operation illegally in many hotels. The room boys in these hotels are attracted towards this flesh trade. Often the hotel management directs them to canvass the customers to stay in the hotels to have sex with the sex-workers. They canvass the customers in front of the hotels, bus stands and railway stations. For this work, the children collect brokerage from the customers and also get tips from the management for each customer brought by them. They become close to the regular sex-workers as the latter depend on the former for certain things to a considerable extent. Taking advantage of this about 10 per cent of the children mostly in the age group of 12-14 years gain access to sexual activities with them. Sometimes, the sex-workers invite the boys to sexual activity.

It is observed that the children and the sex-workers maintain cordial relationship with each other as the two groups depend on each other for certain things. For instance, the sex-workers depend on the children because the former get customers mostly through the latter. In a similar way, the latter depend on the former for two reasons: they get tips from the sex-workers and they want to experience sexual pleasure with these women.

It is interesting to note that on certain occasions, sex workers prefer grown up and good-looking boys in the age group of 14-16 years for sexual activity because they are not satisfied with the elderly customers who are unable to entertain them according to their expectations. In such circumstances, a few old age customers derive pleasure by making the sex-workers have intercourse with the boys in front of them within the room itself. These are all favorable situations for the children for sexual activity.

It is relevant here to present a case study pertaining to a 14-year-old boy employed in a Type III hotel at Shenkottai. The boy describes his sexual intimacy with a 23-year-old sex-worker visiting the hotel regularly.

> I am assigned to canvass customers to stay in the hotel by referring to several facilities including the service of the sex-workers. I am able to bring at least two or three customers every day. This would indeed benefit the sex-workers economically. Therefore, they are very friendly and kind to me. Often I wish to be with a particular sex-worker who is very affectionate to me. Knowing my desire, one day, she entertained me sexually in the hotel room. Afterwards, she continues to do so at least once a week.
>
> At one point of time, I was affected by venereal disease. I approached a local doctor and had treatment for a week. Now I have stopped the practice because the doctor warned me strictly to avoid it, because the disease would result in death. However, I would like to have sex with her again. Since she knows my health problem, she does not want to entertain me as she did previously. Meanwhile, my hotel manger came to know my problem and as a result of this he scolded me in filthy language. Since he knows my father, he warned me not to repeat it; otherwise I would be sent out of the hotel.

It is found that about 15 per cent of the children have contact with sex-workers as brokers. A small proportion of them (about 10%) have sexual contact with these women. The children's contact with them varies with the types of hotel as shown in Table 9.37.

Table 9.37: Respondents by Types of Hotel and Contact with Sex-workers

Types of hotel	Contact with sex-workers			Total
	As brokers	Sexual contact	None of them	
Type I (Boarding only)	14 (6.1)	8 (3.4)	207 (90.3)	229 (100)
Type II (Boarding and lodging only)	26 (21.4)	18 (14.8)	77 (63.6)	121 (100)
Type III (Lodging with Canteen)	32 (25.6)	23 (18.4)	70 (56.0)	125 (100)
Total	**72 (15.1)**	**49 (10.3)**	**354 (74.5)**	**475 (100)**

$\chi^2 = 60.7$ df = 4 $P < 0.05$.

The owners of hotels located in tourist places and corporation limits allow the sex-workers to entertain the customers on their premises. Mostly child workers are used as brokers to run this business. They get tips from the owners, customers and sex-workers. The monetary benefit that the children get from this business turns them into regular brokers.

Out of 229 children in Type I hotels, only 6.1 per cent have contacts with sex-workers as brokers, and only 3.4 per cent have sexual contact with them. In Type II hotels, out of 121 children, over one-fifth (21.4%) have contacts with sex-workers, and 14.8 per cent have sexual contact with them. In Type III hotels, out of 125 children, over one-fourth (25.6%) have contact with sex-workers, and nearly 18.4 per cent have sexual contacts.

Mostly Types II and III hotels are located in tourist places, corporation limits and taluk headquarters. Normally well-to-do customers stay in these hotels and have sex with sex-workers. In some cases, the children are compelled to work as brokers besides working as room boys.

The supply of sex workers to the customers through brokers is common in Types II and III hotels. It is interesting to note that the hotel owners and managers are involved in this activity because they think that they would get more profit from their wine shops and bars through prostitution. For this, they use children as brokers. Thus innocent children fall a prey to unhealthy habits.

Especially in the tourist places, the children from Type II and Type III hotels are used as brokers by the management. The children approach the customers in front of the hotels or in the bus stand and try to get their preference with regard to the sex-workers. They also inform the customers of the cost per night and other details.

In Courtallam, one of the beautiful tourist places in Tirunelveli district, hotel owners invite sex-workers from Kerala and Karnataka besides those from Tamil Nadu. They provide them with good accommodation and food. As the children perform the role of brokers, they move with the sex-workers freely and crack sex jokes with them. As a result of this, sometimes the sex workers entertain the children with sex in the hotel rooms.

Newly married couples, lovers and call girls stay in Types II and III hotels in tourist places. The room boys see their sexual activities through keyholes. Sometimes, they drill holes in windows to watch such activities. This stimulates them to sex with those women. It is found that out of 49 children who have sex with them, 16.3 per cent have contracted venereal diseases. For this, they take allopathic treatment.

It is relevant to discuss a few case studies detailing the children's contacts with sex-workers. A 14-year old room boy in a hotel at Courtallam explains his experience.

> In the morning and in the evening, I supply tea and coffee to the customers staying in the hotel rooms. If the customers ask for liquor, cigarettes and eatables, I get them for them. I get Rs. 5 to 20 per room as tips. My manager is kind to me. He has earmarked two rooms on the first floor to accommodate the customers who wish to stay with sex-workers. My co-workers and myself see the bedroom scene clearly through the keyhole after 11.00 p.m. after putting off the lights in the veranda. In two other rooms, such scenes are viewed by us through a small gap between double doors. On certain occasions, we spend sleepless nights mainly to see this. Sometimes, my master and a few adult co-workers join us.

Pouring out their bitter hearts to the researcher

A statement given by a 14-year-old room boy in a Type II hotel is as follows:

> This hotel has bar facility. We get liquor from the bar and supply it to the customers in the evening after 7.00 p.m. Besides, the sex-workers are brought in to entertain the customers. We watch through a wide gap between the double doors. The customers do not put off the light while having sex with the sex-workers. Almost every night we see such activities.
>
> I get an average of Rs. 30 per day as tips from the owner, customers and sex-workers. We are paid a salary of Rs. 300 per month along with food. The owner does not pay the salary since my mother has already borrowed a sum of Rs. 5000. I am happy in this hotel. I smoke and drink with friends working with me.

It is relevant here to refer to a study on child labour by Walter Fernandes. He mentions that many children working in wayside *dhabas* are attacked physically and also abused into using vulgar words or forced to be pimps for the underworld or other gangsters.[6]

Prakash's study supports the present study. He says:

> Some young boys are employed in sleazy B and C grade hotels and lodging houses where, besides getting a hopelessly inadequate salary and leading a miserable life, they are also faced with a sense of insecurity.
>
> In these circumstances, they are exposed to sexual abuses, for in the hotels and lodging houses where they work, eat and sleep, they are exposed to sexuality in abundance. Call girls are regular visitors and in case of a quarrel, the patron or the call girl can often be seen running out of the room into the corridor semi-nude. Peeping through the keyhole and seeing a man of 50 or 60 copulating with a young call girl, the teen aged hotel boy identifies himself physically and mentally more with the young girl. The girl, in turn, also identifies with the hotel boy whom, more often than not, she regards as a substitute. The hotel boy may also be used by the patron to satisfy his sex urges if the call girl is not available. One case that came was of a boy whose mother used to ask him to keep a lookout for his father while she gave herself to someone else for the sake of a little extra money. Canteen boys who may be serving or carrying out orders for patrons in all male lodging houses are often subject to sexual abuse.[7]

Another study by Antony Cruz also supports the present study. He reports that a majority of the working children in hotels have been used as mediators or brokers for prostitution in the hotels. Later these children have sexual contact with prostitutes.[8] In course of time, they are affected by Sexually Transmitted Diseases. Later on, it may lead to AIDS. Several hundred children below the age of 15 die miserably because they are affected by Sexually Transmitted Diseases.

It is found that there is a relationship between the age of the working children and their sexual contact with sex-workers in the hotels. This is clearly represented in Table 9.38.

Table 9.38: Respondents by Age and Contact with Sex Workers

Age group (in years)	Contact with sex-workers			Total
	As brokers	Sexual contact	None of them	
8-10	5 (3.9)	– (–)	121 (96.0)	126 (100)
10-12	20 (10.3)	9 (4.6)	164 (84.9)	193 (100)
12-14	47 (30.12)	40 (25.6)	69 (44.2)	156 (100)
Total	**72 (15.1)**	**49 (10.3)**	**354 (74.5)**	**475 (100)**

The data in the above table show that out of 126 children in the age group of 8-10 years, only 3.9 per cent have contact with sex-workers as brokers. None of them in this age group has sexual contacts with the sex-workers. Out of 193 children in the age group of 10-12 years, about one-tenth (10.3%) have contacts with sex-workers as brokers, and 4.6 per cent have sexual contact with those women. Out of 156 working children in the age group of 12-14 years, nearly one-third (30.2%) have contacts with them as brokers, and about one-fourth (25.6%) have sexual contacts with them.

The data clearly show that the higher the age group of the children, the higher their proportion with regard to sexual contact with the sex-workers. The primary reason for this is that the owners and managers engage certain experienced children in the age group of 12-14 years as brokers. The second reason is that they get more *beta* and tips so that they will be able to spend money to meet their needs. The third reason is that the owners and managers would send out some insincere and inactive children who, after sometime, establish links with the sex-workers and help them as brokers in their flesh trade.

It is observed that there is no significant relationship between the experience of the children and their sexual contact with the sex workers in the hotels. This is exhibited in Table 9.39.

The data disclose that there is a slight variation in the contact of the children with sex-workers as brokers. When the working children complete one year of experience in the hotels, usually they are compelled by the owners and managers to act as brokers. Especially the experienced children get more tips and *beta* and therefore spend a sizeable portion of the money to meet some of their needs.

Table 9.39: Respondents by Experience and Contact with Sex-workers

Experience (in years)	Contact with sex-workers			Total
	As brokers	Sexual contact	None of them	
Less than 2	16 (11.8)	13 (10.0)	106 (78.5)	135 (100)
2-4	56 (16.4)	36 (10.5)	248 (72.9)	248 (100)
Total	**72 (15.1)**	**49 (10.3)**	**354 (74.5)**	**475 (100)**

$\chi^2 = 1.57$ df = 2 P > 0.05.

It is noted that there is a significant relationship between the background of the working children and their sexual contact with the sex-workers in the hotels. Table 9.40 shows this relationship.

Table 9.40: Respondents by Background and Contact with Sex-workers

Background	Contact with sex-workers			Total
	As brokers	Sexual contact	None of them	
Rural	48 (13.2)	21 (5.8)	293 (80.9)	362 (100)
Urban	24 (21.2)	28 (25.0)	61 (53.9)	113 (100)
Total	**72 (15.1)**	**49 (10.3)**	**354 (74.5)**	**475 (100)**

$\chi^2 = 35.8$ df = 2 P < 0.05.

The data show that out of 362 rural children, 13.27 per cent have contacts with sex workers as brokers, whereas only 5.8 per cent have sexual contacts with them. Out of 113 urban children, over one-fifth (21.2%) have contact with sex- workers as brokers, and one-fourth (25.0%) have sexual contact with them. The data clearly show that the proportion of children who have contacts with sex workers as workers and who have sexual contact with them from the urban area is higher than the proportion of such children from the rural areas. The former type of children may not hesitate to move with the sex workers, whereas the latter type may because of rural ideas of goodness.

The data shows that there is a significant relationship between the frequency of changing the hotels by the respondents and their sexual contact with sex-workers. This is clearly represented in Table 9.41.

Table 9.41: Respondents Changing of Hotels and Contact with Sex-workers

Frequency of changing the hotels	Contact with sex-workers			Total
	As brokers	Sexual contact	None of them	
Twice	47 (14.2)	27 (8.1)	256 (77.5)	330 (100)
More than twice	15 (41.6)	16 (44.4)	5 (13.8)	36 (100)
Not changing	10 (9.1)	6 (5.5)	93 (85.3)	106 (100)
Total	**72 (15.1)**	**49 (10.3)**	**354 (74.5)**	**475 (100)**

$\chi^2 = 84.21$ df = 4 $P < 0.05$.

The data disclose that out of 330 children who changed hotels twice, 14.2 per cent have sexual contacts with sex-workers. Out of 36 children who changed hotels more than twice, 41.6 per cent have contacts with sex-workers as brokers and 44.4 per cent have sexual contacts with them. Out of 106 children who did not change hotels, 9.1 per cent have contact with sex-workers, whereas only 5.5 per cent have sexual contact with them.

It is evident from the analysis that the proportion of children who changed the hotels twice as well as more than twice is significantly higher than those who did not with regard to their role as brokers and having sexual contact with the sex workers. Those who changed hotels have worked in hotels at Chennai, Bangaluru and Thiruvananthapuram. They are more exposed to the urban way of life than their rural counterparts.

It is observed that the location of the hotels is an important factor, playing a vital role in establishing sexual contact with sex-workers. This is clearly shown in Table 9.42.

Table 9.42: Respondents by Location of Hotels and Contact with Sex Workers

Location of hotels	Contact with sex-workers			Total
	As brokers	Sexual contact	None of them	
Tourist place	57 (17.2)	42 (12.7)	231 (70.0)	330 (100)
Non-Tourist place	15 (10.3)	7 (5.0)	123 (84.8)	145 (100)
Total	**72 (15.1)**	**49 (10.3)**	**354 (74.5)**	**475 (100)**

$\chi^2 = 11.88$ df = 2 $P < 0.05$.

It is understood from Table 9.42 that out of 330 children from the hotels located in tourist places, 17.2 per cent have contacts with sex workers as brokers. On the other hand, 12.7 per cent have sexual contact with them, whereas only five per cent of them from the hotels situated in non-tourist places do so.

Generally sex-workers have their business in the tourist places. A large number of customers and tourists visit these places for enjoyment. Hotel owners are inclined to earn more profit. In this situation, they compel the children to work as brokers. This would slowly lead the children to gain close access to the sex-workers. Ultimately the latter invite the former for sexual activity because the former depend on the latter to get some of their needs fulfilled. On the other hand, a few sex-workers prefer to have sexual contact with grown up and handsome children willingly on certain occasions besides their regular flesh trade with the customers.

It is evident from the discussion that the hotel owners assign the older children (12-14 years) to be brokers to invite the customers to the hotels. These experienced children, in course of time, tend to have sexual contact with the sex-workers.

Besides the socio-economic factors involved in the deal between the sex-workers on the one hand and the children on the other hand, it is relevant to analyse the relationship between the two groups based on the social exchange theory from Peter Blau's point of view. The application of Social Exchange Theory already discussed in Chapter 2 Review of Literature is supported by the quantitative as well as qualitative data. The exchange between the sex workers and the children is discussed in this chapter based on relevant tables.

In the hotels, the children who act as brokers bring an appreciable income to the sex workers benefiting them to a notable extent. The sex workers get money from the customers and in turn they satisfy them sexually. This exchange rests on a formal contract that specifies the exact quantities to be exchanged between them. On the other hand, the social exchange between the sex workers and the children is mostly based on unspecified personal obligations.

Moreover, this exchange is more personalized than economic exchange. Sex workers give the children tips at their will mainly to recognize their services. Nevertheless, it is a personal obligation on the part of the former to give the tips to the latter liberally or moderately. In addition to this, once in a while the sex-workers voluntarily entertain the children sexually. The children, highly motivated by this, make sincere efforts to bring the customers regularly for the benefit of the sex-workers. Thus, Blau's theory of social exchange holds good with respect to the deal between the sex-workers and the children.

It is rather heart-rending to note that the children below 15 years of age are getting spoiled because of their contact with sex-workers. Child workers in the other sectors have certain problems, which may not pose a challenge to their moral life. But child workers in hotels are vulnerable to several unhealthy practices including sexual contact with sex-workers. Thus, they easily become prey to such practices even at the age of 13 or 14 years.

It is interesting to note that of six categories of persons, two are predominant in introducing the children to those unhealthy practices, as compared to the other categories. This is presented in Table 9.43 and Fig. 9.1 & 9.2.

Table 9.43: Respondents by Unhealthy Practices and Types of Introducers

Sl. No.	Types of unhealthy practices	Types of person introducing children to the unhealthy practices								Total
		Managers and supervisors	Head Cooks and Asst. Cooks	Adult Co-workers	Peer Groups	Customers	Self/ others	Total children with unhealthy practices	Without these Habits	
1.	Smoking	24 (5.0)	70 (14.7)	121 (25.4)	88 (18.5)	11 (2.3)	36 (7.5)	350 (73.6)	125 (26.3)	475 (100)
2.	Using drugs and intoxicants	81 (17.0)	127 (26.7)	102 (21.4)	62 (13.0)	22 (4.6)	11 (2.3)	405 (85.2)	70 (14.7)	475 (100)
3.	Drinking	72 (15.1)	97 (20.4)	71 (15.0)	25 (5.2)	46 (10.0)	10 (2.1)	321 (67.5)	154 (32.4)	475 (100)
4.	Reading Sex Books	35 (7.3)	121 (25.4)	122 (25.6)	36 (7.5)	16 (3.3)	12 (2.5)	342 (72.0)	133 (28.0)	475 (100)
5	Seeing Blue Films	95 (20.0)	48 (10.1)	96 (20.2)	48 (10.1)	17 (3.5)	24 (5.0)	328 (69.0)	147 (30.9)	475 (100)
6.	Masturbation	5 (1.0)	7 (1.5)	24 (5.0)	24 (5.0)	5 (1.0)	10 (2.1)	75 (15.7)	400 (84.2)	475 (100)
7.	Sexual contact and brokering with sex workers	48 (10.1)	22 (5.0)	14 (2.9)	21 (5.0)	10 (2.1)	6 (1.2)	121 (25.4)	354 (74.5)	475 (100)

The cluster analysis for the above data was carried out by using the Average Linkage Method between Groups. The Agglomeration Schedule shows the following results:

The cluster combination between Managers/Supervisors (Cluster 1) and Head Cooks/ Asst.Cooks (Cluster 2) has a high Cluster Co-efficient of 25472.000. Then, the Cluster Combination between Manager/Supervisors (Cluster1) and Peer Groups (Cluster 4) has a Cluster Co-efficient of 12809.333. The Cluster Combination between Peer Groups (Cluster 4) and customers (Cluster 5) has a Cluster Co-efficient of 8458.000. The Cluster Combination of Head Cooks-Asst. Cooks (Cluster 2) and Adult co-workers (Cluster 3) provides the Cluster Co-efficient of 6560.000. The Cluster Combination between Customers (cluster-5) and Others from outside (Cluster 6) gives a Cluster Co-efficient of 2148.000. It is inferred from this that the unhealthy practices are mainly caused by the Cluster Combination between Managers/Supervisors and Head Cooks/Asst.Cooks. Next to this, the Cluster Combination between Managers/Supervisors and Peer Groups mainly contributes to the unhealthy practices among the children.

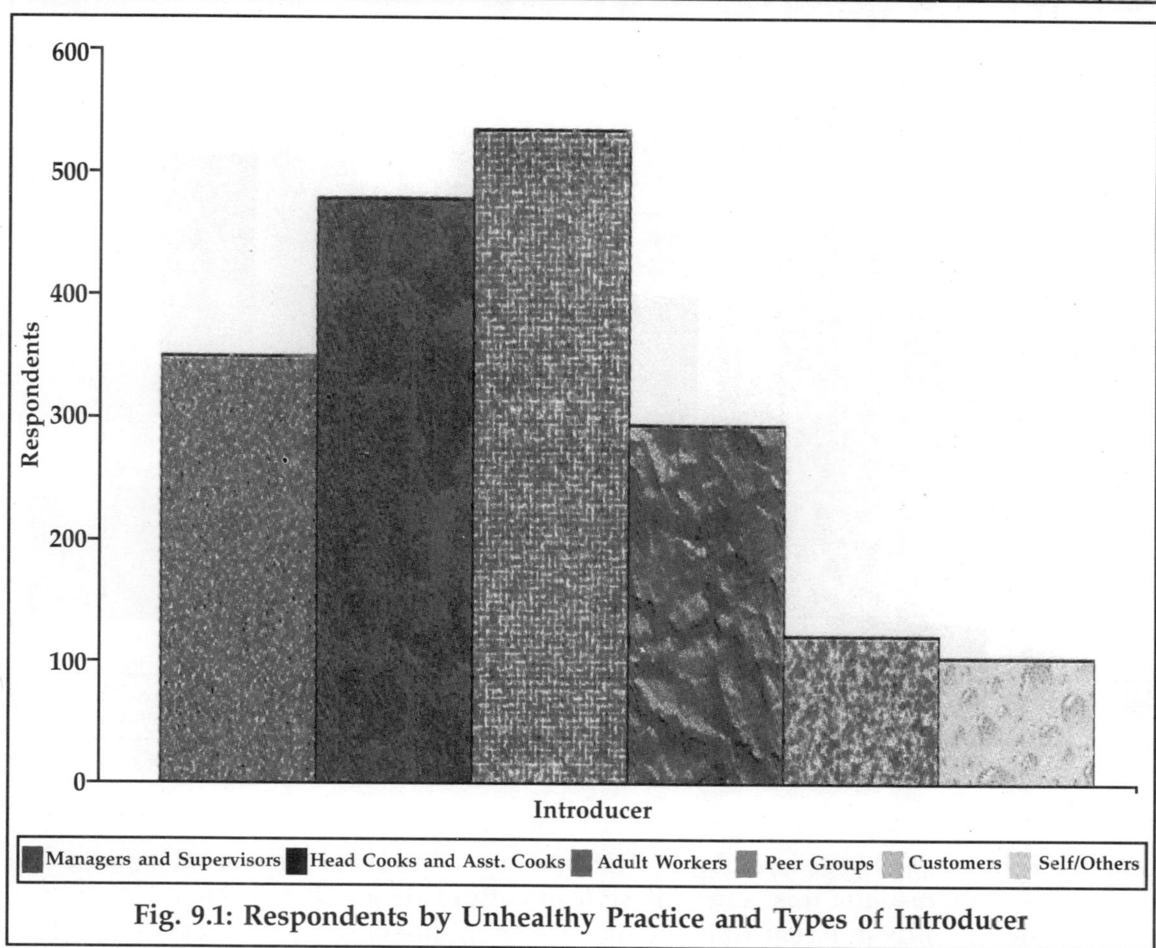

Fig. 9.1: Respondents by Unhealthy Practice and Types of Introducer

It is relevant here to consider some contrasting sub-cultural theories in order to explain delinquency among the hotel employees including children. The delinquent subculture as already discussed in Chapter 2 Review of Literature, gets reflected in the group of hotel employees.

The adult employees in hotels share similar values and lifestyle and follow similar practices, which violate the legal norms. They drink liquor, use intoxicating drugs, see blue films, read pornographic literature and indulge in masturbation and homosexual activities and also indulge in sexual intercourse with sex-workers. They hand down these practices to the children who come mostly from rural areas where there is very limited scope for such practices.

All the hotel employees except managers share a single common room to rest and sleep. They together while away the time gossiping and playing cards and sex-related games. It is found that they have absolutely no privacy. The activities of an employee are transparent to every one of his co-employees. This physical proximity and their

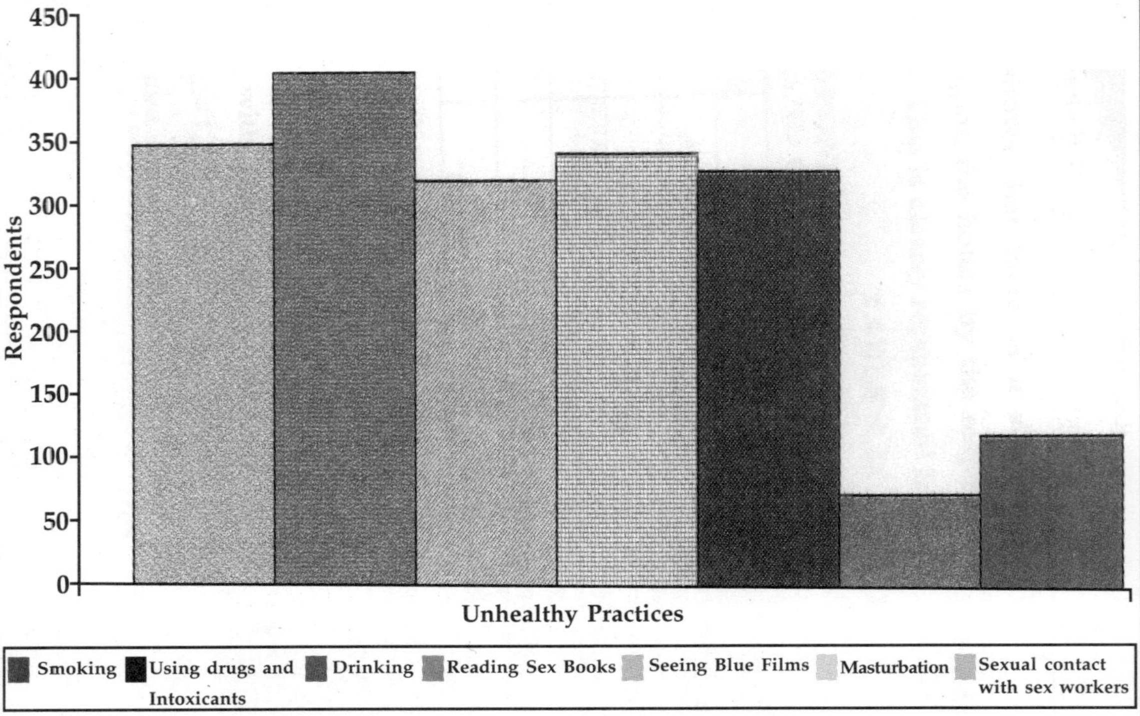

Fig. 9.2: Respondents by Types of Unhealthy Practice

common and accepted practices play a vital role in uniting them for mutual support and obligations. As a result of this, a new lifestyle or culture among them is bound to emerge, which is significantly different from the lifestyle or culture of the dominant culture. This culture of these working-class people may be called a subculture. Since it is represented by the employees whose activities are of criminal as well as non-criminal nature, it may also be called a delinquent subculture. It may be concluded that the employees as a working class in hotels form a delinquent subculture.

CONCEPT OF DELINQUENCY

"Delinquency" signifies deviant behaviour a behaviour pattern that violates institutional expectations, i.e., expectations that are shared and recognized as legitimate within a social system. The term has been preferred for use, with respect to children, while excluding the use of terms like "*crime*", "*criminal*" and "*offence*" from the purview. The object is to view the 'problem child' from a broader perspective of social behaviour that the child encounters with legal intervention but with a liberal, welfare-oriented approach.

There has been unanimity of opinion in the usage of the word "delinquency"

- It frees juveniles from the stigma of "crime", "criminal" and other negative and deterrent labels.
- It addresses a broader range of behavioral problems of children.
- It provides a common platform for social workers and functionaries involved in the administration of justice.
- Technically, juvenile (offending) behaviour is different from adult criminal acts.
- Delinquent behaviour has less individual responsibility compared to adult criminality.
- Overall, it embodies a correctional system, where penal sanctions have no validity.

Juveniles resort to delinquency often because of social factors. They are children for whom life is full of drudgery, abuse and exploitation. In most cases they are victims before they become perpetrators, and hence get entangled in a vicious cycle. They are forced to become deviants due to factors such as poverty and lack of a normal home life.[9]

It is evident from this that class is, in a way, linked to social values. It can lead to violation of the law. What distinguishes the offender from the non-offender is not social class itself, but a set of values that are associated with social class.

It is reported that out of 121children acting as brokers, 52 (10.9%) were arrested by the police at different times while raiding the lodges situated in tourist places including Tirunelveli Corporation limits. Therefore, the children involved in this crime are, in a way, criminals who have a set of rules for the pursuit of material gain by means of acting as brokers. Moreover, sometimes, they gain access to sex with the female sex-workers at the age of 13 or 14 years.

The children buy varieties of alcoholic beverages from nearby wine shops for the customers. As they do it frequently, they are tempted to taste the alcohol. The encouragement that they get from the customers to drink is also there. Consequently, they become regular drinkers over a period of time. While buying liquor mostly for the customers and sometimes for themselves especially on the birth days of Mahathma Gandhi, Lord Mahaveer and Periyar E.V. Ramasamy, a few of them were arrested under the Tamil Nadu Prohibition Act 1937, 4(1),(k) (as amended up to August 1999) because these leaders were crusaders against alcoholism. In a similar way, 15 out of 475 children have been arrested by the police while buying *ganja* mostly for their masters and adult co-workers and sometimes for themselves. The hotel owners have to face difficulties and take immediate action to get the arrested children released.

It is inferred from the analysis of data that most of the activities of the children observed during the fieldwork are of a criminal nature. Nevertheless, a few of their activities may be of a non-criminal nature. For instance, smoking may not be a criminal act, whereas stealing is undoubtedly a criminal act. It is reported that five of the sample children were caught red-handed by the owners and managers while attempting to steal money from the customers staying in the lodges. Similarly, six children were caught by the managers when they absconded with money given to them to clear electricity and grocery bills. Likewise, nine children were subjected to corporal punishment when they made an attempt to steal certain grocery items from the storerooms.

However, it is not right to conclude that all the sample children commit at least one or two criminal activities. Probably the new entrants from rural areas, at the age of eight or nine years, may not be aware of such criminal activities in the beginning. But after one or two years, they slowly pick up such activities. It is, therefore, concluded that a child worker at the age of 14 years has ample chances to become delinquent as he is exposed to several criminal activities during his experience of at least four to five years in hotel jobs. It is, thus, evident that the Differential Opportunity Structure theory of Cloward and Ohlin explains the criminal subculture of the hotel employees including the children.

It is relevant here to understand the criminal behaviour of children employed in hotels. For this, Sutherland's Social Learning Theory seems to be useful. He explains that when an individual is exposed to more criminal than non-criminal activities in his intimate personal group, his chances of violating the law increase to a great extent. In other words, if he is exposed to more law abiding situations than law-breaking ones, then his chances of being law abiding would increase to a great extent. Of the nine propositions of his theory, the first three are applied to understanding the criminal behaviour of children.

The first proposition is that criminal behaviour is learnt. Children acquire criminal behaviour by their frequent interaction with members of their subculture. Learning the criminal activities from these members enables them to commit crimes. Therefore primarily criminal behaviour is learnt but not inherited. In hotels, the children closely observe the behaviour and various activities of adult co-employees such as smoking, drinking, taking intoxicating drugs, reading pornographic literature, seeing blue films and the like. This would motivate them to commit such activities at one time or another.

The second proposition is that the criminal behaviour is learned in interaction with other persons in the process of communication. The children employed in hotels interact frequently with the adult employees for one reason or another. Even if they do not have adequate time to interact with them during their working hours, they have sufficient time to interact with them in the common single room allotted to them for rest and sleep. Especially, the sex-jokes and vulgar discussions on sex-related matters of the adult employees fascinate the children. Sometimes, they introduce pornographic literature to the children and tempt them to read. They also take them to theatres showing blue films at mid-night. They also motivate them to use *ganja,* and to drink. Moreover, they may approach, persuade or force them for homosexual activity. Thus, the behaviour of adult employees spoil the children and sometimes turn them into delinquents.

The third proposition is that the principal part of learning of criminal behaviour occurs within intimate personal groups. This is applicable to the children working in hotels who learn criminal behaviour from among their intimate personal group of co-employees. It is important to mention that the children employed in hotels associate with the intimate personal group of all employees except managers. However, the children from a peer group inadvertently share joys and sorrows with every one of them. Several times, such interactions relieve them from personal and family problems. It is also important to note that there is no disparity among the children in terms of their age and experience. The children in the age group of 8-10 years have close association with their counterparts from the age group of 12-14 years. They organize themselves into peer groups. Nevertheless, all the children and their co-employees together form an intimate personal group. The children learn criminal activities from the adult employees and turn to be delinquents over a period of time. Subsequently they from a part of delinquent subculture and draw new children joining them into this sort of culture in course of time.

REFERENCES

1. N. Meenakshi, S.V. Mehta, Prabhu and H.N. Mistry, *Types of Physical Health Problems in Working Children,* in Child Labour and Health Problems and Prospects, ed. Usha S. Naidu, Kamini R. Kapadia, (Mumbai: Tata Institute of Social Science, 1985) p. 143.

2. Walter Fernandes, "Child Labour and the Process of Exploitation", *The Indian Journal of Social Work*, (April 1992): p. 186.

3. Chandragupt S. Sanon, *Working Children: A Sociological Analysis*, (New Delhi: APH Publishing Corporation, 1998) pp. 144-145.

4. *Ibid.*

5. Prakash Kothari, Sexual Exploitation of Working Children, in *Child Labour and Health*, ed. Usha S, Naidu, Kamini R. Kapadia, (Bombay: Tata Institute of Social Sciences, 1985) p. 143.

6. Walter Fernandes, *Child Labour and the Processes of Exploitation*, The Indian Journal of Social Work, (April 1992): 186.

7. Prakash Kothari, ed. Usha S. Naidu, Kamini R. Kapadia, *op.cit.*, p. 91.

8. Antony Cruz, "Veethikku Vanthu Velichathai Tholaitharkal", *Dinamalkar* (Special Issue May 27, 2000), p. 16.

9. *Convention on the Rights of Child*, India, First Periodic Report 2001, (New Delhi: Department of Women and Child Development, Ministry of Human Development, 2001), p. 341.

CHAPTER 10

Conclusion and Suggestions

Child labour is neither entirely a new phenomenon nor unique to India. Over the decades India has been increasingly facing the problem of child labour. Every third labourer in India is a child. In fact, since ancient times, it has existed in all organized and unorganized sectors in India with varying degrees and magnitude. Children continue to constitute an important source of cheap labour supply. They are either required to help their parents in domestic work, grazing cattle and farming or to earn for their parents in the labour market.

It is reported that about three-fourths of the children are employed on low wages. Several thousands of children are put to work from dawn to dusk. They are deprived of their rights to study and play; they are deprived of their right to health - to put it in a nutshell the present of childhood is snatched off and the future of their manhood is debilitated, and they become martyrs to their families mostly, and also victims to their own weaknesses. Sending the children to work and putting them to domestic work is a violation of child rights.

Child labour has assumed monstrous proportions in India and other developing countries since the economic needs of these countries force the children to work. It is estimated by the International Labour Organization that a third of Asia's 38 million working children belong to India. It is reported that in India the state of Tamil Nadu accounts for a large proportion of children employed in hotels, in match work and firework industries and in *beedi* and hosiery industries.

All over India including Tamil Nadu a considerable proportion of child labour is seen in all types of hotels. The parents and children mostly prefer hotel jobs, because the basic needs like food, shelter and dress are provided by the owners besides the wage. In addition to this is the possibility for the parents to get an advance of money by pledging their children.

CONCLUSIONS

This study deals with child labour (up to the age of 14 years) working and staying in hotels located in some of the urban centres, in Tirunelveli District of Tamil Nadu.

For the study, a sample of 475 children who are working and staying in hotels was drawn from 95 big hotels situated in nine taluk headquarters of Tirunelveli District. On the basis of a simple random sampling, a sample of not less than five (more or less 50 per cent) child workers was drawn from each sample hotel by the Tippet's Table. The data were collected from the child workers, their parents, adult co-workers and hotel employers and employees, by administering a carefully constructed interview schedule. In addition to this, observation and case study methods were used to collect data.

The study discloses that most of the children come to the hotel jobs around the age of eight. In Tirunelveli district, the number of hotels falling under the classification of Type I (boarding only) and Type III (lodging with canteen) is larger than number of Type II hotels (boarding and lodging). The study also shows that a majority of the children in the age group of 8-10 years (56 per cent) join Type III hotels (lodging with canteen). After gaining some experience for an year or two, they shift to Type I hotels. Owing to better prospects like wage, security and food they normally prefer Type II hotels (boarding and lodging). Therefore, a majority of the children in the age group of 12-14 years (62.9%) are found in Type II hotels (boarding and lodging) than in the other types.

The study also shows that a low majority of the children (69.4%) are employed in hotels located in tourist places. A considerable proportion of them (48.6%) work in hotels situated within the Tirunelveli Corporation limits. This is mainly due to the reason that these hotels provide more facilities, salary and tips than the hotels located in non-tourist places outside the corporation limits. Moreover, the children from the tourist centres secure hotel jobs relatively more easily.

It is found that a majority of the children (54%) have studied up to IIIrd Standard (semi-literates) and the rest (46%) up to Vth Standard (literates). The economic status of their families, due to their size and due to unemployment and or underemployment, does not allow them to be keen on education for these children. In Type III hotels (lodging with canteen), the proportion of semi-literates is higher than in type I (boarding only) and type II (board and lodging) hotels, because Type II hotels prefer children with at least education up to the primary level to facilitate easy communication with the customers.

The study shows that a great majority of the children (76%) are from rural areas. The main causes for their migration are poverty and non-availability of earning sources in their native places. Most of the rural parents prefer hotel jobs for their children for obvious reasons like the availability of accommodation facility, security and food. They send their children to towns and cities to secure jobs in hotels.

The study shows that a great majority of the children (89%) employed in all three types of hotels are Hindus. Very low proportions of Muslim and Christian children are employed in them. The Hindus form the majority among the population of the district. In the beginning, most of the Hindu children were engaged in agricultural operations. The failure of the monsoon coupled with a necessity of supplementing their family income forced them to work in hotels. Only a limited number of Christian children are found in hotels owing greatly to the efforts taken by the Christian Missionaries to educate the children by establishing a number of schools in Tirunelveli District. Only a limited number of Muslim children are found in hotels because a great majority of them are engaged in *beedi*-making with their parents in their homes.

Nearly two-thirds of the children who approach hotel owners for jobs come from the Most Backward Castes and Backward Castes. The other third are from the Scheduled Castes. A negligible proportion (4%) belong to the Forward Castes. In Tirunelveli District, the parents from the Most Backward and Backward Castes do not mind their children doing menial jobs in hotels like cleaning the dining tables, washing the plates, tumblers, spoons and sweeping. But the parents from high castes do not want their children to do such jobs.

The study shows that nearly three-fourths of the children earn Rs. 500-1,000 per month. Their average monthly income works out to Rs. 685. This is a substantial contribution to their family income. The average monthly income of their families is Rs.1,686 which includes the income of the children. The contribution of the children is 40 per cent. This clearly shows that the livelihood of the families partly depends on the earnings of the children.

It is found that nearly three-fourths of the children have shifted their jobs twice from one hotel to another hotel. The reason is that the hotels are not so lucrative to the children in all seasons. Besides they have to reckon with the problems caused by their masters, owners and adult co-workers. After some time, they want to switch over to other hotels. The children's tendency of shifting to other hotels is facilitated by the employment potential in the industry.

A great majority of children come from medium and large size families for hotel jobs. Large families supply more child workers than small families. The parents of large families expect their children to support them economically. According to them, more children in the families mean more hands to fetch an income.

An overwhelming majority of the children who are employed in Type I (boarding only) and Type III (lodging with canteen) hotels like their hotel job. This is mainly because Type I and Type III hotels provide them with food, shelter and security. Two-thirds of the children working in Type II hotels (board and lodging) like the job as against one-third who dislike them. This type of hotel also provides the children with similar facilities, but a considerable proportion of the children do not like the job because in these hotels the workload and working hours are relatively higher.

The children's age, experience and rural-urban background have a bearing on their liking and disliking the hotel job. The proportion of children who like their job is much lower among the high age group which has more experience. The reason is that normally the beginners in the age group of 8-10 years like the job, but after serving two years, they feel that it is rather heavy and tough. When they gain experience for more than a couple of years, they experience the same feeling. However, a majority of rural children like hotel jobs for the simple reason that they get food three times a day, shelter and wages.

The study discloses that in the hotels most of the children work for 14 hours a day. Especially, in Type I (boarding only) and Type II (board and lodging) hotels, more or less half the children work for 14 hours a day. Similarly, in hotels situated in tourist places, about half the children are forced to work 14 hours a day. These types of hotels are busy through the day. As the employers want to cater to the needs of the customers to the maximum possible extent, they extract more work from the children by assigning them various types of work for 12-14 hours a day.

In Type I (boarding only) and Type II (board and lodging) hotels, the owners force the children to shoulder a heavy workload. In Type I hotels, two-thirds of the child workers do more than three types of work:

(i) carrying water;

(ii) bringing in firewood;

(iii) cleaning and washing the floor and tables;

(iv) attending room service; and

(v) supplying tea or coffee to nearby shopping centres.

In Type II hotels, three-fourths do more than three types of work, When the children join hotel jobs, the owners, managers and supervisors assign them one type of work, but after a week or a month, they start assigning more work continuously. Since the employers extract more work from the children for hours together, many children run away. However, in the first instance, the children work for not less than two years in hotels.

The study shows that the long duration of work and the heavy workload vary with the children's age, experience, rural-urban background, sources of recruitment and the location of the hotels. It is observed that a majority of rural children from the high age group have more experience, and are recruited mostly through brokers and are employed mostly in hotels located in tourist places and that they shoulder a heavy workload and work for long duration. This is mainly due to the fact that they are given more than three types of work. This tendency of giving heavy workload is perhaps due to the reason that they are above 12 years of age and have more years of experience (2-4) and hence are able to do it. Those who are recruited through brokers also have a similar experience because the employees feel that they are in no way responsible for their recruitment. Therefore, they are not so liberal to these children as they are to those who are recruited through them. Since the hotels located in tourist places are generally crowded most of the time, the employers give them heavy workload.

It is found that in hotels, the owners, managers, supervisors, masters and adult co-workers exploit the working children by getting their personal work and domestic work done by them. The personal work includes fetching cosmetics, *pan-parag*, liquor, cigarettes and the like. Especially the owners send the children to attend to work related to their domestic affairs such as purchasing provisions from ration shops, bringing gas cylinders, buying vegetables and grocery items, carrying drinking water from outside and carrying clothes to laundry shops and bringing pressed dresses. An overwhelming majority of the children attend to the domestic work of their owners and a majority of them attend to the personal work also of their managers, supervisors and masters. Over a third of them attend to the personal work of their adult co-workers. Thus, the employers and employees exploit the working children. This is absolutely extra work for the children who are expected do it without any return either in terms of money or in kind.

The extra work given to children such as attending to the personal work of employees and the domestic work of employers is influenced by the age and experience of the children and also the sources of their recruitment. It is observed that a greater number of younger children with less than two years of experience and recruited mostly through brokers are compelled to attend to the personal work of the other employees and owners. But the number is less in the case of older children with more than two years of experience and recruited directly by the employees themselves. The children within the age of ten years and with less than two years of experience are beginners. They are very obedient to the employees, especially the managers, supervisors, masters and servers, and willingly attend to the personal work of these employees. Moreover, nearly half the children secured the hotel jobs only with their help. Hence it is, in a way, obligatory on their part to attend to the personal work of those employees. They attend to the domestic work of their owners out of fear; otherwise they might lose their job.

The study discloses that the hotel management makes them work for several hours in order to get more profit but pays them very low wages. Especially the children from the hotels located in tourist places work more and get less. A majority of the children earn Rs. 600-900 per month, which is just half the earning of an adult worker. Thus children are subjected to economic exploitation.

However, the income earned by the children is significantly related to the duration of their working hours and the location of their hotels. The proportion of children in hotels in tourist places working for a longer duration is higher than the proportion of those in hotels in non-tourist places. Therefore, their income is relatively higher than that of their counterparts from the non-tourist places.

The children are subjected to punishment by their owners, managers, supervisors, masters and adult co-workers. If they do not perform their work as expected, they are scolded or punished corporally. A great majority of them are punished by the owners. A majority of them are punished by managers, supervisors and masters and over one-third of them are punished by adult co-workers. Punishment includes scolding with brutal and filthy words, beating with firewood and bowls. They resort to this type of punishment in order to extract more work from them.

The punishment meted out to children depends on their age, experience, rural-urban background and location of the hotels. Older and more experienced children are subjected to less punishment. Beginners in the hotel job are mostly unskilled workers and hence they are subjected to more punishment.

The practice of pledging the children to hotel owners is a serious problem. The parents get an advance amount of Rs. 2,500-5,000 while pledging their children for a period of two years. About one-third of the children are pledged to the hotel owners. It is reported that there is no hesitation on the part of the parents to pledge their sons. This is an easy way for some parents to get money in thousands at any time of crisis. Owners do not allow the pledged children to leave the job. This also checks the tendency for asking for any increase in wages. It is a violation of child rights but the parents are not punished by the law. It is understood that both the parents and the employers are equally responsible for the pledging system in the hotels.

It is found that 11 per cent of the children were subjected to sexual exploitation. The other employees try to persuade the children to oblige them in homosexual activities and often coerce them into it. Over two-thirds of those children approached in this way yielded to their masters, supervisors and co-workers. It is heart-rending to note that innocent children are induced to homosexual activities by employees and adult co-workers. This is mainly because a majority of those employees are away from their families and some of them are bachelors. In such a situation, they find homosex a convenient alternative for sexual gratification. On the other hand, the children are left with only recreations like seeing blue films, reading pornographic literature, playing cards, gossiping, loafing and playing sex-related games. These activities tempt them sexually, but do not offer them guidance to live decently. Gradually this results in kindling their sexual urge. Consequently, some of them yield to the persuasion or compulsion of their employees. Moreover, they are respectful and obedient to their fellow employees, especially the masters. Close to a majority of the children approached to engage in homosex were approached by their masters. This unhealthy practice spoils not only the health of the children but also their character in the years to come.

The sexual exploitation of the children differs with respect to their age, rural-urban background, sources of recruitment and the location of hotels. The proportion of rural children from the low age group, from hotels located in tourist places and recruited through brokers, is significantly higher with regard to homosexual activity than the proportion of their urban counterparts from high age group, from hotels located in non-tourist places and recruited through hotel employees.

Normally the younger children from rural areas introduced by brokers do not know anything about this sort of unhealthy practice and therefore, they are more vulnerable to such exploitation by the employees. On the contrary, the older children from urban areas introduced mostly by hotel employees have more than two years' experience in urban life. They know something about such practices. They are less afraid of the employees and they do not yield easily.

The study shows that the children are poor in self-hygiene. A majority of them do not brush their teeth regularly. It is found that a high proportion of children from Type II hotels (board and lodging) brush their teeth regularly as compared with their counterparts from Type I (boarding only) and Type III hotels (lodging with canteen). These hotel managements do not give importance to the welfare and neatness of the children because their main aim is to extract more work from them. But in Type II hotels, customers from affluent families often visit the hotels if they are clean and neat. Therefore, the hotel management takes special care to maintain the standard in boarding and lodging, which in turn leads to compulsory hygienic practices to be followed by the children.

It is found that the proportion of children from Type II hotels is higher than the counterparts from Type I and Type III hotels. Type II hotels are located in tourist places and corporation areas because there is more scope to get more profit in such places than in non-tourist and out-of-corporation areas. Employees are here provided with facilities like bathroom, toilet and uniform. The hotel owners take concerted efforts to attract the customers in order to increase their revenue.

A majority of the children state that they get inadequate food. It is reported that the food prepared thrice a day for the children, suppliers and masters is poor in quality because the hotel management supplies cheap rice, grocery items and vegetables. Most of the time the head cooks, assistant cooks and adult co-workers appropriate a large quantity of food for themselves after preparation. Consequently, sometimes the children do not get sufficient food. More than half the children report that they do not take food in time due to work pressure. Especially, the children from Types I (boarding only) and II (boarding and lodging) hotels located in corporation limits and tourist spots have to attend to the assigned work without delay, because there is an unending flow of customers from morning to late evening. In these hotels, the workload is rather heavy, whereas it is less in Type III hotels (lodging with canteen). The children who are not allowed to take food on time contract health problems such as acidity, ulcer, etc.

A majority of the children report that they do not sleep comfortably during night. The hotels open at 6.00 a.m. and close after 10.00 p.m. In accordance with this timing, the employees are expected to get ready in time and work actively till the closing time. That is why they sleep only for 4-5 hours. In most of the hotels there is only one rest room allotted for the workers. In moderately big hotels, at least 25 workers occupy a fairly big room. All cf them put their luggage in that room and sleep there within the available space. Those who sleep in storeroom or kitchen do not sleep comfortably, because the cooks normally start preparing the tiffin items from 3.30 a.m. As a result of this, they are not able to work actively during the daytime. Due to heavy workload and long duration of work and inadequate sleep, they develop body pain, headache, giddiness and other such problems. This is obviously an act of negligence on the part of the employers.

More than half the children report that they have diseases. They suffer from problems like amebiasis, scabies, fungus, skin diseases, body and joint pain. More of the children in Type I (boarding) and Type II (board and lodging) hotels have such diseases as compared to their counterparts from Type III hotels (lodging with canteen). The reason is that the children have heavy workload for hours together. Most of the time they are busy with cleaning and washing vessels with a chemical powder. This results in scabies, fungus and other skin diseases. In addition to this, they take inadequate food and do not have comfortable sleep. All affect their growth. The prevalence of nutritional anemia reduces their weight.

The study indicates that the diseases among the children are influenced by their age, experience, rural-urban background and location of hotels. It is observed that diseases like amebiasis, scabies, skin diseases, fungal infections and body and joint pain affect more rural children in the high age group with more than 2-4 years of experience than their urban counterparts from the low age group with less than two years of experience. Generally, hotel owners, managers, supervisors and masters prefer rural children for cleaning the vessels and dumping the wastes in the backyard because they are active and sincere in their work. Hence, their hands and legs are wet during the working hours. In addition to this, the owners and other employees make use of their services for their personal and domestic work. Consequently, they have to work harder and longer. That is perhaps why more rural children than their urban counterparts suffer from diseases. Similarly a greater proportion of children in the tourist place hotels than those in the non-tourist place hotels are affected by diseases. This is perhaps because the children in the former hotels have to shoulder a heavier workload and work for longer duration.

A great majority of the children take treatment in private hospitals. The owners send the sick children immediately to these hospitals to get them treated, so that they would resume work as early as possible. The main concern of the owners is that the work should not be affected due to the prolonged illness of the children. Some children prefer indigenous medicines, which are often provided by their masters and assistant cooks.

The study discloses that 40 per cent of the children smoke regularly, and 33 per cent of them smoke occasionally. The proportion of smokers is high in Type I (boarding only) and Type II (board and lodging) hotels as compared to their counterparts in Type III hotels (lodging with canteen). In these hotels, the managers, supervisors, cooks, assistant cooks and adult co-workers smoke in the kitchen and in the rest room. The working children start imitating them as they happen to be with them most of the time.

Owners and employees send the children to fetch *beedis* and cigarettes from nearby shops. The adult co-workers (servers) play a vital role in introducing the smoking habit to the children. This affects the children economically in the sense that they spend at least Rs. 2.50-5.00 per day on this. It also affects their health in the long run causing cough, lung cancer, heart disease, loss of sense of taste and blindness coupled with nutritional anemia.

The smoking habit of the children differs with respect to their age, experience, rural-urban background, tendency of changing the hotels, and location of hotels in which they are employed. The proportion of urban children who are older, experienced, employed in tourist place hotels and have changed to at least two hotels is high with respect to smoking than of their rural counterparts who are younger, less experienced, employed in non-tourist place hotels and who have not changed the hotels.

The study shows that a majority of the children drink liquor. Over a fourth of them drink once a month and over a third of them, twice a month. The proportion of those who drink twice a month is higher in Type II (board and lodging) and Type III (Lodging with canteen) hotels than of their counterparts from Type I hotels (boarding only). In the former types of hotels, about three-fourths of the employees (adult co-workers, masters and supervisors) consume liquor often. Especially, those working in kitchens drink regularly in order to get rid of fatigue. They make use of the children to buy liquor from nearby wine shops. Sometimes they offer the children a small quantity of liquor to drink. Another reason is that many of the hotel owners have a wine shop licence and run the shops on their hotel premises or near their hotels. The room boys buy liquor for the customers whenever they need it. For this they get more tips from the customers. Moreover, the children get free leftover liquor, especially in parties or social gathering in Type II and Type III hotels. Those who had worked already in wine shops turned out to be regular drinkers.

The drinking habits of the children vary with their age, experience, rural-urban background, tendency of changing hotels and the location of the hotels. A higher proportion of urban children, of older children, of the more experienced, or those employed in tourist-place hotels or who have changed at least two hotels drink alcohol, compared with their rural counterparts, or those who are younger, or less experienced, or employed in non-tourist area hotels or have not changed hotels.

The study shows that about one-third of the children have the habit of smoking *ganja*, and half the children have the habit of taking *pan parag* and *beeda*. The head cooks and their assistants take such items that cause mild intoxication. The habit of taking tobacco is common among them. Whenever they are in need of such items, they send the children to buy them from nearby shops. Making use of such chances the children taste those items out of curiosity and, in course of time, they get used to them. If they are not able to get them, they steal them from the bags of other employees. The habits of smoking *ganja*, chewing *pan-parag* and tobacco affect them both mentally and physically. This habit can also result in mouth and lung cancer and mental disorder.

The children's habit of taking intoxicating items differs with respect to their age, experience, rural-urban background, and tendency of shifting hotels and location of hotels. A higher proportion of urban children who are older, more experienced, employed in tourist place hotels or have changed at least two hotels, take intoxicating items than their rural counterparts who are younger, less experienced, employed in non-tourist-place hotels or have not shifted the hotels.

The significant relationship between the act of smoking, drinking and taking intoxicating items by the children on the one hand and their age, experience, rural-urban background, tendency for changing hotels and location of hotels on the other hand, may be explained as follows. The older and more experienced children get more bata and tips than the younger and less experienced children. Therefore, the former spend more money on smoking, drinking and intoxicating items. Especially the urban children smoke, drink and take intoxicating items regularly because of the anonymity of urban life, whereas the rural children are reluctant to do so as they are afraid of their parents and the employers and those who introduced them to the hotels. In a similar way, the children who changed the hotels more than twice initially worked in hotels in big cities where they contracted those habits. So they turn out to be regular smokers, drinkers and drug addicts at the age of 12 or 13 years. Likewise, the children working in tourist place hotels are widely exposed to varieties of customers from across India as well as the world. Their interaction with them and other employees in the hotels encouraged those habits in them within a year of joining such hotels.

It is found that nearly three-fourths of the children habitually read pornographic books. The proportion of children who read such books is high in Type I (boarding only) and Type II (board and lodging) hotels, because there are more employees in such hotels who supply those books to them. As a matter of fact, the children have no chance for recreation except reading mostly pornographic literature and playing cards. The children have easy access to such books. They borrow them from adult co-workers who in turn buy them from the shops. This would pollute their mind and induce them to homosexual activities.

The habit of reading pornographic books varies by their age, experience, rural-urban background, tendency of changing hotels, and location of hotels. A higher proportion of urban children, those who are elder, more experience, employed in tourist place hotels and have changed at least two hotels, read pornographic books than their rural counterparts, those who are younger, less experienced, employed in non-tourist place hotels or have not changed hotels.

This may be explained by the older and more experienced children having no fear towards their senior employees. They have close access to the adult co-workers who supply such books freely, whereas the younger and less experienced children are afraid of being caught reading those books. Since the urban children are very much exposed to urban culture, they are in search of those books within the hotels and are also prepared to buy them from shops. Similarly, those who shifted hotels more than twice developed this habit while working in city hotels as they had easy access to such books. Likewise those working in tourist place hotels got used to this as they regularly interacted with various customers from different cultural backgrounds.

The study discloses that a majority of the children (55%) see blue films in theatres and a small minority also watch television programmes in their manager's room. The reason is that most of the time the children join adult co-workers as they need their support to go to theatres. When the children unexpectedly see this sort of film for the first time, they are embarrassed. Later they develop an eagerness to see such films, especially with their peer group. Sometimes they get chances to see those films on television in their manager's room. Their habit of seeing blue films spoils their childhood, pollutes their mind and jeopardizes their soul and body. This habit would also lead to frequent homosexual as well as heterosexual activities affecting their healthy activities. They are affected by the Sexually Transmitted Diseases (STD) and AIDS. The adult co-workers and other senior employees are partly responsible for taking the children in a clandestine way to theatres showing blue films.

The study shows that the children's seeing blue films depends on their age, experience, rural-urban background, tendency of changing hotels and location of the hotels. A higher proportion of urban children – those who are older, more experienced, employed in tourist centers and have changed at least two hotels – see blue films than their rural counterparts – those who are younger, less experienced, employed in non-tourist area hotels or have not changed hotels.

The variation in the proportion of children seeing blue films regularly may reflect the fact that more experienced children have worked in various hotels and established cordial relationships with different adult co-workers. Further the urban children have more exposure to several unhealthy practices including seeing blue films compared with their rural counterparts. As a matter of fact, urban culture accommodates such practices that would attract young people, especially teenage boys and girls. Likewise, the children who changed the hotels more than twice had this sort of experience in cities. Similarly, those working in hotels in tourist centres have similar experience because of their regular interaction with heterogeneous customers.

The study shows that 16 per cent of the children have the habit of masturbation. As has already been stated, their world admits very few entertainments. During rest time and night they read pornographic and yellow books, play cards and gossip with other workers. Through co-workers and such books they learn about masturbation. For instance, when the adult co-workers play with them, and jovially touch their genitalia, they are stimulated to masturbate.

It is evident from the study that the habit of masturbation differs with respect to their age, experience, rural-urban background, tendency of changing hotels and location of hotels. A higher proportion of urban children who are older, more experienced, employed in tourist place hotels and have changed at least two hotels, masturbate than their rural counterparts, those who are younger, less experienced, employed in non-tourist area hotels or have not changed the hotels.

The older and more experienced children have this habit because of their acquaintance with this over a period of more than two years. Similarly, in this respect, the urban children have an advantage over their rural counterparts mostly due to the prevalence of several unhealthy practices in urban areas and the anonymity of urban living. Likewise, those who change the hotels and work in tourist place hotels might have developed this culture because of their greater exposure to a complex cultural setting.

The study discloses that one-fourth of the children have business contact with sex workers in hotels. Of them, 10 per cent have sexual contact with them. The proportion of children who have sexual contact with them is high in Type II (board and lodging) and Type III (lodging with canteen) hotels as compared to those in Type I hotels (boarding only). In the first two types of hotels where lodging facility is available, the managements invite sex-workers to entertain the customers in order to make more profit. The owners mostly use the child workers as brokers to run this business mainly to avoid arousing suspicion among the police and outsiders. The boys get tips from the owners, customers and sex workers for extending their co-operation and service. The monetary benefit that the children get from this business encourages them to be regular brokers. This slowly leads them to close access to the sex workers. They fall to the extent of sexual contact with those sex-workers even at the age of 13 or 14 years.

The extent of this practice among the child workers varies according to their age, experience, rural-urban background, tendency of changing hotels and location of hotels. The proportion of children with this habit increases with the increase in their age and experience, because they have a chance to have such experience over a period of two or three years. In this regard, the proportion of urban children is higher than the proportion of their rural counterparts. This is mainly due to the exposure of the former to urban culture for several years. The proportion of the children with the habit who changed the hotels more than twice during their service is higher than those who did not do so. Those employed in hotels located in tourist places are more prone to this practice than those working in hotels at non-tourist places. This may be because the children from these backgrounds are exposed to the organized trade of sex workers.

Besides the socio-economic exchange between the sex workers and customers, there is a social exchange between the former and the children. The children who act as brokers bring an appreciable income to the sex workers. Thanks to them, the sex workers eke out their livelihood and in turn they satisfy the latter sexually. This exchange does not rest on a formal contract that specifies the exact quantities to be exchanged. The social exchange between the sex workers and the children is mostly based on unspecified personal obligations. Moreover, it is more personalized than economic exchange. Sex workers give the children tips at their will mainly to recognize their services. Nevertheless, it is a personal obligation on the part of the former to give the tips to the latter liberally, sometimes moderately. In addition to this, the sex-workers may voluntarily entertain the children sexually. The children who are highly motivated by this take sincere efforts to bring the customers regularly.

This social activity may be explained in terms of the exchange theory from Peter Blau's point of view. According to him, social life is a *market place* in which, for instance, two actors engage in social activity in order to make a gain, a material benefit or psychological satisfaction. While receiving the benefits, they are obligated to reciprocate in order to continue receiving them in future. Blau's theory holds good with respect to this activity.

It is evident from the discussion that the duration of working hours of children, their workload, attending to personal and domestic work of employers and employees, the punishment meted out to them, their diseases, their habit of smoking, drinking and taking intoxicating items, their habit of reading pornographic literature and seeing blue films, their habit of masturbation and practice of sex with sex-workers all vary according to their age, experience, rural-urban background, tendency of changing hotels and location of hotels in which they are employed. In other words, these socio-demographic variables influence the activities of the children. Thus, it may be concluded that these variables play a vital role in bringing about the differences and changes among the children to a notable extent.

Nevertheless, these activities of the children seem to have shown the difference between them and other children under the direct control of their parents. One way or another, the former children may be called social deviants because they acquire various habits or practices over a period of time.

It may be remarked here that the children who are under the direct control of their parents do not easily slip into the habits. The family does not provide the atmosphere of conspiracy and complicity that so much attracts adolescents. The family's influence is an inhibiting or restraining influence on deviant behaviour. The need for money which drives most of the parents to sending their children to jobs would not however allow them to countenance such habits in their children. The proximity of other deviants and their influence would be considerably counterbalanced by the family and the presence of the parents and others in the family. The parents and other elders would also restrict their spending any extra earnings on any other expenditure.

Boys who pick up these habits violate the assumed social norms for children of their age. To that extent they are deviants. But the groups with which they work is dominantly used to those deviant habits by themselves, and they form an occupational adult group. These young deviants are gradually absorbed by this groups into their groups. Thus they become part of an adult *outré*.

At one point of time, these activities of the children become habitual practices. Therefore, it may be concluded that the children who mostly resemble deviants form a sub-culture, which is distinct from the larger culture.

As they deviate from established norms of society, they may also be called delinquents. They form a subculture, which is a *delinquent sub-culture*. It has its roots in working class culture. This is mostly common among the children employed in hotels.

Moreover, the employment of children in hotels provides them with large scope to develop into delinquents or social deviants. It is no doubt a social menace. A boy who joins a hotel is exposed to several unhealthy examples and practices which mostly resemble social problems.

In the first instance, the boy learns smoking and after sometime takes intoxicating items. Afterwards, he starts drinking occasionally. He might end up a drunkard. In addition to this, he has the opportunity for sex with sex-workers because he is assigned the role of a broker. He also sees blue films and reads pornographic literature. It is, thus, evident that the social atmosphere in hotels spoil the children and provide them with ample chances to become delinquents. Taking the seriousness of child labour into consideration, the Government has to take effective measures to control this problem.

SUGGESTIONS

While suggesting viable strategies to eradicate child labour from India, the following measures may be taken into consideration:

1. The Hotel Industry and Catering Establishments Act, 1958, has not brought about the expected changes in the hotels, as it has not been enforced stringently. The Government should strictly enforce it.
2. The Government should issue identity cards to all workers including children. Then the children need not move from one hotel to another in search of a job. The workers will register their name with the District Welfare Board. The Board in turn would provide death compensation, provident fund and pension. Thus the future life of the child workers would be protected.
3. The Central and State Governments should prepare various schemes for the child labour in hotels. They need to be provided with free education and scholarships. Similarly, poverty relief has to be provided to their families. Besides the Government should publicize such schemes among the people.
4. Only large hotels come under the purview of the Hotel Industry and Catering Establishments Act, 1958, the Child Labour (Prohibition and Regulation) Act, 1986, and the Shop and Establishments Act, 1947. Small hotels, *dhabas*, tea stalls, canteens, wineshops have to be brought under the purview of these Acts.
5. The Government and the NGOs should set up short stay homes (Counselling and Training Homes) for the child workers in hotels in all metropolitan cities, corporations, tourist places and taluk head quarters. These homes should provide them with non-formal education, life skill education, vocational training, apprenticeship, health care services, sports and recreational activities, and value education.
6. The Government should raise the upper age limit of children up to 18 years. Compulsory education should be extended to all children up to 18 years.

7. The Government should initiate steps to prevent strictly the employment of children in wine shops, lodges, hotels located especially in tourist places, metropolitan cities and corporation areas.

In India and abroad, several scholars have studied the problems of child labour in various organized and unorganized sectors. They have also given suggestions to eradicate child labour. The child labour eradication programme can be implemented in rural areas with the support of panchayats, schools and the people. The following suggestions will be helpful in eradicating child labour in India.

1. The Government evolved a programme, *Sarva Shiksha Abiyan* in 2002, mainly to combat the problem of child labour. It is a measure to universalize elementary education by community-ownership of the school system. It is to provide useful and relevant elementary education for all children in the age group of 6-14 years by 2010 in order to complete eight years of schooling. In course of time, this would eradicate child labour.

2. Enacting a stringent Act relating to compulsory, free and quality primary education could be an effective measure to put an end to this problem. In addition to this, the primary schools across India should be provided with infrastructural facilities. The quality of primary education has to be improved by appointing young and motivated teachers. This has to go with the implementation of modern methods of teaching and supplying of free books and notebooks to woo the children so that they would gain interest in pursuing studies at least up to middle school. The eradication of child labour is linked to compulsory primary education. In this aspect, the local panchayat should be given the responsibility of making hundred percent enrolment in the primary schools.

   (i) Since the developing countries such as Indonesia, Sri Lanka, South Korea and Taiwan have already made education compulsory, they have been successful in eradicating this problem. A few other countries like Algeria, Kenya, Tanzania, Zambia, Malaysia, Philippines and Thailand aggressively implemented policies designed to universalize primary education and achieve a high retention rate. Therefore, they have also been successful in eradicating this problem to a great extent. India can also follow a similar strategy to eradicate child labour.

   (ii) Creating awareness among hotel owners, children and people about the plight of children engaged in hotel work is also an important measure to counter the problem of child labour. In this regard, the voluntary service organizations, the National Social Service Schemes of various colleges and universities and other social and religious organizations should come forward to sensitize the people. This can be done by street plays, film shows, campaigns and rallies. A series of awareness campaigns that would also bring about positive changes among the people should be organized by the Government as well as non-Governmental organizations. To put it in a nutshell, it should be a joint venture.

(iii) Income generation by creating more employment opportunities for the families that send children to the hotels is also a suitable measure to counter the problem. In order to generate income, those families should be given loans with subsidies under the Integrated Rural Development Programmes or Self Employment Schemes to start a business or to start a dairy farm by buying milch cows. Moreover, the parents should be prepared to sacrifice something for the betterment of their children, and not harm the children's future.

If these measures are implemented effectively they will yield the desired results. The entire nation should take concerted efforts to tackle the problem if not in one stroke, at least in a phased manner. No civilized nation on earth can watch with unconcern the plight of millions of children toiling not only for their survival but also to sustain the livelihood of their families. It is paradoxical to note that India has made remarkable progress in science and technology, but has allowed this problem to grow to a monstrous size. It is the need of the hour to fight child labour with determination so that this social evil is rooted out once and for all.

Bibliography

BOOKS

Ahamed Shah, Nazir. *Child Labour in India.* New Delhi: Anmol Publications, 1992.

Adler, Freda. Mueller, Gerhard O.W. and Laufer, William S. *Criminology.* New York: McGraw-Hill, Inc, Publishers, 1991.

Burra, Neera. *Born to Work.* Bombay: Oxford University Press, 1995.

Blau, Peter M.*Exchange and Power in Social Life.* New York: John Wiley & Sons., Inc, 1964.

Chakravarthy, B. *Education and Child Labour.* Allahabad: Chugh Publications, 1989.

Conklin, John E. *Criminology.* New York: Macmillan Publishing Co., Inc, 1981.

Devi, Laxmi. *Child Labour.* New Delhi: Anmol Publications Pvt., Ltd., 1999.

Dag, Larsson. *Child Labour: Impact Assessment.* New Delhi: NARAD, The Royal Norwegian Embassy, 1994.

Encyclopedia of Social Sciences, (1930) Vol. III, New York, S.V. Hotel.

Encyclopedia Americana, 2ed, (1972) S.V. Hotel.

International Encyclopedia of the Social Sciences, 10ed, (1972), S.V. Delinquency: Sociological Aspects.

Giri, V.V. *Labour Problem in Indian Industry.* New Delhi: Asian Publishing House, 1960.

Gupta, Manju, and Voll, Klaus. *Young Hands at work: Child Labour in India.* Delhi: Atma Ram & Sons, 1987.

Hirwany, Indira. Cottya, Jacqui and Pandya Pushkar. *Towards Eradication of Child Labour: An International View.* New Delhi: Oxford & IBH Publishing Co. Pvt. Ltd., 1991.

Jain, Mahaver. *Child Labour in the Gem Polishing Industry in Jaipur.* Noida: National Labour Institute, Child Labour Cell, 1991.

Jo, Boyden, and Pat, Holden. *Children of the Cities.* London: Zed Books Ltd., 1991.

Kanbargi, Ramesh. *Child Labour in the Indian Sub-Continent: Dimensions and Implications.* New Delhi: Sage Publications. 1991.

Kohli, A.S. ed. *Social Welfare.* Delhi: Anmol Publications, 1997.

Krishna Kumari, M.S. *Child Labour in Bangalore City.* Delhi: P.S.P.C.K, 1985.

Kulshreshtha, J.C. *Child Labour in India.* New Delhi: Ashish Publishing House, 1978.

Mustafa, Mohd, and Sharma Onkar, *Child Labour in India: A Bitter Truth.* New Delhi: Deep & Deep Publications, 1997.

Mittal, Mukta. *Child Labour in Unorganised Sector.* New Delhi: Anmol Publications, Pvt. Ltd., 1994.

Mohenty, Pragati. *Hotel Industry and Tourism in India.* New Delhi: Ashish Publishing House, 1994.

Mendelievich, Elias. *Children at Work.* Geneva: International Labour Organisation, 1979.

Mishra, G.P, and Pande, P.N. *Child Labour in Carpet Industry.* New Delhi: A.P.H. Publishing Corporation, 1996.

Nangia, Parveen. *Child Labour Cause – Effect Syndrome.* New Delhi: Janak Publishers, 1987.

Naidu, Usha S, Kabadia, Kamini, R. ed. *Child labour and Health Problems and Prospects.* Bombay: Tate Institute of Social Sciences, 1985.

Pandhu, M.K. *Child Labour in India.* Calcutta: Indian Book Exchange, 1979.

Pati, R.N. *Rehabilitation of Child Labourers in India.* New Delhi: Ashish Publishing House, 1991.

Phillips, W.S.K. *Street Children in India.* Jaipur: Rawat Publications, 1994.

Rao, Koteswara, M. *Exploited Children: A Comprehensive Blueprint For Child Labour Rehabilitation.* New Delhi: Kanishka Publishers, 2000.

Rajalakshmi, N. *Tamil Nadu Economy.* Mumbai: Business Publication, INC, 1999.

Singh, Musafir. Kaura, V.D.; and Khan, S.A. *Working Children in Bombay – A Study.* Delhi: National Institute of Public Co-operation and Child Development, 1980.

Sekar, Helan, R. *Child Labour Legislation in India: A Study in Retrospect and Prospect.* NOIDA: V.V. Giri National Labour Institute, 1997.

Sahoo, Basudeb. *Labour Movement in India.* New Delhi: Rawat Publications, 1999.

Sahoo, U.C. *Child Labour in Agrarian Society.* New Delhi: Rawat Publications, 1995.

Sharma, B.K, and Mittan, Vishaa. *Child Labour and Urban Informal Sector.* New Delhi: Deep & Deep Publications, 1990.

Singh, A.N. *Child Labour in India: Socio-Economic Perspective.* Delhi: Shipra Publications, 1990.

Singh, I.S. *Child Labour.* New Delhi: Oxford & IBH Publishing Co. Pvt. Ltd., 1992.

Singh, Surendra, and Verma, R.B.S. *Child Labour in Agriculture.* Lucknow: Print House, 1987.

Sinha, S.K. *Child Labour in Calcutta: A Sociological Study.* Calcutta: N.P. Sale (P) Ltd., 1991.

Srinivasnan, Kamala. Veena Gandotra. *Child Labour-Multi Dimensional Problem.* Delhi: Ajanta Publications, 1993.

Sumangala, M, and Nagarajan, B.N. *Economics of Childlabour and Fertility: Study of Peninsular India.* Delhi: B.R. Publishing Corporation (P) Ltd., 1993.

Sanon, Chandragupt S. *Working Children: A Sociological Analysis.* New Delhi: APH Publishing Corporation, 1998.

Tripathy, S.N. *Migrant Child Labour in India.* New Delhi: Mohit Publications, 1997.

Tripathy. S.K. *Child labours in India.* New Delhi: Discovery Publishing House, 1989.

Tripathy, S.N. *Child Labour in India: Issues and Policy Options,* New Delhi: Discovery Publishing House, 1996.

Varandani, G. *Child Labour and Women Workers.* New Delhi: Ashish Publishing House, 1994.

Weiner, Myron. *The Child and the State in India.* Delhi: Oxford University Press, 1991.

Wood, B. Stephen. *Constitutional Politics in the Progressive Era: Child Labour and the Law.* Chicago: The University of Chicago Press, 1968.

Williams, Katherine, S. *Criminology.* New Delhi: Oxford University Press, 2001.

Mir. A. *Child Labour: With Special Reference to Carpet Industry of Kashmir: A Social – Legal Study.* Unpublished Ph.D, Thesis, Kashmir University Library, Srinagar, 1991.

Shah, N.A. *A Study of Child Labour in Unorganised Sector in Srinagar, Kashmir.* (Unpublished Ph.D, Thesis, Kashmir University Library, 1991.

Sutherland, Edwin, H. and Cressey, Donald R. *Criminology.* New York: J.B.Lippincott Company, 1978.

JOURNAL ARTICLES

Amerijit Singh and A.N. "Child labour in India". *The Indian Worker,* 29 (October 1980): 15-27.

Anandharajakumar, P. "Child Labour – A Contemporary Social Evil". *Social Action,* 48 (Jan-Mar 1998): 7-17.

Arimpoor Joe. 'Profile of the Child Worker. Social Action", 48 (January-March 1998): 59-68.

Ahmed, Iftikhar. "Getting Rid of Child Labour". *Economic and Political Weekly,* 34 (July 1999): 1815-1822.

Bhanumathi, R. and Sushila Srivastva, *"Child Workers in Forming Domestic and Catering Sectors". Social Welfare* 41 (October 1990): 24-26.

Chattoraj, B.N. and Saxena, Rekha. *"Victimisation of Children: An Urgent Need for Effective Measures." Social Change* 20 (September 1993): 23.

Chandra, Suman. *"Problems and Issues of Child Labour". Social Action,* 48 (Jan-Mar 1998): 19-33.

Daniel, J. Christopher. *"Child Worker has come to Stay". Social Welfare,* 14 (November 1976): 6.

Francis, C. *"Eradication of Child Labour Need for an Integrated Approach". Social Action,* Vol. 46 (Oct – Dec, 1996): 455-466.

Fernandes Walter, *"Child Labour and Procesess of Exploitation". The Indian Journal of Social Work* (April 1992): 171-190.

Karunanithi, G. *"Health Risks of Beedi Making". Social Welfare* 44 (June 1997): 9-11.

Karunanithi, G. *"Plight of Pledged Children in Beedi Workers". Economic and Political Weekly* 33 (Feb 1998): 450-452.

Kothari, Smithu. *"Child Labour in Sivakasi". Economic and Political Weekly 2* (July 1983): 119.

Lal Geetha. *"Child Labour in India: An over view". Social Change* 27 (September-December 1997): 3-4.

Mohsin, Nadeen. *"Poverty-Breeding Ground of Child Labour". Mainstream* 18 (February 1980): 29-30.

Murthy, G.K., and Rani, T.J. "Wages of Child Labour". *Yojana,* 27 (March 1983): 12-14.

Rodgers, Gerry and Standing, Guy. *"Economic Roles of Children: Low Income Countries". International Labour Review* 120 (January-February 1981): 12.

Ravi, Aparna. *"Combating Child Labour with Labels: Case of Rugmark". Economic and Political Weekly* 36 (March 2001): 1141-1147.

Sundaran, Satya. *"Child Labour: Facing the Harsh Reality", Social Action* 44 (July-September 1994): 39-45.

Sahoo, U.C. *"Agrarian Dynamics and Child Labour". Mainstream* 22 (September 1989): 25-26.

Sahoo, U.C. *"Child Labour in Surat Textile Industry"*. *Social Change* 20 (September 1993): 36-37.

Sathyamurthy, T.V. *"Children's Work"*. *Economic and Political Weekly* 30 (April 1995): 807.

Sharma, A.M. *"Child Labour in Indian Industries. Indian Journal of Social Work* 40 (March 1979): 345–352.

Srivastava, Sushila and Sheriff. H. *Child Labour in Madras and Vellore Social Welfare* 38 (September 1991): 14-17.

Shobhana, M.V. *"History of Legislation on Child Labour in Colonial India"*. *Social Action* 48 (January-March 1998): 1-6.

Saini, Debi S. *"Children of a Lesser God, Child Labour Law and Compulsory Primary Education"*. *Social Action* 48 (January-March 1998):1-13.

Sooryamoorthy, R. *"Child Labour in Kerala: Work and Working Conditions of Child Labourers in three major Cities"*. *Social Action* 48, (January-March 1998): 47-57.

Videk Jan. "World's Working Children: Need Protection against Exploitation". *Eastern Economist* 18 (October 1978): 822-823.

MAGAZINES

Anna Davin. *"Child Labour: The Working Class Family and Domestic Ideology in 19th Century Britain"*. *Development and Change,* November 1982.

Sadu, A.N. and Singh, Amerjit. *"Child Labour in India"*. *The Indian Worker,* October 1980.

REPORTS

Baskar Paul, *Resting Centre for Restaurant Child Workers.* Dindigul: Peace Trust, Annual Report, 1997.

Child Labour :Challenge and Response. A Status Report on India. Initiatives towards the Elimination of Child Labour, Noida: National Resource Centre on Child Labour, V.V. Giri National Labour Institute, 1996.

Convention on the Right of the Child. World Declaration and Plan of Action from the World Submit for Children, UNICEF, Indian Country Office, 1991.

Das, Rijani Kanta. *Child Labour in India.* Geneva: International Labour Organisation Press, 1934.

Gurupathasamy. *Report on Child Labour.* New Delhi: Ministry of Labour, 1979.

Karunanithi, G. *Report an Assessment of the Status of Primary* Education in Selected Blocks of Kamarajar and V.O.C. Districts of Tamil Nadu. Madras: United Nations Children Education Fund, 1993.

Karunanithi, G. *Report on Child Labour in North Arcot Ambedkar District: An in-depth Study in pledged Children in Beedi Works*. New Delhi: Indian Council of Social Science Research, 1993.

Karunanithi, G. *Report on Child Labour in Beedi Industry in Tirunelveli-Kattabomman District of Tamil Nadu*. New Delhi: Ministry of Labour 1995.

Karunanithi, G. Report on A Status of Primary – Middle School of Education and Child Labour in Two Blocks in Tirunelveli District of Tamil Nadu. Tirunelveli: Manonmaniam Sundaranar University, 1997.

Mandakini, Khandekar. *A Report on the Situation of Children and Youth in Greater Bombay.* Bombay: Tata Institute of Social Sciences, 1970.

Mishra, G.P., and Pande P.N. *A Study on Child Labour in Glass Industry, Ferozabad.* New Delhi: Indian Council of Social Science Research, 1992.

Mendelievich, Elias *Introduction – Children at Work.* Geneva: International Labour Organisation, 1979.

Pandian Soundra, M. *A study on Working Children in Hotel Industry in Chennai,* Proceedings of Workshop on Street Children. Department of Sociology, Gandhigram Rural Institute – Deemed University, 1999.

Report of the Director General, International Labour Conference, 6th Session, Genera: International labour Organisation, 1983.

Report of the Committee on Child Labour, Government of India: Ministry of Labour, 1979.

Study of the Working Children in Urban Delhi: A Report New Delhi: Indian Council of Child Welfare, 1977.

Vidyasagar, R. *A Status Report on Child Labour in Tamil Nadu.* Madras: United Nations Children Education Fund, 1995.

NEWSPAPERS

The Hindu, March 4, 1997, August 11, 1998, July 23, 1998.

Dinamalar, May 27, 2000.

Malai Murasu, February 24, 2000.

Malai Murasu, March 19,2000.

CENSUS

Census of India, 1991, 2001, *Census of Tamil Nadu,* 1991, 2001.

Census of Tirunelveli District, 2001.

Index